SOAPS

A PICTORIAL HISTORY OF AMERICA'S DAYTIME DRAMAS

Seli Groves

with the Editors of
the Associated Press

Robert A. Waldron,
Research Consultant

A Norback Book

**AP
Library**

Contemporary Books, Inc.
Chicago

Library of Congress Cataloging in Publication Data

Groves, Seli.
    Soaps, a pictorial history of America's daytime dramas.

    "A Norback book."
    Bibliography: p. 225.
    Includes index.
    1. Soap operas—United States—History—Pictorial works.
I. Associated Press.   II. Title.
PN1992.8.S4G75   1983   791.45′75′0973   83-19005
ISBN 0-8092-5577-4

Photo research: Wendy Davis

Published by Contemporary Books, Inc.
180 North Michigan Avenue, Chicago, Illinois 60601
Manufactured in the United States of America
Library of Congress Catalog Card Number: 83-19005
International Standard Book Number: 0-8092-5577-4

Published simultaneously in Canada by
Beaverbooks, Ltd.
195 Allstate Parkway
Valleywood Business Park
Markham, Ontario L3R 4T8
Canada

SOAPS

Contents

Acknowledgments

Thanks to photographers Bob Deutsch, Ed Geller, and Howard Gray.

Thanks to Joanne Douglas, Charlie Earle, Bob Olive, Ron Scott, The Raleigh Group, Ltd., Jim Warren for their special help.

Thanks also to ABC, CBS, and NBC—whose ever-helpful people have made it possible for me to keep up with the world of soap operas over the years.

Another heaping dollop of thanks to the editors of *Daytime TV*, *Soap Opera Digest*, and *Soap Opera World* for keeping soap operas alive in the imaginations of their readers and for printing valuable source material in their well-produced publications.

And thanks to soap opera actors, producers, and members of the crew who always make life a little easier for those of us who write about daytime dramas.

Most especially, thanks to Ruth Pollack for patience and Jody Rein for understanding.

Introduction:

What Is a Soap Opera?

Most people would say that a soap opera is a television show broadcast during the day between the hours of 11:00 and 4:30, in which the themes are, invariably, love, hate, life, death, good, evil, stupidity, wisdom, generosity, avarice, and, of course, various manifestations of sexual expression—or, sometimes, of sexual repression.

Those with a more technical bent might add that unlike some nighttime varieties (also called soaps, but they really aren't), a true soap opera is a continuing serial with storylines that go on until either the writers or the ratings make it an act of necessity to end the plot or fire the actor or the writer—and sometimes do all three, especially when it's close to contract-renewal time and someone threatens to ask for a raise.

But why call them soap operas, anyway? Perhaps we should get that straightened out before we go any further.

If you saw the film *Tootsie* in which Dustin Hoffman, an out-of-work actor, pretends to be a woman so that he can audition for the role of a female character on a soap opera, you may recall that one of the actors tells Hoffman not to refer to their production as a *soap*, but rather as a *daytime drama*.

Soap operas were aptly named because when they first started on radio more than 50 years ago they were both sponsored and owned by soap manufacturers and were geared to a daytime audience of soap product users. Today many of the televised soaps are still owned by soap manufacturers. For example, "As the World Turns," "Another World," and "Guiding Light," to cite just three, are owned by Procter & Gamble. Some shows are owned by the network. For instance, "Ryan's Hope" (ABC) is such a show.

Back in the days of radio, soap products were introduced and sold through the medium of the serialized daily stories. Duz, with its slogan, "Duz does everything," was one of these products. Rinso presented its share of serials along with the promise that not only would your clothes become Rinso white, you wouldn't ever find yourself sneezing while scrubbing.

"Ma Perkins," one of the most popular soap operas on radio, was introduced in 1933. It may have been the serial that finally decided the fate of the medium as we still experience it. Previous to "Ma Perkins," radio serials enjoyed varying degrees of popularity, and sponsors and/or owners were not necessarily wedded to any one vehicle. But when "Ma" took off, so did sales of Oxydol. Credit a clever Procter & Gamble executive for linking "Ma" with the product. The show was introduced as "Oxydol's Own Ma Perkins" and any woman who valued the wise widow's kindness and helpfulness could hardly be faulted for buying *her* soap powder when she went to the market. "Ma Perkins" remained on the air for 27 years, with an occasional time out. "Ma" was the last of the great radio soaps. Her popularity and viability made the soap opera an advertising force to be reckoned with. If one may be forgiven an irresistible pun here: thanks to the soap operas of the past and present, many a sponsor, writer, and actor has really cleaned up!

So now you know that a soap opera is so-called because of its origins as the property and/or advertising vehicle of a soap manufacturer.

But the question persists: what is a soap opera, *really*—and what makes it unique?

Let's review what we think most people would say are the necessary components of a bona fide soap opera:

1. It must be a daytime program.
2. It must be a serialized program.
3. It must be sponsored and/or owned by a soap manufacturer.
4. It must have lots of sex, greed, love, hate, intrigue (etc., etc.)

But surely there must be more to this than that!

The foregoing line, of course, is the standard dramatic transition gimmick used when someone—usually one of the older core characters—becomes aware that something is not quite right in the affairs of Oakdale, Monticello, Bay City, or Llanview.*

There is something more, indeed: relationships. A soap opera doesn't deal just in the themes of life, death, hate, love, and sex. It deals with them in terms of their impact on human beings. One must love some-

one to be hurt, rejected, proud, pleased, or turned on by what that someone does or doesn't do. One must also hate—for however long—in order to plot, plan, and engage in all sorts of nasty schemes directed against another human being. Someone has to be vulnerable, in some way, to be affected by what someone else does or doesn't do.

Woe to the soap opera that forgets to stress the *relationships* between and among people. Once in a while it's all right to tinker with a science fiction plot line such as the machine that turned Port Charles frigid on "General Hospital" or the lovesick ape that turned up the heat on Delia on "Ryan's Hope," but unless the series gets back to emphasizing the human factor, its ratings will fall quickly.

Soap operas make people important! That is the key to their success. Regardless of how long or short a storyline is, for that length of time the people involved in the plot are permitted to come out of obscurity and show their strengths as well as their weaknesses.

The soap viewer invariably identies with someone on the soap. Soaps make people paramount; soaps, therefore, make the viewers feel important as well.

Occasionally some soaps do forget that Divine Dictum of soap opera success: *Always Keep the Human Quotient High.* For example, some of the recent outlandish escapades of Travis and Liza Sentell on "Search for Tomorrow," including one story involving a ninja, caused a ratings drop because the plot had moved too far into adventure and out of interpersonal relationships. A similar fate befell "Ryan's Hope" in 1982 when it featured its Egyptian-mummy's-curse storyline. The actors on "Ryan's Hope" considered the story a sort of *mummy weirdest* concoction that didn't have the saving grace of sentimentality that made the Delia/ape story—as fantastic as it was—at least a little Fay Wray/King Kongish; unbelieveable but charming. Eventually the story was scrapped; the mummy plot was wrapped up and the series returned to its focus on the Irish-American Ryans.

Anyone who watches soap operas will notice a marked similarity between one series and the next. This is not a coincidence. Soap opera producers recognize a good thing when they see it, and most soaps have certain factors in common:

Setting: With a few notable exceptions, soap operas are set in fictional small towns, many of them in the midwest, and some within a short plane ride of New York. The typical soap opera town is large enough to

---

*The fictional towns found in "As the World Turns," "Edge of Night," "Another World," and "One Life to Live," respectively.

contain a mix of characters from all economic strata but small enough to make it believable when the characters constantly cross each other's paths. To make for the required melodrama, each soap town usually contains at least one hospital, a few restaurants, a baronial mansion or two, some more modest houses and/or apartments, and perhaps a police headquarters; there's also always a courtroom that comes into use whenever a character is caught in the act of some dastardly deed.

Families: For the most part, soap operas have thrived on the two-family setup that is used to create instant conflict. Sometimes these core families are both rich; sometimes one is rich and one is poor; other times one or both are in between. Whatever the case, economics, politics, or some other factor puts the two clans at loggerheads with each other.

Themes: The theme for all soap operas is interpersonal relationships, and most often romance is the main subject. But just about every family-related issue will come up at one time or another. In a few cases in soap operas of today there is a general theme that carries the show. "Ryan's Hope" for example, is about upwardly striving people who have close family ties and much hope for the future. "Edge of Night" is the only soap opera on the air today that has a mystery theme. And new "Capitol," while it is essentially a show about people, as are all the others, is based in Washington, DC, with politics as the theme that ties the characters together and drives them apart.

A notable trend of the modern soap opera is the youthful look many of them have adopted. Certain soaps, such as "The Young and the Restless" and "General Hospital," are considered to focus mainly on young characters, though they do feature older characters as well.

Often the same names—Jenny, Mark, Tony, Jason, Patty, Maggie, Amanda, and Kate—are given to characters on several soaps. One writer told us that there is a great deal of deliberate copying that goes on. If something works on one soap, there is no hesitation in adapting it or blatantly copying it for another series. Names that are particularly descriptive of certain characters on a soap are used to continue that descriptive allusion on another one. Jennys, for example, appear to be women who are good and beautiful but often victimized between their triumphant moments. Cases in point: Jenny Gardner (played by Kim Delaney) on "All My Children" and Jenny Janssen (Brynn Thayer) on "One Life to Live".

As for the situations in common, in almost every soap on the air at this time, these are the elements they're bound to share:

1. Someone turns up as the illegitimate offspring of one of the pillars of the soap community.

2. Someone turns up as the long-lost brother, sister, or half-sibling of one of the characters.

3. Someone is pregnant with a baby whose father is not that someone's husband or even current lover.

4. Someone is a former prostitute who may or may not still be tormented, threatened, or simply just embarrassed by her former pimp.

5. Someone in the family is a doctor.

6. Someone in the family is a lawyer.

7. Marriages that last 20 years or more must face dissolution as one of the partners either becomes disillusioned and leaves because he or she cannot face growing older without having a "fling," or because he or she fears becoming a burden on the other due to a developing disease (which often proves to be a false alarm), or because he or she suspects the other is in love with someone else and won't stand in the partner's way.

8. All such marriages are eventually reinstituted and the partners are more closely united than before.

9. The "mob" or the "syndicate" or the "Washington connection" intrudes into the lives of the people on the soap.

10. Someone is kidnapped.

11. Someone has amnesia.

12. Someone has been unjustly convicted of a crime.

13. Someone faces life-threatening surgery.

14. Some surgeon must perform the operation although he or she hates the patient enough to want to see him/her die.

15. Someone allows her child to be adopted by someone else in town and lives to regret it.

16. Someone is breaking up someone else's marriage.

17. Someone is marrying someone who loves someone else.

18. Someone is marrying someone although he or she loves someone else.

19. Someone is marrying someone because he or she thinks the one he or she loves is dead—but it's not so.

20. Someone is on drugs or drinks too much.

21. Someone is being blackmailed.

22. Someone is hiding his or her true identity.

23. Someone has had plastic surgery, which has

completely changed the way he or she once looked.

24. Someone owns the town's favorite watering place or the most popular restaurant or disco.

25. Someone is an older woman who loves a younger man.

26. Someone is an older man who loves a younger woman.

27. Someone is unscrupulous in business.

28. Someone is a teenager who will not only get into trouble but cause a lot of problems for a lot of people.

29. Someone is pregnant and either doesn't want the baby or is unable to care for the baby. Almost always a miscarriage makes the matter moot.

30. Someone is suing or otherwise plotting to get custody of a child.

31. Someone is getting into bed with someone for the first time and the word virgin won't be used in the dialogue leading up to and following the sex act.

The foregoing standard plot lines that occur over and over in soaps reflect the stuff of which solid entertainment is made. There is no chance of any soap being successful unless it can entertain the audience. Regardless of which soap may be more forthright on matters that affect human relationships, and which drama may emphasize social issues, and which one may take its cast into exotic locales, the essential aim is to *entertain*.

Every writer makes that point over and over again. Douglas Marland, who wrote "Guiding Light" for years and has been credited with introducing the youthful characters that attracted a younger audience and who now writes the new Agnes Nixon soap, "Loving," stresses the entertainment factor as all-important. Marland, a former actor, understands audience reactions. He provides the chemical compounds that cause these reactions to take place. Maggie dePriest, who writes "Days of Our Lives," not only believes in entertaining her audience but says that "Days," because its primary objective is to do just that, is, in her own words, "a classic soap."

One of the reasons so many "standard" plot lines are used in any given number of soaps at any one time is that entertainment is not only the name of the game, but the name of the ratings winners. If Soap A is reaching (that is, successfully entertaining) a large audience because of a certain storyline, then Soap B can't be faulted for "borrowing" the plot in an effort to win (entertain) a share of that audience for itself.

People remain loyal to those soaps whose stories are more *meaningful* (another synonym for *entertaining*) to them. That's where the essential quality of making the relationships work in turn marks the difference between a successful soap opera and one that slides down the ratings roster into oblivion.

How realistic soap operas must be in order to entertain is a subject of longstanding controversy. In the early days of TV soaps little attention was paid to the type of detail that films, for example, use. But this may have been simply a matter of having a low budget. Today, with bigger budgets and a more demanding audience, soaps are forced to pay more attention to detail, and many of them have succeeded in replacing the dull and sterile trappings of the past with more convincing settings.

As to the stories, whether or not they seem realistic is often a matter of personal opinion. Whatever the case, soap opera audiences are not likely to be watching daytime drama because they want to see a documentary, nor do they have an enormous desire to be educated. (Many soaps have, however, succeeded in becoming fairly informative in spite of the fact that that's not their job.) It's not the realism of a scene that's important. It's how each problem represented affects the people involved.

From the beginning the successful soap opera formula contained two absolutes: (1) it involved its characters in stories that made them react as *you* might in the same circumstances; (2) it make *you* care about them. Even if you hated them, you were involved and you needed to know what would happen to them.

Some observers believe that the growing popularity of soap operas, not only in the United States and in Canada but in other countries as well, is attributable to one basic fact of life: that the soaps show us people something like ourselves who go through situations we will never have to endure. Perhaps. But this seems to be a negative appreciation of soap operas. It may well be that soaps have a *positive* factor that is much more to the point. To wit, that above or in spite of everything else, soap operas are darned good entertainment, well-produced, well-acted, well-written, and full of the stuff that makes for universal acceptance. In short, the viewer witnesses and appreciates the human condition in all of its many manifestations.

This book is divided into two sections. Part I includes chapters devoted to each of the 14 current network soap operas, explaining the history of each soap through relating the experiences of central characters.

Original and current cast and character lists for each soap, plus, of course, the many affairs to remember, mysteries and murders will be found in these pages.

Part II is chock-full of inside information on your favorite soaps and soap characters, including motivations for cast changes and plot twists, a discussion of some well-known soap opera gimmicks, a look at the life of soap opera actors, the backgrounds and past and present accomplishments of soap stars of yesterday and today, the Emmys awarded since 1974, and even some hints about what to expect from the soaps of the future. Chapter 18 lists trivia questions and answers for those who really want to test their knowledge of soap mania.

Finally, in the Appendix you will find complete lists of all the TV and radio soaps through 1983.

Before delving into the story behind each of today's soap operas, read the following chapter, which sums up the major events that have made soap operas what they are today.

SOAPS

1

A History of Soaps

RADIO: IN THE BEGINNING WAS THE WORD

The first radio serials, including the legendary *Amos and Andy*, were released around the time of the Depression and were light and amusing in nature. The oldest soaps were written as much for humor as for the "soapy pathos" quality. Even when a character in a radio soap was in the thickest of emotional quicksand, some form of comic relief was introduced, usually right before the commercial.

Fibber McGee and Molly (their real names were Jim and Marion Jordan) starred in the first on-air soap

"Vic and Sade" was the second soap to air on network radio (NBC's Blue Network, 1932). A domestic comedy, "Vic and Sade" was called the best soap opera by Time *in 1943. Photo © Field Enterprises, Inc. Photograph reprinted with permission.*

Early "Guiding Light" cast members rehearse around the ever-present organ. Included here are Ted Corday, Charita Baur, Lyle Sudro, Theo Goetz, and Rosa Rio at the organ. Photo courtesy Corday Productions, Inc.

opera, "The Smith Family," which was originally broadcast in 1925 as a 17-minute show (early television soap operas were on for 13 minutes a day before expanding in length.) It wasn't until a few years later that the tear-jerking soap formula that has lasted 50 years was truly born.

The radio soap hit the air waves on February 15, 1932, when NBC made the first national broadcast of *Clara, Lu 'n' Em.* From then on radio and TV audiences have had a choice of dramatic serials.

And a popular formula it proved to be: by the mid- to late 1930s there was a dizzying selection of 15-minute series. In fact, between 1939 and 1940 a movement began to protest the prevalence of the "drippy" soaps. Needless to say, the protests had little effect, and soap operas have continued to flourish.

The radio soaps also introduced their episodes with a stock line or set of lines. For instance, "Our Gal Sunday": . . . the story of an orphan girl named Sunday from the little mining town of Silver Creek, Colorado, who in young womanhood married England's richest, most handsome lord, Lord Hentry Brinthrope. The story that asks the question: Can this girl from a mining town in the West find happiness as the wife of

a wealthy and titled Englishman?" (The answer was, of course, yes. But Sunday often had to put up the good fight to keep her ladyship from sinking in some heavy emotional weather.)

The secret to creating and sustaining a successful television soap opera was discovered when soaps were introduced to radio audiences around the country. Essentially, the formula follows a pattern that is as old as nature itself. In the way the universe is said to revolve around its own center, in the way planets revolve around their sun, and so on, soap operas move around a set of core relationships.

The core may be a family grouping. Or it may be a sort of extended family situation that takes in people related by various means. The "family" may even be a group of non-related people who work together such as the central staff members of "General Hospital."

Storylines wind and twist around several characters at any given time. But trace enough of them back through their deviations and someone from the central core will be involved in some way. From the appearance of "Clara, Lu 'n' Em" in 1932 through "Best Seller," a 1960 serialized format that involved dramatizing best-selling books, such classics as "Guiding

Light" (1937), "The Road of Life" (1937), "Life Can Be Beautiful" (1938), "Against the Storm" (1939), and "The Right to Happiness" (1939) have used this formula with great success.

It should be noted at this period of raised and rising women's consciousness that the most popular radio soaps almost always involved a woman or women who came out of the home and achieved some success independently of any men in their lives. The radio soaps were awash with female doctors, reporters, mayors, and businesswomen. Soaps in which the female leads lived only for the sake of a child or a husband were less successful (examples: "My Son and I," "Madame Courageous," which lasted less than one year and three months respectively, "Rose of My Dreams," and "Nona from Nowhere." "Stella Dallas," which dealt with a mother's sacrifice for her daughter, would seem to be the exception, lasting from 1938 to 1955. But Stella was a strong woman with a mind of her own and a sense of her own destiny. Stella was always played as someone who knew that one day all would be well.

The post-World War I period produced a generation of women who knew that if they had to they could handle all of the jobs that men could. These women either were themselves ambulance drivers, factory workers, and front-line nurses or kith and kin of same. The radio soaps that came out in the '30s reflected their strong sense of themselves and of their potential.

The post-World War II radio soaps that were successful continued to reflect these strong images. The ladies may have been home caring for husbands and children, but they weren't willing to submerge their own identities completely while soaking laundry or scrubbing floors or frying chicken in Crisco.

_ Not surprisingly, the core character of almost every radio soap was a strong woman—a trend that is still going strong on TV. There was the "Romance of Helen Trent," which opened every show by reminding the listeners that although Helen was over 30, she not only had the gumption to look for romance, but had every expectation of finding it and making the most of it.

As for Mary Noble, the "Backstage Wife," she, too, was a strong woman who, though wed to one of the most successful and desirable actors in the country, not only knew how to keep her man from straying but also how to encourage him to greater successes. When the curtain fell, Mary's husband took direction from her.

In those soap operas in which the woman was not

Charita Bauer, who has played Bert since "Guiding Light's" radio days, is shown here on an early TV set. Bert evolved into the strong matriarch that has been an element of the soap opera formula since 1930. Photo by Howard Gray.

already a well-established personality, such as in "Her Honor, Nancy James," and "Wendy Warren," the ladies all tended to marry into a higher economic and/or social stratum. This was partly the stuff of which dreary Depression or post-Depression dreams were made, of course. But it also reflected what the listeners wanted for themselves.

The American woman was, if one were to consider her choice of radio soap operas indicative, never going to be content with the *status quo* of her situation. Later, the successful television soaps would pick up on this and present their heroines as doers in the outside world.

While virtue was lauded on the radio soaps, a pinch

or two of sin was tolerated. After all, the soap was not a morality play, per se. It was also entertainment. Long after "Big Sister," for example, left the air, devoted fans continued to talk about the love affair of Ruth Wayne and that fine, decent man who wanted to marry her but was too good to divorce his hopelessly insane wife.

The radio soap was also distinguished by the ever-present "Mary Worth" type—a woman who could always be depended on to offer much-needed advice. The "Ma Perkins" character seldom initiated any storyline. But when those lines became tangled webs, one could expect Ma to somehow straighten everything out again. These characters were always older than the other women on the show and were portrayed as wise and deep. More often than not they were blessed with a wonderful sense of humor as well.

Even where men appeared to be the central figures—such as in "Young Dr. Malone"—the men usually reacted while the woman or women precipitated the action.

"Young Dr. Malone" went on television in 1958. It continued on radio until 1960. Although it had been successful on radio, it never really pulled in the viewing audiences.

"Guiding Light" was the only radio-born soap that survived the move to television. Besides "Young Dr. Malone," the other radio-cum-TV series that failed were "The Brighter Day," "Portia Faces Life," "Road of Life," "One Man's Family," and "Kitty Foyle."

Why haven't soaps returned to radio? Media observers say radio is now an excellent money-maker for sponsors. Radio sets that have TV sound station pickups are being sold to listeners who say they like to hear their favorite soaps, especially if they're somewhere where a TV set is not available. So, if people can *listen* to the televised soaps, why not put on made-for-radio versions again?

One answer can be found in the assessment of a soap opera writer who says: "With the advent of television, sex was finally permitted to come out of the imagination and onto the visual field. It's much easier to show a couple slipping into bed and under the sheets than it is to try to find the words and the sound effects you'd need to describe such a scene on radio. The FCC would turn you off for using indecent language."

The writing remains basically the same. The radio soaps were written to a three-count. That is, much of what was said was repeated three times in order for the listener to keep up with the plot movement.

(Changing diapers, cooking, ironing, cleaning, or other distractions always competed for her attention.) Televised soaps continue to use the three-count method when important storyline transitions, for example, have to be made. (Again, someone's daytime hours may often have to be shared with chores or other activities not done in the evening.)

Larry Haines, who plays Stu Bergman on "Search for Tomorrow" made this comment:

"In some ways a televised soap opera, while it concentrates on the visual, is like a radio soap opera. To be successful, it has to have good dialogue. You, the audience, must be able to hear the story. *Seeing* is not enough. The spoken word stimulates the imagination. For radio, it helps create a 'picture' in your mind. It also helps you 'see' more of the visual you're looking at on television. While TV has become more sophisticated and techniques are brilliant, it's still the spoken word that's all-important."

SOAP OPERAS COME TO TV

"Big Sister" was actually the first TV soap to air, going out on the coaxial cables in 1946. But its tenure on the tube lasted only 15 minutes. A year later something called "A Woman to Remember" was aired, but almost no one remembers much about it. Another serial, "The First Hundred Years" aired in 1950 but didn't make it past 100 days.

The first soap opera to make its ultimately successful debut on television is still on the air. "Search for Tomorrow" made its debut on September 3, 1951. Its leading lady, then and now, Mary Stuart, almost didn't get to the telecast on time. She explained her near loss of direction on the day of the telecast, "It wasn't that I didn't know the way to the studio. There was no studio. At least, not in the sense of what most of us think a television studio ought to be. Instead, the producers fitted up a few rooms somewhere in that maze in Grand Central Station. They had cameras and lights and dressing rooms—in fact, the works. The only thing they didn't provide for those of us who were still relatively new was a detailed map showing exactly which corridor led where and, more important, which corridor led to a dead end."

Eventually, Mary did find her way to the *Search* studio for that historic—and *live*—telecast. And the show went on the air.

In her autobiography, *Both of Me*, Mary describes those early TV days: "We were, to a great extent, in

Mary Stuart survived the formative years of TV soaps to become a seasoned veteran and a favorite of "Search for Tomorrow" fans.

blackness. Because of the way the lights and the cameras had to operate at that time, black walls, black surroundings were necessary. Also, we were a live show. Therefore, we moved around as little as possible. Anything could happen on a live show, and usually did. So we did our best to minimize the risks wherever possible."

Among the problems that the televised soaps had to contend with were the following:

Movement: In the radio studio almost no one except the sound effects man moved around too much. On TV the story had to be told with movement added.

Rehearsal: On radio a good actor needed very little rehearsal time. A quick read and then a run-through with the cast was usually sufficient. The most important thing was knowing how to move the pages of the script without letting the microphones pick up the sound. With television, live TV, time had to be set aside for the actors to learn their scripts and their camera marks.

New Technical Challenges: In the 1950s wonderful programs were being wired on live television. "Playhouse 90," "Studio One," and "Kraft Theater" were nighttime shows that established many fine actors, directors, and writers. Fortunately, many of the technicians who worked with these shows also came to do the soaps, bringing with them the finest technical qualities available.

Makeup: Color television hadn't yet arrived, but makeup for the early TV soaps was another problem that had to be solved. Actors had to wear clothes and makeup in accordance with what the cameras would pick up. For example, if a shirt was to appear white, it had to be blue!

The Evolution of TV Soaps

As mentioned in the beginning of this chapter, soaps have remained successful partly because they've adhered to a formula hit on in the early '30s. But so much else has happened to soap operas that it's worth taking a look at the major changes that have made them what they are today.

When soaps made the switch to TV the ubiquitous, and often irritating, narrator of radio soaps was eliminated. The visual dimension added by TV also rendered the soliloquies gimmick used on radio ineffective.

Perhaps in keeping with social changes, the tone of the shows gradually became less righteous and moralistic. An example of this trend could be found in "Guiding Light," which at first featured a minister but later, a few years before its move to TV, dealt with the problems of an all-American middle-class family. The Bauer family did, however, espouse the values preached by Reverend Rutledge.

Interestingly, "GL" did hold on to one soon-to-be vestige of radio soaps in having its core family headed by a pair of immigrants who had settled in California. Later soaps quickly drifted away from the ethnic emphasis that could be found in such popular radio series as "The Goldbergs" and toward all-WASP casts of characters. There were no black principals on soap operas until 1968.

While soap operas often reflect the mores of their time, even today they rarely trailblaze in broaching ticklish subjects. Soap operas of the '50s, '60s, and early '70s preached the values of motherhood, the

Stefan Schnabel portrayed Dr. Stephen Jackson during "Guiding Light's" early and middle television years. Photo by Howard Gray.

family, and religious faith, and errant characters were almost invariably punished for their evil ways. Today characters are more likely to be multidimensional: most have a good side as well as a bad side.

Still, soap operas, in their goal of entertaining, protect their viewers from things they might not want to see or hear. They give them just enough scandal to titillate but not enough to shock. Interracial romance, battered wives, homosexuality, and incest have barely been touched on. When "Days of Our Lives" incorporated a kiss into a romance between a white man and a black woman in a 1975 storyline, the viewers responded so negatively that "DOOL" was forced to abort the affair and quickly sent the wayward young man back to his family and the arms of a "suitable" white girl.

Sometimes it's not easy to predict what will be accepted by viewers. The audience seems to love the increased amount of tape shot in the bedroom, though nudity and the sexual act are only implied. But sex in soaps almost always mean romance, which is exactly what the viewers want.

Picking upon one gimmick established during the radio era, soap operas of the '70s began to hire celebrities as guest stars. The familiar faces of Joan Crawford and Kim Hunter have appeared in daytime

dramas. Along with stars came more entertainment: suddenly soap opera characters began breaking out into song in the middle of the action, and to this day many a soap opera star has belted out a tune. More glitter was added to soaps when soap weddings were featured. Besides adding a festive touch, these weddings brought viewers into the intimate lives of the characters they loved.

One of the most significant and controversial of all changes in the soap form was the inclusion of violence in many storylines. The number of murders, domestic battles, blackmail schemes, rapes, and underhanded plots that are used by soaps would seem to give them a decidedly disturbing air. But many viewers find them less offensive than the type of violence they see in nighttime programs. The violence in soap operas is mostly implied and is based on suspense. The audience is supposed to be titillated by implied threats of impending doom, not shocked by blood and gore. Most soap writers feel that, compared to nighttime shows, daytime series avoid gratuitous violence. Someone is murdered, for example, not to frighten the audience with the mere violence of the murderous act but to intrigue them about the repercussions that will affect the characters.

Here are some additional trends noticed in soap

Jayne Meadows and Virginia Graham guest-starred on "Texas."

opera plots over the years.

As TV serials become more popular with daytime viewers, the networks began to experiment with variations on the genre. One of the most remarkable daytime shows to come out during the 1960s was "Dark Shadows." While it had its soap opera-ish share of fleshly pursuits and emotional *angst*, it also boasted a decidely supernatural theme. Vampires were redeemed but remained no less chilling figures. Ghosts were stirred by the sounds of music box melodies and came to life in the 20th century.

The series, directed by Dan Curtis, who would direct and produce "Winds of War," a 16-hour mini series for ABC in 1983, nearly fell back into its own crypt when it made its debut in 1966. However, by giving its vampire "hero," Barnabas Collins (played by Jonathan Frid), a poignant, human quality, Curtis was able to turn a monster into a sex symbol and saved the series for a four-year run.

Another departure from the norm of the day was "Edge of Night," which made its debut in 1956. "Edge of Night" proved far more durable than "Dark Shadows," and to this day it is the only daytime drama dedicated to the proposition that crime is a constant. Its characters are forever involved in some manifestation of mankind's darker nature.

"EON" has remained successful most likely because it has for the most part continued to reflect the external fluctations of society, as all successful soaps must. Even today Agnes Nixon, who has created or helped create such important soaps as "All My Children," "Another World," "Search for Tomorrow," "One Life to Live," and the new series "Loving," is said to scan the newspapers before sitting down at her typewriter. Consequently, she's done shows at present medical, scientific, and social changes.

During the mid-70s almost all the daytime series featured murders and seemed especially fond of long trial scenes. In fact, the theme eventually was overused and in the early '80s trials are usually held off screen.

Many people feel the exotic plots of the late '70s and early '80s, have reached their peak, forcing soaps to return to some of the more traditional subjects. With divorce so common in real life, soap characters are always battling for child custody. In mid-1983 there was a renewed trend toward paralysis in the soaps. During the first half of 1983 Marie Curtis of "Days of Our Lives" was paralyzed, as were Luke Spencer of "General Hospital," Greg Nelson of "All My Children," Thomas McCandless of Capitol," and Jack Abbott of "The Young and The Restless."

When soap operas started injecting more adventure into their episodes, viewers were again treated to many versions of the same story. During the early '80s "Another World," "As the World Turns," and "One Life to Live" all ran mystery plots in which the characters made a movie that led one of them to commit murder and mayhem in order to keep some secret the film would reveal. "All My Children" and "The Young and the Restless" featured stories involving black-market videotapes. Several other series featured abusers of cocaine and speed.

SOAPS: YESTERDAY, TODAY, AND TOMORROW

Core families, love stories, and melodrama notwithstanding, a lot has changed in the world of soap operas since they were introduced to TV viewers in 1951. Much progress has been made, but there was a period of time not long ago when no self-respecting adult would admit to being hooked on the goings-on in Henderson, Bay City, or Port Charles. Until soaps really came out of the closet in the late '70s, when college students and men began to watch, too, soap opera viewers were stereotyped as being bored matrons who had nothing better to do than while away the hours in front of the tube.

Soap operas were considered such low-brow entertainment that jokes about them and parodies of them abounded. Radio listeners may remember, for example, the hilarious parody of "Mary Noble: Backstage Wife" created by veteran comedy team Bob and Ray. This popular pair called their "soap opera" "Mary Backstage: Noble Wife," and they incorporated into it all the foibles radio soaps were scorned for: long pauses in dialogue, loud organ music, and episode endings that were supposed to leave listeners begging for more but usually left them puzzled about whether or not anything had actually happened. In the mid-70s Norman Lear made fun of soaps in his nighttime show starring Louise Lasser, "Mary Hartman, Mary Hartman." Again, all the earmarks of soapdom were there, but Lear's approach was more satirical, with a touch of serious commentary often underlying the plot. A third entry parody was the recent nighttime program entitled simply "Soap."

Despite the controversy surrounding soap operas over the years, today's audience is made up of upscale adults in the 18-to 35-year-old age bracket that the advertisers love. Many soaps have also managed to hold on to their traditional audience of housewives, but as early as 1976, "All My Children" boasted an audience that was 30 percent male, and all across the country college students could be found crowded into their student unions to watch daytime dramas at lunchtime. Today more than 30 million people watch the soaps every day. Famous personalities who admit to being hooked on soaps include Fred Astaire; Carol Burnett; Sammy Davis, Jr.; Olivia Newton-John; Dean Martin; and Betty Ford.

Such widespread popularity adds up to big bucks for all involved. While soaps aren't cheap to produce, in 1951 it cost producers about $8,650 a week to produce daily 15-minute TV episodes, which was more than twice what radio serials cost. Only a few years later that $8,650 would pay for only one episode, and the costs have kept rising over the years—fortunately, ad revenues have more than kept pace with expenses. According to a 1983 TV Guide article, 1981 ad rev-

"Love of Life" introduced teenage girls to soap opera casts in the early '70s, as the percentage of young viewers increased. Cindy Grover played Stacey Corby, the character on which many subsequent teen characters were modeled. Photo by Howard Gray.

enues from daytime TV amounted to $1.4 billion out of a total $5.6 billion for the three networks. A full 50 percent of ABC's network profits were coming from daytime TV. And a 30-second spot on daytime was likely to run an advertiser $29,000. Time magazine reported in 1976 that a Kojak episode cost the network $250,000 but returned only $200,000 in revenue. "Days of Our Lives," on the other hand, cost $170,000 a week to produce but brought in ad revenues of $120,000 per day.

The networks aren't the only ones to benefit financially. Major actors can make in excess of $100,000 a year on daytime dramas, and more and more well-known actors and actresses are appearing on soaps because, as one star said, the money may not be great, but it's steady work and guest appearances on night-time shows are paying less than they used to. The creators and writers of soap operas also cash in big on their babies: headwriters can make a quarter of a million dollars a year, while senior writers under them may earn $100,000.

Daytime drama is so demanding of its writers, actors, and everyone else involved that they easily earn their money. A typical day on a soap opera set begins at 7:30 A.M. and rarely ends less than 12 hours later. Actors must go through makeup, wardrobe, and dress rehearsal before the final shoot. Every time someone flubs a line the scene must be taken from the top. For a one-hour show such as "GH," actors might have to memorize a 64-page script for the next day. Shows are taped about a week ahead of air date.

With so many soap operas on the air, and so much imitation among them, many viewers of the '80s were becoming saturated with suds. In fact, during mid-1983 the most highly rated daytime show was "The Price Is Right," a game show.

Have the network TV soap operas reached a dead end? Will the young viewers of today demand more and more sensationalism until they can get it only from the more risqué cable TV ventures? Only time will tell. One thing is pretty certain: Whatever they're like, the more successful soaps will (1) entertain, (2) retain the best of the past, and (3) reflect the times.

(For more information on the outlook for the soaps of the future, see the Appendix.)

PART I:
The Soaps

2

All My Children (ABC)

The times they were still a-changing in America when "All My Children" made its debut on January 5, 1970. The ferment of the 1960s had not yet been dissipated. The war in Vietnam was still raging. College campuses were still afire with youthful dissent and rebellion. But an awareness of peace was beginning to be sensed in the land. Change was coming and change was being called for. However, voices were no longer so strident. Tones were lowered; cries were muted. People were beginning to ask questions of themselves as often as they had demanded answers from others.

It was out of this seething restlessness of the '60s and the growing promise of introspection in the dawn of the '70s that "All My Children" was created.

The creator was Agnes Nixon, one of the most prolific writers of soap operas. She's won awards for her writing and is known as a writer who observes social movements and translates them into relevant drama.

Fate almost kept "All My Children" from premiering on television. Agnes Nixon began working on the outline back in 1965, while still writing for a Procter & Gamble soap. While on vacation, she lost the suitcase containing her "AMC" manuscript. Since Nixon didn't have a carbon copy, she thought the manuscript was lost forever. A few months later, however, the suitcase resurfaced, with the manuscript still safely tucked away inside. Finishing work on the presentation, Nixon presented "All My Children" to Procter & Gamble, which immediately took an option on it. Not long after, the company dropped its option, claiming there was no available network time slot for the series. The writer mistakenly assumed that Procter & Gamble just didn't think her story was good enough, so she filed the manuscript away.

A few years later, after she had made "Another World" a top-rated series, ABC asked Nixon to create a new soap. Rather than use "All My Children," Nixon

Agnes Nixon (center), creator of "All My Children," with Susan Lucci (Erica) and Ruth Warrick (Phoebe), stars of the popular soap opera. Mrs. Nixon was the first woman to receive the coveted Trustees Award of the National Academy of Television Arts and Sciences.

created an entirely new soap, "One Life To Live." "One Life To Live" quickly became a ratings success, and the network solicited her for yet another series. But Nixon claimed she didn't have any ideas for a new soap. At that point her husband reminded her of "All My Children," which she reread and decided to submit.

When "All My Children" debuted in 1970, ABC was making an assertive move to compete with CBS and NBC for ratings. Besides "All My Children," "The Best of Everything" and "A World Apart" (whose cast included Susan Sarandon), were introduced. After a

year and a half, only "All My Children" had survived. "All My Children's" initial ratings weren't spectacular, but the show did manage to build an audience through the star appeal of Rosemary Prinz, who had left her major role on "As the World Turns" and had agreed to return to the soaps via "All My Children." Prinz played liberated woman Amy Tyler for only a short time, but "AMC" had built its own group of loyal fans by the time she left the cast.

Why has "All My Children" stayed near the top through the '70s and early '80s?

Since those early days "AMC" has presented its

fans with a fascinating combination of family values, idealism, and glamor. "AMC" conveys a sense of variety and contrast that attracts a broad audience and helps keep the pace lively in each episode. Fans of the show are whisked from Phoebe Tyler's mansion to the local hospital to Palmer Cortlandt's mansion to the office of Cortlandt Electronics to the elegant penthouse in which Erica lives. Viewers know that whenever that New York skyline flashes onto the screen something exciting is likely to occur. Will the frenetic Erica be lunching at Kirby's today? Will she have cocktails at Nexus, gathering place of the beautiful people? Will we see her masterfully complete a modeling shoot in some of the world's most exquisite clothes?

Back in Pine Valley, the anxious audience is often treated to some of the most heartwarming romantic scenes the soaps can conjure up: ultraclean Greg and Jenny vowing their undying love for each other at Pine Valley's skating pond on a beautiful winter night; Erica being lured to a storybook southern mansion to meet Kent Bogard, her secret admirer; Brooke and Tom reconciling passionately in an isolated mountain cabin after an enthusiastic pillow fight.

What probably makes romance so appealing on "AMC," however, is that it's not limited to the young characters. Who can forget the years in which Mona Kane and Charles Tyler patiently waited for Charles to get his freedom from Phoebe? And what about the guilt-ridden affair between upstanding Paul Martin and Ellen Shepard while Paul's wife Ann was still confined to a mental hospital? The mountains of approving fan mail that poured in when Phoebe and Langley got together proved that "AMC" could give its characters many sides—including humor. Watching Phoebe fall—hook, line, and sinker—for the slippery Langley, vowing her love with tears in her eyes, delighted, touched, and tickled the viewers.

WELCOME TO PINE VALLEY

The Citizens

Characters and families have come and gone in Pine Valley since it was conjured up by Agnes Nixon in 1970, but the action has always centered around two core families: the Tylers and the Martins. In a slight departure from the rich family–poor family setup often used in other soaps, both families are far from destitute. The Tylers represent the quintessential Philadelphia Mainline family, with matriarch Phoebe never

missing a chance to remind those in the valley of her DAR background. The Martins, also an old and respected family in the valley, espouse more modest values than the Tylers. Where the Tylers represent the idle rich, the Martins represent the Protestant work ethic and the attitude that family, honesty and fairness, and integrity are worth a million Tyler fortunes. Where the Tylers are the arbiters of good taste in the valley, the Martins are the arbiters of good sense. And, to make the conflicts between the families more believable, the writers have set up the Martins as just about the only residents of Pine Valley who really don't feel either intimidated or envious of the Tylers.

Not all of the Tylers and Martins live in Pine Valley, but they're all connected with the show. Here is a rundown of the major families in "AMC":

The Tylers

Phoebe: Snooty aristocrat par excellence. Phoebe presides over her mainline mansion as if it were Buck-

Ruth Warrick (Phoebe Tyler Wallingford) is the doyenne of Pine Valley. Photo by Ed Geller.

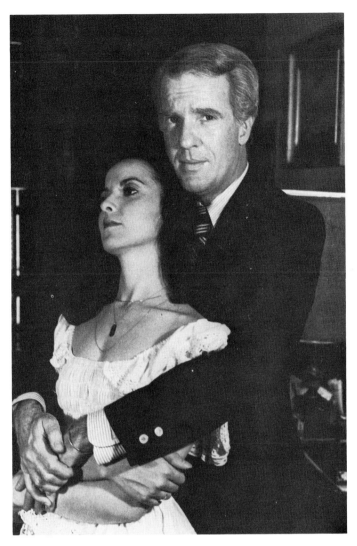

Francesca James and Peter White played the lovers, Kitty and Linc (and later Kelly and Linc) for years. They return occasionally when the Tyler family marks an important milestone. Photo by Bob Deutsch.

ingham Palace and she the queen of England. Always trying to manipulate her family's loves and lives so that they conform to her idea of what is proper and best, she nonetheless has a heart of gold.

Charles: The good doctor, former husband of Phoebe, really just wants to live out a peaceful life in modest surroundings with current wife Mona.

Amy: A liberated woman, Amy was Phoebe and Charles' daughter-in-law and Ruth Martin's sister. Was written out 6 months after "AMC" premiered, when Rosemary Prinz left.

Ann: Frail daughter of Phoebe and Charles, Ann was married to Paul Martin before she died in the early '80s.

Lincoln: Phoebe and Charles' son, attorney Linc is sensible and smart; married to Kelly, he and his wife moved to escape the disapproval and meddling of Phoebe.

Chuck: Grandson of Phoebe and Charles; unlucky in love.

Brooke: Not actually a Tyler, Brooke is Phoebe's niece.

The Martins

Kate: Matriarch and grandmother of the Martin clan, she seems to do little but bake cakes and cookies and treats everyone with the utmost kindness.

Joe: Kate's doctor son, one of the leading figures in Pine Valley.

Ruth: Joe's second wife, a nurse; Amy Tyler's sister.

Jeff: Joe's son from his first marriage, also a doctor; moved to California during the late '70s and hasn't been seen since.

As Dr. Joe Martin, Ray MacDonald heads the Martin family. Photo by Howard Gray.

William Mooney plays attorney Paul Martin.
Photo by Bob Deutsch.

A Tour of the Valley

While Pine Valley is hardly a real place, as is "Ryan's Hope's" setting, it does bear a strong resemblance to real Philadelphia Mainline towns. Pine Valley and its aristocratic residents take great pride in its pre-Revolutionary War origins and in the quality of life one can find there. Pine Valley's location makes it possible for characters to run in to Philadelphia to shop or fly off to New York, where Erica now lives. One of the most curious aspects of Pine Valley's locale is its obvious proximity to "One Life to Live's" Llanview, another southeastern Pennsylvania town.

Pine Valley Motivations

Things can become so complicated in the world of the Tylers and Martins; there is, however, one aspect of the show that provides many of the characters with their primary motivation: social caste.

When Phoebe and Mona were fighting over Charles, Phoebe's anger with Mona was that much greater because Mona sprang from simple stock, while the Tylers were descended from *important* families. More recently the social classes of Pine Valley have clashed among the younger citizens. Greg, who comes from the right side of the tracks, loves Jenny, Opal's daughter. Naturally, his mother, Enid, is furious and has continued to do what she can to encourage Liza and other more socially acceptable young women to torment Jenny and to pursue Greg. The character of Jesse, a nephew of the late Dr. Frank Grant, has also been introduced into the class rivalries among the young. When Jenny made friends with Jesse, Opal, Jenny's backwoods mother, objected only because he was black; it didn't matter that he was the nephew and ward of a doctor. As if that wasn't enough, Jesse was hated by the father of Angie, whom he had secretly married, because lawyer Les didn't want his daughter involved with a "street kid."

It seems notable that "All My Children" in recent years has introduced numerous plots that focus on the excitement of big business. We watch characters like Ellen Dalton and Nina Cortlandt proving that women can make it as executives, and to its credit, "All My Children" has been among those soaps that attempt to show women as capable creatures who, although they would love to have a man as lover, mate, friend, admirer, or patron, are not completely dependent on any male for any length of time.

Paul: Joe's brother, Paul often serves as attorney for characters on both "AMC" and sister soap "One Life to Live."

Mary: A Martin by marriage to Jeff; died long ago.

Tara: Daughter of Joe; she was a major character 10 years ago but left town to move to the northwest with her new husband.

Tad: Adopted son of Joe and Ruth; his natural mother is Opal Gardner.

In the early days of "AMC," many viewers complained that there were too many characters to keep track of. When the show was premiered some of the more important other characters included the Brents; Mona Kane and her trying daughter Erica; Jason Maxwell, who was killed in the series' first murder plot; the Hoffmans; the Grants; and the Kennicotts.

Larry Lau and Kim Delaney play Greg and Jenny, young people from opposite sides of the track who are in love. Photo by Ed Geller.

We also see power-mongers Palmer Cortlandt and Lars Bogard trying to outdo each other in the realm of the huge cosmetics industry and the high-cost world of thoroughbred horses. We see the tough side of modeling through Jenny Gardner and brother Tad Martin. "AMC's" Pine Valley and environs is a thoroughly modern world.

A PEEK AT THE PINE VALLEY ARCHIVES

Cast members—those who have left and those who have stayed—have had a lot to do with what's hap-pened in Pine Valley. Susan Lucci, who plays Erica Kane, almost missed her audition for the soap because it was raining. Larry Keith, another popular actor on "All My Children" during its early years, was supposed to be written out after six months. However, headwriter Nixon found his portrayal of Nick Davis so electrifying that she decided to keep the character around.

Karen Gorney, extremely popular as the first Tara Martin, was dismissed from the series in 1977, when she began taking up precious rehearsal time to make fun of what she felt were poorly written scripts. Interestingly enough, Gorney had just returned to the

The Four Faces of Tara:

Tara No. 1: Karen Gorney, who went on to star in the film Saturday Night Fever, *originated the role of Tara Martin. Photo by Howard Gray.*

Tara No. 2: Stephanie Braxton. Photo by Howard Gray.

Tara No. 3: Nancy Frangione.

Tara No. 4: Mary Lynn Blanks, who currently appears in "As the World Turns" as Dr. Annie Stewart Ward. Photo by Ed Geller.

series a year earlier to take over for Stephanie Braxton. When Gorney was permanently released, Nancy Frangione (now Cecile Cory on "Another World") took over the part and played it until 1979. A year later Mary Lynn Blanks (now Dr. Annie Stewart Ward on "As the World Turns") was cast as Tara, and she played the part until 1981, when the character was written off.

When "All My Children" premiered in 1970, Joe Martin had two sons, Bobby and Jeff. Six months into the show, Bobby left on a skiing trip and was never heard from again. His unexplained departure from the series was a constant source of amusement for the cast during the first few years. If a sudden unexplained noise was heard on the set during rehearsals, Ray MacDonnell, who plays Dr. Joe Martin, would call out, "Bobby, is that you?"

One notable aspect of "AMC" has always been its well-researched storyline. Social and medical issues such as child abuse and the eye problems related to diabetes were presented with much attention paid to accuracy of detail. Nina Cortlandt's eye exams were researched and filmed at Johns Hopkins University Medical Center.

Another memorable storyline focused on a battered wife. Curt was a wife-beater. Leora was a victim. Agnes Nixon, with the keen eye of a social observer, emphasized the *victim* syndrome to the point where it was agonizingly accurate. Beaten wives often come to believe that they get what they deserve, and Leora was no different. There are those who said that the Curt-Leora story should have finished on a grand gesture: either Leora should have beaten or even killed Curt when he came to hurt her again, or she should have humiliated him in some fashion in retaliation for what he'd done to her. Instead, the story simply ended when Leora fled to a women's shelter and Curt fled to Chicago. Perhaps the story treatment was much closer to realism than the more outraged viewers would like to believe.

As often happens in daytime drama, Pine Valley activity has gradually shifted away from core families. In this case it is the staid Martins who have been pushed somewhat to the sidelines, with more trendy characters such as Opal Gardner (who started out as a temporary character but quickly won the hearts and funnybones of the viewers and the support of the network) taking the fore. In the '70s we watched various denizens of the valley seeking out the Martins for advice on just about everything. When they censured

James Mitchell and Taylor Miller (Palmer Cortlandt and his daughter, Nina Cortlandt Warner) brought an important new family to Pine Valley in the '80s. On camera Mitchell plays a (usually) ruthless man. Off camera he's anything but.

As Tom Cudahy, Dick Shoberg plays Erica's ex-husband.

reconciled with her. (It is not unusual in "AMC" to see nice guys finishing first for a change; this may be one of the ways that "AMC" so successfully makes its fans sympathize and identify with its characters.)

In 1982 Jacqueline Babbin took over the producer's job for "All My Children," and the show's look was altered even more. Babbin has concentrated on giving the characters more now-sounding dialogue and on giving the show a more realistic look, matching the clothing, for example, to the characters' situations.

Though "AMC" has moved into the exciting worlds of modeling and tycoons, it has never lost sight of the romance that daytime audiences want. Over the years "AMC" has delivered to the viewers more love, and complications thereof, than they could keep track of. One way "AMC" keeps things hopping is by featuring love triangles. It seems that hardly a relationship has begun and ended without the intervention of a third party. Some of the most famous "AMC" triangles have included:

Phoebe-Charles-Mona

Dack Rambo, as Steve Jacobi, complicated the love lives of Cliff and Nina Warner when he came to Pine Valley to work for Cortlandt Electronics.

the wayward Erica, so did the rest of the town. In the '80s, however, we're more likely to hear Opal condemn the Martins as dull.

The new family to take the forefront of "AMC"—and, in many instances, the opposing stance against Phoebe—is the Cortlandts: tycoon Palmer, beautiful daughter Nina, prodigal wife Daisy/Monique, and Nina's grandmother and the Cortlandt housekeeper, Myra. The Cortlandts represent the powerful world of big bucks and big business that characterizes the latest look of "AMC."

Along the way several other important characters have been penned into the "AMC" scripts. The Cudahy boys—retired football star turned restaurateur Tom and his charming get-rich-quick younger brother Sean—have proved a significant Pine Valley force. Though Sean has disappeared after being convicted of manslaughter, the storyline he dominated was one of the longer and more earth-shattering in recent years. Tom still figures prominently in the plot, playing the nice guy who was hoodwinked into marriage by Erica, then married Brooke, only to be separated and then

Palmer-Chuck-Donna
Estelle-Benny-Billy Clyde
Paul-Ann-Nick
Tara-Chuck-Phil
Jenny-Liza-Greg
Nina-Steve-Cliff
Nina-Cliff-Sybil
Donna-Chuck-Tara
Monique (Daisy)-Palmer-Lars
Erica-Silver-Kent

The Many Loves of Erica

If there is one character whose love life has always been featured on "AMC," it is Erica.

Erica Kane was introduced to "AMC" fans as the daughter of Mona Kane and ex-husband Eric, who was living in Hollywood directing movies when she arrived in Pine Valley to live with her mother. Pine Valley has never been the same. Erica's first conquest was Ted Brent, who died trying to prove that Erica was not the vicious harpy everyone had pegged her as. Even at this early point in "AMC" history it was obvious to viewers that Erica was seeking love from every man she met to try to make up for her father's rejection of her. She next infiltrated the staid Martin family by eloping with their ingenuous son Jeff. When Erica became pregnant and had an abortion, one of "AMC's" most memorable storylines was launched.

Characteristically, Erica was lured away from her dull life with Jeff by dashing Jason Maxwell, who wanted to turn her into a top New York model. (Curiously, a later storyline was almost identical.) Erica fell hard for Jason, asked Jeff for a divorce, and then Jason was murdered, leaving Jeff the apparent culprit. In another twist that was repeated later in "AMC" history, Erica was also suspected of the crime at one point.

When Phil Brent returned to Pine Valley he fell right into the clutches of Erica when he found out Tara

Cheryl Tiegs, Lee Godart (Kent Bogard), and Susan Lucci (Erica Kane) on the set of "All My Children."

In real life, Susan Lucci is married to restauranteur Helmut Huber. They have two children. Photo by Bob Deutsch.

had married Chuck. Again, Erica was dissatisfied, and soon she fell in love with Phil's father, Nick Davis— quite a twist since she had always despised him. Through her need to feel loved and wanted, Erica began to be obsessed with marrying Nick, who loved her but wanted no part of marriage to her. After reneging on his promise to marry Erica, made while she was supposedly on her death bed, Nick fled to Chicago and a new job.

Fortuitously, Tom Cudahy arrived in Pine Valley to open the Goal Post Restaurant as soon as Nick had boarded a plane out of town. Erica laid her sweetness-and-light act on Tom as she never had before, and the sweet ex-jock married her believing that he'd settle down to a perfect life with a perfect wife and lots of kiddies. But, no, Erica had other ideas. Again she was lured to the Big Apple to become a model. When Tom discovered that she had been taking the pill and had no intention of giving up a promising career to have babies, his eyes were opened and he divorced her.

In the meantime, in a rerun of the Jason Maxwell

Larry Keith, as Nick Davis, was one of Erica's earlier loves. Photo by Bob Deutsch.

plot, Erica began to fall for her boss, Brandon Kingsley of Sensuelle, who convinced her he was single so he could get her into bed. During a long battle for Brandon between Erica and long-suffering Sarah Kingsley, Kent Bogard initiated a secret-admirer campaign, complete with expensive anonymous gifts, to lure her into bed and into the lap of the Bogard empire. When Brandon and Sarah took off together for Hong Kong, Erica gave her heart to Kent, who was then the president of Sensuelle. Again, Erica had trouble talking Kent into marriage, and the situation became even more complicated when a con artist named Connie arrived in New York claiming to be Erica's destitute half-sister Silver. Erica took the ugly duckling under her wing, and when ambitious "Silver" turned herself into a swan, she developed a hunger for everything else that was Erica's, including her job and her man. Silver began sleeping with Kent, and when the truth was revealed to Erica, she threatened to kill herself in front of Kent, who was accidentally shot in a struggle for the gun. Eventually, charges of murder were dropped against Erica after "Silver's" story that it had been cold-blooded murder was discredited. Viewers had a good time in the meantime, though, watching the snobby Erica forced to mingle with "hardened criminals" while she was in jail—and to disguise herself as a nun before she was caught.

Erica swore that Kent had been the love of her life, but viewers probably wouldn't bet on that. In mid-1983 she was faced with a man who may not be so easy to push around—the ghostwriter for her upcoming autobiography, who (gasp!) hadn't even heard of Erica before being assigned to the job.

AFFAIRS TO REMEMBER

"AMC's" first two major romances involved characters of disparate ages. Youthful love and youthful disillusionment (Phil Brent and Tara Martin) were contrasted with the middle-aged romantic problems of Charles and Phoebe Tyler and "office wife" Mona Kane. In a switch from the usual setup, it was Mona who played the sympathetic character and Phoebe who denied her husband the basic human needs of warmth, love, and feminine companionship. By the time Phoebe finally agreed to a divorce and freed Charles to marry Mona, the mail from viewers supporting the divorce and remarriage would have made it obvious to any social historian that divorce was no longer anathema to the American public, that the public had become tolerant in ways that weren't apparent

Phil Brent was originally played by Richard Hatch (left), shown here with "All My Children" parents Ruth (Mary Fickett) and Ted (Mark Dawson). Photo by Howard Gray.

earlier. This was a reflection of the growing feelings of social acceptance for situations previously considered intolerable by many. Agnes Nixon caught the sense of change in the land and translated it into a powerful story involving a loveless marriage and loving woman and love-starved man who found each other.

With a vengeful glee in their eyes, viewers soon watched Phoebe fall for a charming con man who presented himself as a scholar. The viewer's knowledge that Phoebe has been hoodwinked made them feel that Phoebe had been punished for her treatment of Charles and Mona and also made the imposing matriarch much more human.

As Ruth Warrick, the veteran actress (she was Mrs. Kane in *Citizen Kane*, among her many other films) put it in her book, *True Confessions of Phoebe Tyler*, describing the turn-about in character:

"Phoebe was no longer a young girl. Life was passing her by. She could either continue to resist what life offered or she could start to live. I'm delighted that we could show that an old woman such as Phoebe is capable of adjusting to change if necessary and that we could also show her as someone who could change her mind about sex. Not very easy for young people sometimes and, certainly, quite difficult for older people.

"When Phoebe went to bed with Langley before they were married, I received mail from women all over the country who told me how happy they were for her and how much they appreciated the fact that

Louis Edmonds, now playing Langley, was Roger Collins on "Dark Shadows." Photo by Ed Geller.

Star-crossed young lovers, Phil and Tara, were played originally by Richard Hatch and Karen Gorney. Photo by Bob Deutsch.

Jack Stauffer originated the role of Chuck Tyler, the third side of the Phil-Tara-Chuck triangle. Photo by Howard Gray.

the show could present such a good case for sex in the lives of older women.''

Phil and Tara's teenage romance had dire repercussions. Tara and Phil slept together before he was shipped off to Vietnam, and by the time he was reported to be an MIA, Tara knew she was pregnant with his child. Torn between her still-painful love for Brent and her need to give her baby the security of a real home and of two parents, she agreed to marry Chuck Tyler, Phoebe and Charles' grandson.

The sad case of Devon, who drank too much, marked an important story that ran through much of 1981 and 1982. A night in a motel room with a young man named Wally was meant to cure her of her inexperience and turn her into the woman with whom Dan would fall in love. Instead, the night turned Devon into a pregnant woman who was carrying an unwanted child.

Devon and Wally were eventually married and she began to care for her baby. Not yet the mature person

she wanted to be, Devon became resentful of the impositions her child made on her life. She turned to drink for an instant resolution and thereby added still another problem to her long list of emotional tribulations.

Ellen Dalton would not become anyone's victim. Married to Mark Dalton, Erica Kane's half-brother, Ellen is very much her own woman. Too bad her daughter, Devon, couldn't have been more like her.

Ellen and Mark have both had love affairs. Mark, a handsome college professor, often finds himself pursued by his female students. Ellen and Mark are invariably involved in marital problems. They obviously love one another. In their case, the road to true love wasn't smooth before they were married, nor has their bumpy experience been modified by marriage. If anything, marriage has revealed deeper areas of misunderstanding. Ellen is a mature woman reveling in her new career as a computer expert and businesswoman. One gets the feeling that Ellen Shepherd Dalton may be the most liberated lady on the soaps. Mark is an insecure younger man who always seems to find himself lured from the path of righteousness, whether by a nubile young coed or by the thrill of cocaine.

Among the myriad other affairs that have marked the lives of so many "All My Children" characters, the following are the most memorable:

1. Chuck married Donna, a former hooker. They divorced, and Donna married Palmer. Donna had a one-night affair with Chuck, which the sterile Palmer realized when Donna became pregnant. As of mid-1983 Donna and Palmer were divorced and she and Chuck were warming up to each other while cooing over their baby boy, who has since died. (Chuck had married and been left by Carrie Sanders.)

2. Youngsters Jenny and Greg love each other but keep letting circumstances split them up.

3. Brooke, once wed to Tom, has returned to Pine Valley and to Tom.

4. Mary and Jeff were in love and were married, but Mary died and Jeff later married a doctor named Chris, with whom he moved to San Francisco.

5. When Opal arrived in Pine Valley she tried to seduce the reserved Paul Martin but failed dismally. Then she had a hilarious affair with sex-starved Langley, who conned her into believing he would marry her when Phoebe died of a terrible disease in the near future. When she found out the truth about Langley, Opal fell in love with electrician Sam Brady who eventually made it clear to Opal that she was a lot of fun but he was in love with Opal's daughter, Jenny. Opal has developed from a character who thought the way to wealth was marriage into an ambitious businesswoman. Opal left Pine Valley in fall 1983.

MURDER/MAYHEM/MYSTERY

"All My Children" has had its share of mystery and violence, though the first murder plot didn't take place until about three years after the series began. Among the more memorable instances are the following:

Mark LaMura (Mark Dalton), off the set.
Photo by Bob Deutsch.

- The first murder ever on "AMC" was the murder of Jason Maxwell, as discussed under Erica's history. The guilty party turned out to be none other than Mona Kane, who had accidentally shot him in a struggle over a gun and blocked it all out until she took an injection of truth serum to get accused Jeff Martin off the hook. (Curiously, in two later incidences on the show, a character was killed accidentally in a struggle over a gun.)

- Another older mystery plot involved Lincoln Tyler and his loves. Lovely Kelly Shea was indicted for drug trafficking and was defended by Linc, who married her after clearing her of the charges.

- During the late '70s the character of Ray Gardner returned to Pine Valley to exact revenge against the Martins, who had "stolen" his son Tad from him and adopted him. Ray raped Ruth Martin and was sent up for the deed but was released through a lucky accident that made him seem a hero. Again he returned to Pine Valley for vengeance against the Martins. A plan to blow up the entire Martin household failed when Ray was killed trying to retrieve the bomb because he found out that his daughter Jenny was inside the house.

- In 1982 the plot that involved Brooke English and her parents' drug smuggling came to a sad end. When Brooke's father (Phoebe's brother) died sud-

Peter Bergman (Dr. Cliff Warner) and Taylor Miller (Nina Cortlandt) during the filming of their TV wedding on "All My Children." The "bride" is obviously being playful in the second picture.

A toasting crowd at Nina Cortlandt's (Taylor Miller) short-lived marriage to Dr. Cliff Warner (Peter Bergman) that took place in 1980. The wedding was taped at Waveny, an estate in New Canaan, Connecticut.

denly, Brooke was told that her father had been a drug runner and, unless she and Tom agreed to take over for him, Brooke's mother, Peg English, would be killed. The plot, in which Peg was kept from the awful "truth" about her husband, was engineered by a mystery voice that gave the name Cobra. As it turned out, Peg was actually Cobra, and it had been Brooke's father who had been an innocent pawn. To make this all easier for Brooke to take, Brooke learned through a hidden letter left by her father that Peg wasn't really her mother at all. Peg was killed trying to murder Brooke, so at least Brooke was relieved from the anguish of trying to under-

stand why her own mother would try to kill her.

- During the late '70s and early '80s Ann Martin was released from a mental hospital and she and Paul, after some struggles, decided they could make a go of their marriage. It all seemed like hearts and flowers for the reunited pair until Ann was killed by a car bomb intended for Paul, who had been cracking down on local drug pushers.

- Concurrent with the rise in importance of the Cortlandt family was the reappearance of Nina's supposedly dead mother Daisy, alias Monique. Daisy secretly made friends with Nina and dallied with some of the local men, including young Sean Cud-

Julia Barr (Brooke English Cudahy).

ahy. Daisy was forced to reveal to Nina who she was when she had to turn evidence against Sean to clear Nina's husband Cliff of the murder of Sybil Thorne. Sean, as in previous "murders," had accidentally shot Sybil in a struggle over the gun he had brought to Sybil's apartment to scare her into keeping quiet about Sean's plans for Nina.

- One very brief "mystery" storyline of the early '80s threatened to reveal Langley's long-kept secret about his past. Ever since the character of Langley was introduced, viewers have been anticipating the fireworks that would fill the sky if Phoebe ever found out that her "professorial" husband is actually Lucky Lenny, the con man. This secret was almost blown when Verla Grubbs, played by the inimitable Carol Burnett, showed up in Pine Valley looking for her long-lost father. Who else could it have been but Lenny/Langley? The martyred Verla agreed not to blow her father's cover, even though she was devastated by her father's unwillingness to acknowledge her.

MILESTONES

"All My Children" was the first soap opera that dealt openly with the most pervading social phenomenon of its time despite the fact that the United States had begun its involvement in Vietnam almost a full decade before the soap's debut. One of the original male characters (Phil Brent) was drafted into the army, sent to Southeast Asia and disappeared. He became an MIA (Missing in Action) statistic. Later Brent was found alive and returned to Pine Valley, USA, but in the meantime the audience had been made to experience through a daytime drama what so many people had already experienced in real life.

"All My Children" not only acknowledged the reality of the war in which every American at the time was involved in one way or another, but it gave recognition and, therefore, subtle but sure approval of the peace movement. One of the characters, Phoebe Tyler (played by Ruth Warrick, of course), spoke sympathetically about the peace movement, while another character actually became involved in the Mothers March for Peace.

Medical Firsts

"All My Children" projects a sense of involvement with the audience that often reaches into the doctor's office and very often into the operating room. A case in point involved the 1974 on-camera plastic surgery procedure followed by a daily on-camera recovery report.

When Eileen Letchworth (Margo) approached Agnes Nixon about having her face done, Nixon broke tradition and suggested that she have the operation on camera and allow the viewers to share the daily examination of her healing face. Some quoted Letchworth as having said at the time that her sense of drama overwhelmed any other hesitation that she might have had. This would be, after all, a first, and what actor could pass up that chance?

Another medical "first" was the dramatization of the tragedy of infant "crib death." Beth, the tiny daughter of Paul and Ann Martin, was found dead in her crib. Her death stunned her parents and nearly shattered their lives. Guilt was assumed. Blame was leveled. Accusations were made.

The response from the public was overwhelming. People whose families endured the agony of losing children in this manner wrote to thank "All My Chil-

Carol Burnett appeared on her favorite soap, "All My Children," for three weeks during April 1983. Here she poses with some members of the cast. Photo by Ed Geller.

dren" for helping to alleviate guilt and for sharing this tragic experience with so many who may have felt so alone in their grief.

Back when Erica was married to Jeff Martin she became pregnant and had an abortion. To minimize the effects of culture shock among those viewers who were still not so sure about some of the more relaxed attitudes of the '70s and to reassure the sponsors that there would be no backlash in the supermarket from outraged audiences, Agnes Nixon arranged for Erica to find a mental copout for her actions. She was permitted to have a loss of conscious memory about her experience. She told herself that she had had a miscarriage. But Agnes Nixon knows that no lie is as disturbing as the lie we tell ourselves. In time Erica had to face the truth. When she did, the audience approved. The abortion was accepted by the viewers and by Erica and another breakthrough was marked.

WHO'S WHO IN PINE VALLEY

Original Cast

Actor	*Character*
MICHAEL BERSELL	**Bobby Martin**
MARK DAWSON	**Ted Brent**
PAUL DUMONT	**Lincoln Tyler**
MARY FICKETT	**Ruth Brent**
HUGH FRANKLIN	**Dr. Charles Tyler**
KAREN GORNEY	**Tara Martin**
RICHARD HATCH	**Phillip Brent**
HILDA HAYNES	**Lois Sloane**
FRANCES HEFLIN	**Mona Kane**
LARRY KEITH	**Nick Davis**
SUSAN LUCCI	**Erica Kane**
RAY MAC DONNELL	**Dr. Joseph Martin**
ROSEMARY PRINZ	**Amy Tyler**
JACK STAUFFER	**Chuck Tyler**
CHRISTINE THOMAS	**Kate Martin**
DIANA deVEGH	**Anne Tyler**
CHRISTOPHER WINES	**Jeff Martin**

First Air Date: January 5, 1970

Write to "All My Children" c/o ABC-TV, 1330 Avenue of the Americas, New York, NY 10019.

A Directory of Recent Characters*

Kent Bogard: Co-owner of Sensuelle Products; son of Lars; killed by the gun Erica was threatening to use on herself. *Lee Godart*

Lars Bogard: Co-owner of Sensuelle; competing with Palmer Cortlandt over Daisy; interested in Erica. *Robert Milli*

Liza Colby: A rich daughter of unhappy parents, Liza once competed with Jenny for Greg; involved with Tad. *Marcy Walker*

Daisy Cortlandt: Palmer's former wife and mother of Nina. *Gillian Spencer*

Donna Cortlandt: Former hooker; ex-wife of Chuck Tyler, also divorced from Palmer Cortlandt; had a child by Chuck when wed to Palmer. *Candice Earley*

Palmer Cortlandt: Wealthy and ruthless but charming; he's Nina's dad and Daisy's and Donna's ex. *James Mitchell*

*The actors/actresses who currently play these major roles are in italics.

Erica Kane Brent Martin Cudahy: Top model and former spokeswoman for Sensuelle; former wife of Phil Brent, Jeff Martin, and Tom Cudahy; daughter of the late Eric Kane and Mona Kane Tyler; half-sister of Mark and Silver. *Susan Lucci*

Brooke English Cudahy: Phoebe's niece; formerly involved with Dan Kennicott; reconciled with husband Tom Cudahy; a top reporter. *Julia Barr*

Tom Cudahy: Once wed to Erica and now to Brooke; brother of Sean. *Richard Shoberg*

Sean Cudahy: Tom's brother; formerly Daisy's lover; Sybil Thorne's killer. *Alan Dysert*

Mark Dalton: Erica's half-brother; a composer and pianist married to Ellen Dalton. *Mark LaMura*

Ellen Dalton: A business woman married to Mark; mother of Devon; grandmother of Bonnie. *Kathleen Noone*

Myrtle Fargate: A former carny woman who knows the true identity of Langley Wallingford; she owns a boutique. *Eileen Herlie*

Eileen Herlie (Myrtle Fargate) appeared with Richard Burton in Hamlet.

Jenny Gardner: A teenager who has launched a modeling career; Opal and Ray's daughter; loves Greg; Jesse and Angie's best friend. *Kim Delaney*

Opal Gardner: Formerly a maid at the Wallingford home; owner of a beauty parlor; Jenny's mother. *Dorothy Lyman*

Carl Grant: Young son of Nancy and the late Dr. Frank Grant. *Billy Mack*

Nancy Grant: Carl's mother; Frank's widow; a social worker; Jesse's aunt by marriage. *Lisa Wilkinson*

Jesse Hubbard: An orphaned teenager; Carl's cousin; Frank's nephew; Jenny's friend; divorced from Angie. *Darnell Williams*

Steve Jacobi: Lawyer who works for Cortlandt Industries; lives with Nina. *Dack Rambo*

Silver Kane: Posed as Erica's half-sister (real name was Connie). *Deborah Goodrich*

Joe Martin: A doctor; husband of Ruth; father of Joey, Jeff, and Tara; Paul's brother; adoptive father of Tad. *Ray Mac Donnel*

Paul Martin: A lawyer; widower of Ann Tyler Martin; Joe's brother. *William Mooney*

Ruth Martin: Joe's wife, a nurse; adoptive mother of Phil and Tad; mother of Joey. *Mary Fickett*

Tad Martin: Son of Opal and Ray, adopted by Joe and Ruth. *Michael Knight*

Myra Murdoch: Daisy's mother; Nina's grandmother; Palmer's housekeeper. *Elizabeth Lawrence*

Enid Nelson: Greg's mother. *Natalie Ross*

Greg Nelson: Rich teen in love with Jenny. *Laurence Lau*

Benny Sago: Estell's widower; father of Emily; Phoebe's chauffeur; a reformed gambler. *Vasili Bogazianos*

Carrie Sanders: Chuck's former wife. *Andrea Moar*

Charles Tyler: A doctor; Mona's husband; ex-mate of

Mary Fickett (Ruth Martin), here with Larry Parks.

Phoebe; father of Lincoln and the late Ann Tyler Martin; Chuck's grandfather. *Richard Van Vleet*

Langley Wallingford: Phoebe's husband; formerly carny con artist "Lucky Lenny;" pretends to be a professor. *Louis Edmonds*

Phoebe Tyler Wallingford: Langley's wife; ex-wife of Charles; Chuck's grandmother; Lincoln's mother; mother of the late Ann Tyler Martin; aunt of Brooke English Cudahy; Pine Valley's *grand dame. Ruth Warrick*

Cliff Warner: A doctor; divorced from Nina Cortlandt; father of Bobby through his affair with the late Sybil Thorne. *Peter Bergman*

Nina Cortlandt Warner: Divorced from Cliff; Bobby's adoring adoptive mother; Palmer and Daisy's daughter; involved with Steve Jacobi. *Taylor Miller*

Lisa Wilkinson is Nancy Grant.
Her singing talent was incorporated into a 1980s storyline.

Ellen Dalton, sometimes called soap's most modern woman, is played by Kathleen Noone. Photo courtesy Daytime TV *magazine.*

Larry Fleischman played Benny.

3

Another World (NBC)

On May 4, 1964, the National Broadcasting Company aired the first segment of "Another World." Set in the fictional town of Bay City, the soap told the story of the Matthews family and their relationships with the Baxters. William Prince, the fine film actor, played Ken Baxter, and Nicholas Pryor was Tom Baxter. In time the Baxters faded from the scene but the Matthews clan continued strong.

When "Another World" premiered the announcer opened with, "We do not live in this world alone, but in a thousand other worlds." "Another World" was one of the last shows created by Irna Phillips. Assisting Irna Phillips in the creation of "Another World" was William J. Bell, who went on to create "The Young and the Restless" in the mid-70s. Coincidentally, the show's first producer, Allen Potter, is also its current producer (he has also produced "Guiding Light"). Tom Donovan, who went on to produce "General Hospital" during the mid-70s, just before Gloria Monty took over,

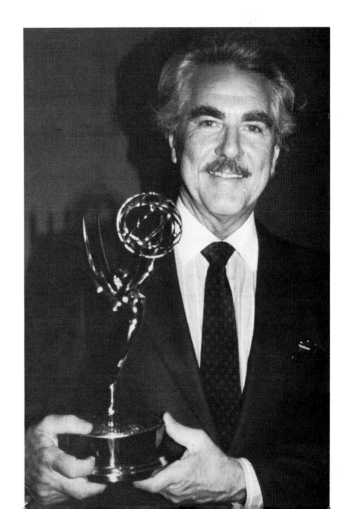

Douglass Watson won an Emmy for his portrayal of publishing tycoon Mackenzie Cory. Photo by Bob Deutsch.

was "Another World's" first director, along with Norman Hall.

"Another World" was born into a less innocent time than its predecessors. John F. Kennedy had been assassinated less than six months earlier. The conflict in Vietnam was heating up. There was talk, again, of Cuba's growing involvement in South American politics. The so-called apathy of the 1950s was turning on itself to produce a growing dissent against the status quo in civil rights and the developing military ethos.

Since rapid change invariably becomes a wind that scoops up all lagging social forces in its path, several issues were beginning to demand recognition and resolution. The growing women's liberation movement produced a demand for the right to regulate one's own reproductive capacities. Abortion, long a part of the medical netherworld, was becoming a matter of open discussion and demand.

At the time, a critic of daytime soaps recalled: "This soap opera ("Another World") will either be yanked off the air within a year or it will be a rousing success . . . .(It) has the ability to make someone mad at it some of the time. . . ."

WELCOME TO BAY CITY

The Citizens

There's been such upheaval on "Another World," especially in the last several years, that it would be impossible even to list all the so-called major characters here. Of the core families that have been featured, the Matthews and the Corys are probably the most exemplary.

Although men figure rather well in "Another World," this soap has never lost touch with the realization that strong women make for strong soap opera stories.

The Corys

There are several interesting younger men on "Another World," but the dominant male remains the silver-maned old lion, Mackenzie Cory, played by stage veteran Douglass Watson. A publishing tycoon, he either directs or becomes involved in the experiences of most of the characters on the series, including the young lions: Sandy, his beloved illegitimate son; and Jamie, his equally beloved stepson (offspring of Steve and Rachel Frame). Mac, as he's called on the show,

is also the stepfather of Rachel's son, Matthew, born of a rape in which Rachel had become Mitch Blake's bed partner in an effort to get information that would free Mac of a threat to his life. Mac is the sire, also, of the lovely Iris Bancroft Carrington.

Sandy and Jamie are as fond of each other as if they were flesh and blood siblings. For a while each thought he was the father of the child born to the soap's currently reigning young bitch, Cecile. Each was prepared to accept the possibility that the other brother was the father. Stout fellows, they.

The Matthews

Irna Phillips' original conception of the Matthews family called for the "AW" clan to be friends of "ATWT's" Hughes family. When "Another World" became an NBC soap the plan to make Bay City a neighboring town of Oakdale had to be scrapped.

The NBC Matthews clan was headed by two brothers, William and James, and their families. The cast included other relatives as well, but these peripheral characters—Grandma Matthews, for example—were phased out quickly.

James and William both work for an accounting firm, but while William's family was rich and classy, James and his family fell into the middle class. William and wife Liz had two children, who were left fatherless when William died long ago. Not long after, this branch of the Matthews family was written out, leaving Jim and family to lead the "AW" action.

Jim and Mary had three children—Alice, Pat, and Russ, who became a doctor. As fans will remember, Alice became the most fascinating member of the family in the '70s through her stormy triangle with Steve Frame and Rachel Davis. In recent years, the Matthews family has all but vanished from Bay City.

Other major characters have included John Randolph (Pat's husband), and his daughter Lee; attorney Mike Bauer, and his daughter Hope; salt-of-the-earth Ada and Ernie Downs, and Ada's brother Sam; Missy Palmer; Steve and Jamie Frame; Walter Curtin; Eliot and Iris Carrington; Gil and Tim McGowan; Willis Frame; and many others. Rachel Davis, who later became a major part of "AW" and the wife of Mac Cory, is discussed in full in Bay City history.

More than any other soap at the time, "Another World's" characters were tailored specifically to fit the personalities of the actors playing the parts. When Harding Lemay took over as headwriter in 1971 he

Constance Ford plays Ada.

dispensed with this practice and began providing the characters with psychological motivations for their behavior. Actors who weren't able to meet the new demands put on them were quickly dismissed, regardless of their popularity with the viewers.

This attitude was markedly different from that of writers for many other series. On "Ryan's Hope" the writers, with lots of contributions from the actors, have gradually developed a picture of the ideal Mary, Siobhan, Pat, and Frank; when they had the right person for the right part, they knew it. On many other daytime dramas certain actors and actresses have become such stars that they have been frantically restored to scripts after heated protests from fans who couldn't bear to part with their favorite soap people; in other cases temporary roles have become as permanent as soap characters get, and peripheral characters have

been brought into the center of the action. When actresses such as Jacqueline Courtney and Beverly Penberthy were released from "AW" the fans were horrified—and mystified. (For more inside information on these cast changes, see Chapter 15, Behind the Scenes.)

BAY CITY HISTORY

Bay City might be nicknamed "the city with many faces." There have been so many different personalities or looks to this show since it premiered that viewers of today undoubtedly wouldn't recognize the "typical" happenings of the old Bay City. Briefly, these are the significant events that molded "Another World" into what it is and has been:

1. Irna Phillips' interest in tailoring characters to meet the personalities of the performers set the pattern for "AW" for many years.

2. During Agnes Nixon's tenure as headwriter, she created the famous Alice/Steve/Rachel triangle.

3. When Harding Lemay took over as headwriter many of Phillips' star actors and actresses were removed from the cast.

4. "AW" was expanded to an hour in length.

5. The writers and producers decided to turn the show's focus on Rachel and made the character sympathetic.

6. The show was unsuccessful in expanding to 90 minutes.

7. Beverly Penberthy, who provided continuity as the only link to the show's past, was fired.

Without relating all the details contained in the Bay City archives, we can take a look at the complex lives of Alice and Rachel, the two female stars that served as the focus of Bay City activity for years. Jaqueline Courtney played Alice Matthews Frame for 11 years before being snapped up by "One Life to Live" upon her dismissal from "AW," and she was the light of the viewers' life. Like most soap heroines of the '60s, Alice was demure (the blonde hair helped) and lovely— and unlucky in love. In fact, Alice's postponed wedding may have kept viewers on the edge of their seats longer than any other romantic plot.

After Courtney left "Another World" it was revealed that writer Harding Lemay wanted the character of Rachel to become the hub of Bay City happenings. To accomplish this, Rachel had to evolve into a multidimensional character, instead of remaining merely the bitch from the seedy part of town. When

Rachel married Mac Cory, for example, she did an almost complete turnabout to become a sympathetic character. This type of soap opera device would probably never go over with the viewers were it not for the fact that, in this case, the audience was so fond of Mac Cory that fans could believe he would be able to transform his young wife.

When Harding Lemay left "Another World" in 1979 he felt that the producers were trying to emulate the success of such popular youthful soaps as "The Young and the Restless" and "All My Children" by choosing to focus on younger characters. Although "Another World" has undergone a change of producers since then, it seems apparent that, despite the show's occasional low ratings, the producers hope that the younger characters will take "Another World" back to the top.

Agnes Nixon had started writing for "Another World" in 1967. When she created Rachel she based the character on Erica Kane from "All My Children." Although "All My Children" had yet to premiere, Agnes Nixon had begun working on the outline for the show back in 1965, while still writing for another Procter & Gamble soap, "Guiding Light." It was rumored in the early '70s that when Robin Strasser left the role of Rachel for the second and final time, Susan Lucci (Erica Kane) was offered the part.

Thus the stage is set for a look at the loves of Alice and Rachel:

Alice Matthews Frame was played by Jacquie Courtney for 11 years. Photo courtesy **Daytime TV** *magazine.*

Alice Matthews Frame

1. Alice fell in love with Steve Frame, who knew at the time that Alice's sister-in-law, Rachel, was going to have his baby.

2. Alice and Steve were engaged.

3. Alice broke off the engagement when she found out about Rachel's pregnancy.

4. Alice and Steve reconciled and married.

5. Alice was set up by Rachel's father to find Rachel and Steve together.

6. Alice left Steve.

7. Alice stayed away from Bay City for months and left Steve to Rachel's clutches.

8. Alice divorced Steve so he could marry Rachel.

9. Steve discovered the setup engineered by Rachel's father and divorced Rachel.

10. Alice was left alone again after only a few days of remarriage to Steve, who went to prison for bribing a witness in his divorce trial.

11. Alice cracked under the strain of Steve's internment and the secret she had kept from him that she couldn't have children.

12. Rachel told Steve about Alice's secret, and Alice began to return to sanity.

13. Alice and Steve were happily reunited.

14. Steve apparently died, and Alice adopted Sally Spencer.

15. Steve's brother Willis and his lover Carol plotted to rob Alice of the Frame riches, but failed.

16. Alice remarried to Ray Gordon.

17. Alice got involved with Mac Cory.

18. Steve returned to Bay City and he and Alice got together again.

19. Eventually Steve fell for Rachel; when Alice caught on she broke off her engagement with Steve.

It was during this period—when Steve returned to

As Steve Frame, George Reinholt was one of daytime's most popular lovers until both he and Jacquie Courtney (Alice) were dismissed from "Another World." Photo by Howard Gray.

town—that the shift in character emphasis was being engineered. With Steve in love with Rachel, Alice went off to study medicine. And not long after, Steve was killed (for real this time—his body was recovered from a demolished car instead of disappearing in a river, and the viewers were convinced he was gone for good), and as of 1983 there seemed to be little chance that Alice would ever come back.

Rachel Davis Matthews Clark Frame Cory

This is how things developed in Rachel's life:

1. In the beginning, she was married to Russ.
2. She became pregnant by Steve Frame.
3. Realizing Steve was the father of her baby, Russ divorced Rachel.
4. Rachel married Ted Clarke, a drug pusher.
5. Rachel divorced Ted Clarke.
6. Rachel schemed to get Steve back.
7. Rachel contributed to Alice's miscarriage.
8. Rachel succeeded in getting closer to Steve when

Alice left town.

9. Wanting to be closer to his son Jamie, Steve married Rachel.
10. Steve realized Rachel was partly responsible for Alice's miscarriage.
11. Steve divorced Rachel.
12. Rachel met Mac Cory, a wealthy businessman.
13. Rachel fell in love with Mac.
14. Rachel married Mac.
15. Iris, Mac's daughter, tried to break up their marriage.
16. Believing Rachel had been having an affair with Philip, Mac left her.
17. Mac realized he was wrong and won Rachel back.
18. Mac became jealous of Rachel's sculpting career.
19. Mac and Rachel broke up again.
20. Rachel and Mac cleared up their differences.
21. Rachel had a baby daughter named Amanda.
22. Rachel disapproved of Jamie's relationship with Blaine.
23. Rachel broke up their relationship.

Victoria Wyndham as Rachel.

24. Disapproving of Rachel's actions, Mac divorced her.

25. Mac became involved with and married Janice, Steve Frame's sister.

26. Rachel realized Janice was trying to poison Mac.

27. Rachel agreed to sleep with Mitch to confirm her suspicions.

28. Rachel managed to save Mac's life.

29. Rachel and Mac remarried.

30. Rachel discovered she was pregnant by Mitch.

31. Realizing Rachel was pregnant with his child, Mitch tried to resume their relationship.

32. Getting into a fight with Mitch, Rachel was accused of his murder.

33. It was discovered that Mitch hadn't been murdered.

34. Rachel and Mac broke up once again.

35. Mac successfully sued for custody of Amanda.

36. Mac became involved with Alice.

37. Steve Frame returned to town.

38. Rachel and Steve were involved in a construction accident.

39. Rachel and Steve discovered they loved each other.

40. Rachel and Steve made plans to marry.

41. Steve was finally killed in a car accident.

42. Rachel was blinded.

43. Mac helped Rachel accept her blindness.

44. Rachel's sight was restored.

45. Rachel renewed her romance with Mac.

In August of 1983 Rachel and Mac were married in a double-ring marriage ceremony along with Sandy and Blaine.

The only way to summarize Bay City's more recent history is to say that it has been inconsistent. In the late '70s and early '80s this show was revamped so many times that faithful viewers weren't sure they were watching the same drama. "AW's" low point probably occurred when the show began to exhibit the characteristics of a "General Hospital" clone. Besides moving almost entirely away from love stories, which had always been its meat, the show killed off, in one way or another, some of its most popular characters and most critically acclaimed cast members. Perhaps the dismissal of Jacquie Courtney and George Reinholt was prophetic, because by the '80s the Matthews Family, for example, had all but disappeared from the scripts. Courtney has been called the quintessential Alice, and even though the new Steve (David Canary) proved to be popular, the character was axed.

The change began with the death of matriarch Mary

Matthews; also to disappear were Russ and Pat. Beverly Penberthy's Pat was such a good character that all involved were shocked by the writers' and producers' decision to write her out. Finally, Jim Matthews was written out when actor Hugh Marlowe died.

An interesting note on the newer face of "Another World":

Cecile, who always believed she was the daughter of a French nobleman and then found out she's the illegitimate daughter of a charming scamp, is the younger version of what Rachel used to be on the soap: the scheming, conniving, amoral tramp who, when she trips up, seems to fall no farther than into some new admirer's bed.

Beverly Penberthy was so popular as Pat Randolph that she had to hold a press conference to explain to her fans why she had been dismissed from "Another World." Photo by Howard Gray.

"Another World" is facing its 20th year on the air with some anxieties about recent low ratings. In this photo several stars pose with crew members: At right, Steve Schnetzer (Cass) looks over Constance Ford's (Ada) shoulder. In the background (between the man holding the cake and the white-coated woman) is Gail Brown, who plays Clarice Ewing. Left of Gail is Linda Dano (Felicia Gallant), holding Ms. B. B. Dano, her 17-year-old papillon dog, who always goes to work with her. Photo by Bob Deutsch.

AFFAIRS TO REMEMBER

Romantic entanglements have marked each of the soaps 20 years. Some of them include Rachel's passion plays with Russ, Ted, Mac, Mitch, and Steve; Mac Cory's involvements with Rachel, Elena, Alice, and others; Alice's adventures with Steve and Ray, the ex-husband of her friend, Olive, and Alice's desires for Willis, who wound up marrying another Frame, Gwen.

Former prostitutes such as Clarice and Blaine have gone through several bed-hopping experiences. Clarice, however, settled down by marrying Blaine's brother, Larry, while Blaine is finding true love with her husband Sandy. In the past, Blaine was likely to

think of herself as somehow jinxed by Cupid, because each time someone promises something nice, some cad causes the poor lady more problems. Cecile, for example, almost made Blaine believe that she was mad after hiring a nasty woman named Alma to play *Gaslight* tricks on the girl.

Rachel and Mac have had a rough time, as exhibited by the preceding history of Rachel. Each time Mac seems poised to pick someone else out of the pack and forget Rachel forever, he comes back and hovers around her waiting until she agrees to try marriage with him again. Douglass Watson says of Mac's role: "From the point of view of an actor, I wouldn't want it any other way. There's nothing so deadly boring as

Judy Barcroft has played Lenore Curtin on "Another World," as well as Ann Tyler Davis Martin on "All My Children," and Barbara on "Ryan's Hope." She's also served as stand-in on "As the World Turns." Photo by Howard Gray.

a completely contented character. Conflict makes a role and a production interesting. . . . If anything I would like to see Mac involved in more romantic storylines."

Iris Bancroft (Beverlee McKinsey) stirred lots of interest during her tenure on "Another World" and lent some class to "Texas" as well. As the daughter of Mac Cory, she could command and demand. Even discovering the fact that Mac was her out-of-wedlock father didn't diminish her ego one whit. She has done her best to ruin the marriage of her father and Rachel, among others.

Other romances that tantalized the viewers included these:

John and Pat Randolph: In characteristic "AW" fashion, they had many successive break-ups and make-ups.

Bill and Missy Matthews: Bill died, again typical of "AW," shortly after he and his wife had finally found happiness.

Walter and Lenore Curtin: The typical May-December problems plagued them.

Iris and Eliot Carrington: Divorce was inevitable.

Ada and Gil McGowan: Ada was happy with her second husband, a policeman, until he was killed in the line of duty.

MURDER/MAYHEM/MYSTERY

There has been a lot of mayhem—in front of the camera and behind the scenes—in "Another World." Here's a rundown of some of the most mysterious happenings:

• *The murder of Danny Fargo.* Missy, who had fallen in with a desperate character after running away from the truth about her parentage, was accused of

Surgeon Russ Matthews (played by David Bailey) married singer Tracy deWitt (played by Janice Lynde) in a 1980 "Another World" episode.

killing Danny. The real culprit was revealed to be Danny's old girl friend.

- *The playboy and the ex-DA.* The part of Wayne Addison and Walter Curtin engaged in shady deals in Bay City.
- *The death of Wayne Addison.* Lenore Curtin was accused of this murder but acquitted after being defended eloquently by husband Walter, who eventually confessed to her that he had done the deed. He died before he could turn himself in, and his widow kept the secret until she left town much later.
- *The machinations of Iris Carrington.* Iris has always been a troublemaker, and she's never been able to hold onto a man, including her father, Mac Cory. At one point Iris had a breakdown, which conveniently convinced husband Eliot not to go through with charging her with bugging his apartment to spy on him and Alice. Years later Iris hired someone to break up the marriage of her father and Rachel, whom she'd always resented.
- *The death of Mitch.* A few years ago Rachel was accused and convicted of killing Mitch Blake, the man who raped her and fathered a child with her. However, while Rachel sat in jail and thought of life behind bars as her ultimate destiny, it was discovered that the body found in the barn, which Rachel was supposed to have burned down to kill her erstwhile rapist/lover, was *not* Mitch's after all. It was that of a poor vagrant who set a fire to keep warm and accidentally set fire to the entire structure.
- *The death of Kirk.* Iris was suspected of murder, when one of her many lovers, Kirk Laverty, died under suspicious circumstances. Although someone else was brought to trial (and later acquitted), Iris remained a prime suspect until her loyal maid, Vivian, and her always-loving but perpetually cuckolded husband at that time, Brian Bancroft, found the evidence that cleared her completely.
- *The attempted murder of Mac.* Janice Frame, who lured Mac from Rachel and married him, wanted his body interred six feet under so that she could inherit the Cory fortune and share it with her lover, Mitch Blake. Rachel suspected her ex-husband's current wife of having murderous intentions and, with Mitch's connivance, got the evidence that nipped Janice's plan in the bud.
- *The mysterious movie incident.* Jamie Frame wrote a book about Bay City and a movie was produced from that book. The filming took place in town and

Beverlee McKinsey was Iris Carrington on "Texas" after playing the role in "Another World's" Bay City. Photo by Bob Deutsch.

several harrowing experiences occurred until the producer, Milo, was unmasked as the man who was responsible for the problems.

Meanwhile, political corruption emanating from the Mayor's office was tackled by the intrepid pair of Blaine and Sandy (Blaine and Jamie were no longer lovers at this time) and vice was evicted from city hall.

- *The child custody battle.* Vice and visciousness also surrounded Cecile's attempts to gain custody of her daughter by Sandy in order to win control of a fortune left in a trust for the child. During a custody trial Cecile announced that Jamie was the real father, and not until the blood test proved otherwise was she prepared to acknowledge the truth.

Christopher Rich plays Sandy.

BAY CITY MILESTONES

Abortion was not the first social shocker produced by "Another World." Although it wasn't alone in maintaining a prostitution storyline, it did introduce the concept of male prostitution by having the character of Sandy Alexander Cory admit that he was once a call boy in Las Vegas.

On a less shocking level, "Another World" was one of the first soaps to make use of the off-camera talents of one of its stars in on-camera segments. Victoria Wyndham is, in her private life, a well-known sculptor. When one sees Rachel puttering with clay and putty knife on screen, one should know that those sculpted pieces really were made by her in her upstate New York studio.

In 1982 "Another World" introduced the successful middle-aged pregnancy. ("The Doctors" had one of its characters, Maggie, become pregnant in mid-life, but Maggie had a miscarriage.) The character Clarice Ewing underwent amniocentesis to determine whether her unborn baby would be normal. The tests were indeterminate and Clarice faced a choice: abort or risk bearing an abnormal child. Clarice carried her preg-

Two of "Another World's" stalwarts: Gail Brown (left), sister of actress Karen Black, who plays the role of a reformed hooker-turned-conventional wife and mother, Clarice; and Irene Dailey (Liz Matthews), the real-life sister of the late Dan Dailey. Photo by Ed Geller.

In an unusual twist, Nick Costa played Robert Delaney on "Somerset" before taking his character to "Another World," which spawned "Somerset." Photo by Howard Gray.

nancy through and produced a healthy baby.

In 1975 "Another World" was the first soap to expand to an hour. By experimenting with the new format, "Another World" set the tone for subsequent soaps that expanded to an hour. "AW's" milestone move in 1979 to a 90-minute format, while Fred Silverman was president of NBC, was not as successful, however. "Another World" returned to its one-hour format in 1980.

"Another World" is also the first, and only soap, to spin off other soaps. In 1970, "Another World—Somerset" premiered. On the same day that "Somerset" premiered on NBC, ABC premiered "Best of Everything" and "A World Apart." ABC's were quickly canceled. "Somerset" was canceled in 1976 to make way for yet another spin-off from "Another World." This one was created by Harding Lemay and was called "Friends and Lovers." Disappointed by the show's low ratings, NBC temporarily took it off the air. When it returned six months later, it was retitled "For Richer, For Poorer." Less than a year later it was canceled for good. In 1980 "Another World" spun off daytime TV's first original one-hour soap, "Texas." Despite changes in producers and writers, the program's ratings remained consistently low. Finally, in 1983, NBC canceled the show.

Lahoma Vane Lucas was played by Ann Wedgeworth on both "Another World" and defunct spinoff "Somerset." Among her many other credits are a role on CBS's nighttime spoof "Filthy Rich." Photo by Howard Gray.

Jordan Charney played Sam Lucas on "Another World." His other soap credits include stints as Vinnie Wolek on "One Life to Live" and as Dr. Katz on "General Hospital"; he also played a part on "Somerset." In 1983 he was a regular on ABC's nighttime program "Three's Company." Photo by Howard Gray.

WHO'S WHO IN BAY CITY

Original Cast

Actor	*Character*
VERA ALLEN	**Grandma Matthews**
JOHN BEAL	**Jim Matthews**
LIZA CHAPMAN	**Janet Matthews**
JACQUELINE COURTNEY	**Alice Matthews**
SARAH CUNNINGHAM	**Liz Matthews**
VIRGINIA DWYER	**Mary Matthews**
JOE GALLISON	**Bill Matthews**
WILLIAM PRINCE	**Ken Baxter**
NICHOLAS PRYOR	**Tom Baxter**
CAROL ROUX	**Melissa Palmer**
JOEY TRENT	**Russ Matthews**
SUSAN TRUSTMAN	**Pat Matthews**

First Air Date: May 4, 1964.

Write to "Another World" c/o NBC TV, 30 Rockefeller Plaza, New York, NY 10020.

A Directory of Recent Characters*

Brian Bancroft: Iris' former husband, a lawyer. *Paul Stevens*

Iris Bancroft: Mac Cory's illegitimate daughter; former wife of Brian Bancroft; she's been Iris Cory Bancroft Carrington Wheeler. *Beverlee McKinsey*

Cecile dePoulignanc Cory: Jamie's ex-lover; Sandy's ex-wife; Elena's and Louis's daughter; Maggie's mother. *Nancy Frangione*

Mackenzie Cory: Top man of Cory Publishing: Father of Amanda and Sandy; stepfather of Jamie and Matthew. *Douglass Watson*

Sandy Alexander Cory: Mac's illegitimate son; Jamie's step-brother; Amanda's half-brother; Cecile's ex; father of Maggie; Blaine's husband. *Christopher Rich*

Rachel Davis: Four times wed to and three times divorced from Mac Cory; formerly wed to Steve Frame; mother of Jamie, by Steve; mother of Amanda, with Mac; mother of Matthew, by Mitch. *Victoria Wyndham*

Elena dePoulignanc: Posed as Cecile's aunt but really her out-of-wedlock mother. *Maeve McGuire*

*The actors/actresses who currently play these major roles are in italics.

Blaine Ewing: Former prostitute; Jamie's ex-wife; Sandy's wife. *Laura Malone*

Clarice Ewing: Larry's wife. *Gail Brown*

Jean Ewing: Blaine's and Larry's mother finally turned up on screen in March of 1983 and died in August of 1983. *Betty Miller*

Larry Ewing: Blaine's brother; Clarice's husband. *Rick Porter*

James Frame: Son of Rachel and the late Steve Frame; half-sibling to Amanda and Matthew; Sandy's stepbrother; Blaine's ex-husband; Cecile's ex-lover; a writer and film maker. *Stephen Yates*

Sally Frame: Adopted daughter of Alice and Steve Frame. *Jennifer Runyon*

Liz Matthews: Alice's aunt and a reliable confidante; frequent rival of Rachel. *Irene Dailey*

Ada McGowan: Rachel's mother. *Constance Ford*

Nancy McGowan: Rachel's sister; a recurring role. *Danielle J. Burns*

Susan Sher: Liz' daughter; a recurring role. *Lynn Milgrim*

Bill Boggs, daytime talk show host, has appeared on "Another World" as a TV talk show host.

Dorothy Lyman (left), now on "All My Children," and Jennifer Leak were both on "Another World" for several years. Photo by Ed Geller.

4

As the World Turns (CBS)

"As the World Turns" debuted on April 2, 1956. It was the first half-hour daytime series on television. In 1975 it was expanded to a full hour.

The show describes itself as "the day-to-day story of the conflicts and happenings that affect several closely related families in an American community."

"ATWT" has always taken a unique approach to producing a soap opera. When it was introduced to the public by creator Irna Phillips the viewers shunned it, and the sponsors were sure this was due to the utter lack of happenings in Oakdale, U.S.A. Unlike other soaps, the show's storylines stayed completely away from the usual traumas that affect daytime characters: nobody died, nobody got pregnant, nobody came down with an exotic disease. During its first year "As the World Turns' " unique approach was rewarded by abysmal ratings from the viewers. But by its second year it was right at the top and remained there for years.

At first it seemed that the audience would probably prefer an afternoon nap to watching principals Nancy and Chris Hughes drone on about family concerns in their kitchen. But, as it turned out, writer Phillips was correct to follow her instincts and give the female audience what she thought they wanted. Phillips gave those women long closeups of the speakers' faces and left long pauses in the dialogue. And, surprisingly, rather than bore the audience, such techniques proved to fascinate them. Combined with the strict, wholesome midwestern values Phiillips injected into the show, they contributed to an ideal formula. "ATWT" appealed to women who really wanted to become part of the characters' lives—to be in on all their intimate and personal discussions, to catch them in their introspective moments, to read their faces so they could judge their worth, identify with their dilemmas, learn to love or hate them.

Of course, even popular "ATWT" was forced to

Cast members celebrate the anniversary of "As the World Turns" in 1981 (left to right): Ann Sward, Mary Linda Rapelye, Anthony Herrera, and Margaret Colin.

change with the times, so the provincial mores have for the most part been buried along with bobbie socks and James Dean. But "ATWT" probably survived the revolutionary times of the '60s and '70s a little more intact than some of the other older soaps. This is in part attributable to a fine cast and in part to fortuitous changes in writing staffs that have successfully brought "ATWT" in line with the times.

WELCOME TO OAKDALE

The Citizens

It all started with the middle-class, typical, mid-

western family surrounding Chris and Nancy Hughes. Chris and friend Jim Lowell are partners in the law firm founded by Judge Lowell. Nancy is a housewife whose domain over 25 years pretty much remained in the kitchen. In fact, the very first scene of the very first "ATWT" episode showed groggy Nancy in the kitchen, saying "Good morning" to beloved husband Chris. The Hughes family also includes four children: Bob, a physician and a widower at the beginning of the show's long run; Penny, played by Rosemary Prinz for 12 years, from teenage to mature womanhood; Donald; and Susan, who died. Other members of the clan included Tom, the son of Bob and his former wife Lisa; Grandpa Hughes, who lived with Nancy and Chris until his death in 1976; and Edith, wonderfully por-

Zsa Zsa Gabor made a two-week appearance on "As the World Turns." Here she rehearses with Anthony Herrera (James Stenbeck).

from fiction. Eileen Fulton's character, Lisa, so captivated and enraged audiences that she had to be escorted between studio and home to fend off physical attacks. Women who loved to hate Lisa were prone to approach Fulton on the street and slug her with a handbag for all her dirty deeds. And Rosemary Prinz often was berated by irate fans who didn't think Rosemary should do anything that Penny wouldn't have done. Indeed, "ATWT" fans were so wrapped up in the story and characters that they believed they always knew what was best for the characters. During a stormy tenure—from 1956 to 1973—with "As the World Turns," Irna Phillips was prone to unpredictably write characters out or jar the viewers with out-of-character behavior or incredible dialogue. And the show was always taken to task for these moves by an outraged audience.

The Kitchens of Oakdale

Oakdale a typical midwestern town filled with typical midwestern residents. Especially in the early years, viewers saw Oakdale mostly from its kitchens and living rooms. There, ensconced at a kitchen table or

Einar Perry Scott (Nels).

trayed by Ruth Warrick, who is Chris's more eccentric sister. Over the years, Bob Hughes became the unifying force among Oakdale citizens.

Conflict was instantly supplied on "ATWT" by the other original core family, the Lowells. The Lowells were antithetic to the Hughes: wealthy, nonharmonious, and fraught with the usual soap problems ascribed to those who have too much money and not enough love. Main characters Jim and Claire Lowell unfortunately don't love each other, which constantly distresses their daughter, Ellen, who is Penny Hughes' best friend.

In later years the Stewarts became a major family in Oakdale as well.

Probably the most interesting fact about the "ATWT" characters is how convincing—and often infuriating—they were to their fans. Perhaps more than any other current soap, "ATWT" fans really took the show to heart, and numerous incidents proved that they sometimes had a difficult time distinguishing fact

on a comfy sofa, the Hughes would air their worries and their joys. The flavor of this soap opera really made the surroundings unimportant.

Oakdale Behind Closed Doors

When Oakdale appeared on America's TV screens the happenings in the town were fairly predictable and fairly unnotable. The Hughes were a nice family who had ordinary problems. The Lowells, however, were not so nice, and it was implied by the show that money was at the root of all their evil. Nothing seemed to please the middle-class audience more than to have their suspicions confirmed that "money can't buy everything."

Over the years economic class took a back seat as one of the major social issues, and gradually the Hughes climbed the ladder of success to put them on an equal level with the Lowells.

During Irna Phillips' tenure, "ATWT" was plagued by inconsistency. If Phillips was angry enough at a cast member to write the character out in a fit of temperament, carefully crafted storylines had to suffer. Characters were killed off-screen, denying the loyal fans even the chance to bid their Oakdale friends farewell. In the early '70s Phillips' writing became so erratic that the actors and actresses rebelled at reading their lines. In one case Phillips had David Stewart drag his wife Ellen to a bar to get her drunk so he could tell her their son had died. Then the incredibly stoical wife replied without emotion that they had to keep on going, "even in the face of death."

25 YEARS IN OAKDALE

While Irna Phillips was known as impulsive and even vindictive, she has also been called brilliant. And despite numerous snafus involving Phillips' tantrums, it is a tribute to her genius that "As the World Turns" remained vastly popular for so long. When Phillips was finally fired in 1973 she was replaced by Robert Soderberg and Edith Sommer, who had written "Guiding Light" for several years. When the turbulent late '70s and early '80s rolled around, "ATWT" found itself in the same type of trouble that had hit other old soaps. It was just too serious for many of the modern, and often young, viewers of the day.

The writing team most responsible for turning this soap around was made up of Jerome and Bridget

Don McLaughlin and Helen Wagner as Chris and Nancy Hughes. Photo by Victor Petersen.

Dobson. The Dobsons employed techniques that were very successful in making "General Hospital" a top-rated soap. Coincidentally, Bridget Dobson's parents created "General Hospital" back in the '60s. The Dobsons wrote for "General Hospital" during its period before Gloria Monty took over, although there was one writing team (the Pollocks) after them. "As the World Turns' " current headwriters are John Saffron (who has written dialogue for "All My Children") and Elizabeth Levin.

The techniques that worked for the Dobsons on both "GL" and "ATWT" included a faster pace, humor, and fun. All the characters were woven back into the romance and mystery storylines, and new exciting characters that were introduced caught on quickly with the fans. An example of the Dobsons' touch was the turnaround in the weird Mr. Big mystery. When the Dobson team came on board in the middle of this story, it had the unfortunate problem of combining deadly seriousness with a ridiculous situation dominated by a demented midget. The Dobsons made this story funny so that the viewers could accept and enjoy it. They also have helped "ATWT" add younger characters and keep the romance coming at a dizzying pace.

Lisa: The Woman They Loved to Hate

It's easy to see why the fans missed Eileen Fulton so much. Right from the start the young actress injected such depth into the character that the viewers couldn't help but love her at the same time as they condemned her for her naughty deeds. Let's review the havoc she has wreaked in Oakdale.

Lisa arrived in Oakdale on the arm of college student Bob Hughes, whom she'd trapped into marriage. The couple moved in with Nancy and Chris, and Lisa soon had a child. Bored and disappointed with her new life, Lisa soon strayed from home and into the arms of wealthy Bruce Elliot. She divorced Bob hoping that Elliot would marry her and make her a rich young woman. But Bruce got bored with the conniving country girl and dropped her; eventually Lisa left her son Tommy with her in-laws and ran out of town.

When Lisa returned from Chicago not long after, she was given a new sophisticated look. She had married again, and her divorce had left her wealthy. She and social-climber Michael Shea had an affair behind his wife's back, but when Lisa got pregnant, Shea shunned her. Later, his wife divorced him, he became

"As the World Turns's" Eileen Fulton was on that series for 23 years until she left to be replaced by actress Betsy von Furstenberg. Photo by Bob Deutsch.

When Eileen Fulton left because she felt that her character, Lisa, had become too benign, Betsy von Furstenberg took over the role.

attached to his son Chuck, and he proposed to Lisa, who no longer wanted any part of the idea.

When Lisa's older son Tom returned from Vietnam and turned to drugs to forget the war, he tried to rob Dr. Shea's medical supplies and was forced to sign a confession that Shea used to force Lisa to marry him. Their marriage was dismal, and when Shea threatened to take Chuck away from her, Lisa ran away again, only to return in the nick of time to find son Tom confessing to the murder of her husband. The shock gave her amnesia until the real culprit was discovered.

Lisa next had a quick affair with Simon Gilbey.

Lisa finally decided Bob Hughes hadn't been so bad after all, but by now he wasn't available, so she fell for his older brother Donald; they never married.

Lisa was then pursued by three new suitors, Wally Matthews, Jay Stalling, and Grant Colman. The virtuous Colman won her hand and helped her become a more virtuous person herself. Suddenly Lisa became the victim of manipulation rather than the perpetrator when Grant's supposedly divorced wife showed up and tried to prevent their marriage. They were finally wed, but Grant's wife told him she had borne his son a few years ago, and Grant continued to rally to Joyce's side whenever she had a problem. Lisa tried to be patient, but she finally told Grant to get lost. Lisa started seeing Dick Martin, but she and Grant were reconciled when Grant showed up drunk at her apartment one night.

Lisa's marriage to Grant fell apart when he divorced her to run off with a younger woman he had fallen in love with. For a while Lisa dated a younger man, Brad Hollister. However, their relationship was based on mutual loneliness, rather than on love. When Brad left town Lisa took it in stride.

When wealthy businessman Whit McColl came to town, Lisa immediately found herself attracted to him. Besides running an Oakdale newspaper, Whit's also the head of McColl Enterprises. He has two adult sons, Brian and Kirk, as well as an adult daughter, Diana. After a brief engagement Whit made Lisa his wife.

Lisa, however, wasn't married to Whit for long before problems arose. A woman named Charmane arrived in Oakdale claiming to be Whit's wife, thus making Whit's marriage to Lisa illegal. According to Charmane, a former Las Vegas showgirl, five years ago a drunken Whit picked her up and they got along so well that by the end of the night they were married. Not having any recollection of the incident, Whit hired a private investigator to check out Charmane's story. The investigator returned with news that Charmane was telling the truth. Not wanting to jeopardize his marriage to Lisa, Whit has kept the truth about Charmane a secret. As far as everyone in Oakdale knows, at least as of this writing, Charmane is Whit's long-lost sister.

What's happening to the younger set on "As the World Turns"? Here are a few recent storylines:

"As the World Turns" has been turning on a set of villains for years. At one point John Dixon was the nasty man who did everyone dirt. In time he mellowed.

The current villain, James Stenbeck, came on the scene as a mysterious, powerful, rich man with ties to many people in Oakdale. Dark, suave, and almost reptilian in appearance, he had an adversary in Gunnar Stenbeck, who arrived in 1982 to play the heroic, courageous, more honest character who saved James' wife, Barbara, from a miserable marriage.

Coleen Zink (Barbara).

The introduction of a dark, sultry adventuress, Miranda Marlowe, was an exciting note. However, the series removed her from any Mata Hari-esque situations she may have been involved with and married her off to another community pillar, the good (but oft-wed) Dr. Bob Hughes.

In 1983 one of ATWT's newer core families, the Stewarts, welcomed four children into their lives, courtesy of daughter Dr. Anne Stewart and her husband, Jeff Ward. This may well be the first time quads were not only born to a soap character, but were played by real-life quads who fortuitously made their entry into the world at about the same time the soap's youngsters did.

AFFAIRS TO REMEMBER

Oakdale affairs have been numerous. Here are a few other romances to remember:

- In one misdirected storyline involving Dr. David Stewart, the elder statesman of the town of Oakdale suffered from amnesia and fell in love with a much younger woman, Cynthia Haines. Ellen Stewart, his longtime wife, left him. The affair went nowhere. Eventually the Stewarts reconciled, killing the tale in mid-telling.
- Before Anne and Jeff were married and conceived their quadruplets, their affair was threatened by a young woman, Karen (who subsequently married James). Karen, during a period of madness, believed Jeff was in love with her and was determined to do what she had to do to keep Anne from taking him away.
- James, who wound up marrying two of the women he bedded, continued to bed several others, including Dee, the former wife of John Dixon. Dixon not only despised James for winning Dee's body but also for having had an affair with Dixon's beloved illegitimate daughter, Margo.

MURDER/MAYHEM/MYSTERY

"ATWT's" personal theme seemed to make it unnecessary for the show to feature much in the way of mystery. As long as someone occasionally was wrongly accused of a murder, viewers' need for excitement outside the bedroom seemed satisfied. Most of the mayhem through the '50s, '60s, and up to the mid-'70s was motivated by love and lust (and sometimes greed), not by criminal instincts. By the mid-'70s, however, even this staid show began to feature some wild adventures and fantasies. Here are a few of the other recent storylines:

- The series has had several mysteries and murder plots that blew up before coming to some logical conclusion. In 1981-82 the Mr. Big storyline, involving a "nasty dwarf" with a penchant for blowing people up if he didn't get his way, gave a pair of lovers—Margo and Tom—a chance to play amorous adventurers in France and other far-off places, including the Gilette Castle in Connecticut.
- Miranda Marlowe was accused of selling dope on an international scale and was jailed in Paris and finally released when the authorities determined that

she may have been more of a victim than a criminal.

- Dee Stewart had been involved in a mysterious death; her lover, Ian McFarland, died in her bed. Although she was later proved to be innocent of any wrong-doing, the lady did go through some harrowing experiences following the grisly morning after.

- The lovely Lisa was also involved in a murder involving a lover. In this case, the man, Bennett Hadley, had a housekeeper named Hester who loved him and decided to kill his wife. She would also have killed Lisa, but the time hadn't come for the character to be sent away yet.

SOMETHING NEW SOMETIMES HAPPENS

A few firsts courtesy of "ATWT":

"As the World Turns" featured the first marital rape in which the wife—again a Stewart, this time Dee—brought her husband, Dr. John Dixon, to court charging that he had forced himself on her. Dixon did not deny that he had had marital relations with his wife on the night in question. Nor did he deny that he had been rather rough in his advances. His defense was that it couldn't have been rape, that it was simply a healthy desire for a much-loved wife.

This court case might have produced an important landmark (for soaps) verdict. Instead, there was a cop-out: Dee chose not to pursue the matter.

Frank Runyeon (Steven Andropolous).

WHO'S WHO IN OAKDALE

Original Cast

Actor	Character
BOBBY ALFORD	**Bobby Hughes**
ANN BURR	**Claire Lowell**
LES DAMON	**Jim Lowell, Jr.**
WENDY DREW	**Ellen Lowell**
WILLIAM JOHNSTONE	**Judge James T. Lowell**
DON MACLAUGHLIN	**Chris Hughes**
SANTOS ORTEGA	**Grandpa Hughes**
RUTH WARRICK	**Edith Hughes**

First Air Date: April 2, 1956

Write to "As the World Turns" c/o CBS, 51 West 52nd Street, New York, NY 10019.

A Directory of Recent Characters*

Kim Stewart Andropolous: Mother of Betsy; former wife of John Dixon; widow of Nick. *Kathryn Hays*

Steve Andropolous: Kim's brother-in-law; once wed to Carol; loves Betsy; had an affair with Maggie. *Frank Runyeon*

Maggie Crawford: A lawyer; Lyla's sister. *Mary Linda Rapelye*

John Dixon: A doctor; ex-mate of Dee, Kim, and Ariel; dad of Margo by Lyla. *Larry Bryggman*

Bob Hughes: Chris's son; Tom's dad; Lisa's ex-husband, Miranda's husband; has a daughter Frannie. *Don Hastings*

Chris Hughes: Bob's dad; Tom's grandfather. *Don MacLaughlin*

Miranda Marlowe Hughes: Bob's wife; Blain's mother; a woman with a "past." *Elaine Princi*

Tom Hughes: Bob and Lisa's son; wed to Margo. *Justin Deas*

*The actors/actresses who currently play these major roles are in italics.

Betsy Stewart Montgomery: Kim's daughter; Craig's wife; always loved Steve. *Meg Ryan*

Lyla Montgomery: John's former love; mom of Margo, Cricket, and Craig; Maggie's sister; a nurse. *Ann Sward*

Gunnar Stenbeck: Barbara's great love and the heroic opposite of cousin James. *Hugo Napier*

James Stenbeck: Ex-husband of Barbara; wed to Karen; related to Gunnar and Ariel. *Anthony Herrera*

Karen Haines Stenbeck: James' wife; once loved Jeff; Cynthia's daughter; David's lover. *Kathy MacNeil*

Annie Stewart-Ward: David and Ellen Stewart's daughter; Jeff Ward's wife; mother of quads; a doctor. *Mary Lyn Blanks*

David Stewart: A doctor; reconciled with wife, Ellen; dad of Dee and Anne; hates Dee's ex-husband, John. *Henderson Forsythe*

Dee Stewart: Formerly wed to John Dixon; involved with James Stenbeck; daughter of Ellen and David. *Vicki Dawson*

Ellen Stewart: Wife of David; mother of Dee and Anne. *Patricia Bruder*

Jeff Ward: A doctor; Annie's husband; dad of quads. *Robert Lipton*

Elaine Princi played Miranda Marlowe Hughes.

A Word from the Real-Life Miranda—Elaine Princi

"I recall the first day I read for the role. I'd been told that they wanted someone with a foreign accent. I practiced all the dialects and accents I was familiar with and added some new ones. When the time came to read, what came out was not French, nor Spanish, nor Italian. But whatever it was, it was exactly what they had been hoping to hear." Princi felt that this refusal to be too narrow in the conception of a character, to open the character's possibilities instead, gives the show its characteristic penchant for always being willing to try something different.

5

Capitol (CBS)

"Capitol" made its debut over CBS on March 26, 1982. Around the same time CBS let "Search for Tomorrow" switch to NBC, and March 26 was coincidentally the anniversary of CBS's much-watched "The Young and the Restless." A hallmark year for CBS!

"Capitol's" beginning was unusual in several aspects. First, like "Ryan's Hope," the new soap was to be set in a real place. And like "RH's" New York, Washington, DC, certainly holds a lot of possibilities for power and conflict to pepper the plots. "Capitol" was also endowed with a lot of money, and in a daytime first it was premiered as a special nighttime pilot that ran directly after "Dallas." A winning combina-

Constance Towers plays Clarissa McCandless. In real life she is married to former actor John Gavin who is currently Ambassador to Mexico. Miss Towers is a long-time musical star. Photo by Ed Geller.

tion, if ever there was one, and "Capitol" proceeded to capture healthy ratings during its first six months.

There were plenty of reasons for viewers to tune in. It featured some of the more venerable names in show business: the late Carolyn Jones, Constance Towers, Ed Nelson, Anthony Eisley, and Rory Calhoun in the original cast. Richard Egan joined later on.

Creator/writers Stephen and Elinor Karpf were thrilled when they were asked to come up with an idea for a new daytime drama, and they knew exactly what they wanted to do. A longtime fascination with politics and a familiarity with DC made "Capitol" a natural for them, and the network ate it up. But the writers stress that this is not a show about politics; it is a show about people who live in DC and whose lives are entwined with the political scene. Politics on a smaller scale certainly has been touched on by other soaps, but the power that exists in DC lends a certain extra excitement to the show as well as a touch of realism.

A Word from the Producer—John Conboy

Conboy is a former actor and director. He understands what happens when the cameras roll and the action begins.

In 1973 he helped revolutionize soap operas when he introduced "The Young and the Restless" on TV and brought beautiful, young people with problems that were more reflective of the post-60s turmoils than those touched on by most other daytime dramas. He also introduced older people with problems that older people may well experience in real life.

But, essentially, Conboy practices the credo of his art: "Entertainment before anything else," he says. "Television is a viewing medium, but you still have to tell a story; people still 'hear' what they see."

Of "Capitol," he says: "We have created two separate families with two sets of philosophies. Most often they disagree but sometimes they agree. Remember, the two women (Myrna Clegg and Clarissa McCandless) may be adversaries, but once they were friends and their memories of this friendship are always there. They may fight for the rights of their children—or what they feel the rights are. But that is what mothers everywhere do. However, they know who they once were to each other and that's always there, between them.

" 'Capitol' is not about a city; it's about people."

Because this show is about people, not issues, most of the action takes place behind the political scenes, but the undercurrent of national and even international power is always there to titillate. The writers intended to cross cultural and economic lines in their new show, as do most soaps of today.

The core families, the McCandlesses and the Cleggs, have been engaging in a feud for decades, and from there the initial conflict arose. The Cleggs are wealthy and ruthless; the McCandlesses are of modest means and endowed with middle-class morality, and for the most part the families hate each other. That is, except for Tyler McCandless and Julie Clegg, who were introduced to "Capitol" as the Romeo and Juliet of the nation's hub. How the Cleggs attempt to keep the McCandlesses down and the young lovers apart formed the foundation of "Capitol's" initial storylines.

Due to the proliferation of factual fiction that Americans have seen on TV in the last 10 years, it's not surprising that "Capitol's" setting would inspire speculation on the basis for the characters and their actions. There had been some talk that the show's characters would be based on real people. Producer John Conboy said, "It's based on whomever you think." The power struggles that go on are not limited to any one person or group of people in the political milieu in which "Capitol" is set.

Considering what it started with, "Capitol" has reason to anticipate a bright future.

WELCOME TO DC

The Citizens

On soaps, even the male-powered world of DC is a matriarchal society. The fundamental conflict between the Cleggs and the McCandlesses lies between the mothers of the two clans: Clarissa McCandless and Myrna Clegg. Myrna's meanness began when her once-close girlhood friend, Clarissa McCandless married the man she, Myrna, adored. The families both have sons with political ambition; each hopes their lad will sit in the White House one day.

Clarissa is the strong but vulnerable mother who raised and supported five kids on her own while working in her father's law office. Like many soap heroines, she's blonde. Myrna, a fiery brunette, is the antagonist, and she'll do anything to put Clarissa down, including pushing son Trey Clegg into a political battle for power with Tyler McCandless.

To give the Romeo and Juliet scenario an extra

president may remind some of the late Ambassador Joseph Kennedy's plans for his sons. The mellowing of the once fiercely ambitious personality that Trey first showed could also be Kennedyesque, reminding us that the Kennedy brother considered the most determined of all, Robert, lost his hard edge over time.

Judson Tyler is Clarissa's father, played charmingly by Rory Calhoun. The part of Dr. Tom McCandless was phased out for a while, but "Capitol" is in the process of recasting it and returning the good doctor to DC. Other McCandlesses include Matt and Wally. On the Clegg side of the fence, Myrna's husband Sam II is the only person who can intimidate his single-minded wife and his ambitious son.

DC Sightseeing

"Capitol" fans get a bonus when they watch this show: visually, there might not be a better backdrop

The late Carolyn Jones was the original Myrna Clegg. A serious illness forced her to leave "Capitol" in April, 1983. Marj Dusay replaced her. Photo by Ed Geller.

Nicholas Walker plays ambitious Samuel Clegg III (Trey). He was formerly seen as a young doctor on "The Doctors."

dimension, the Dennings have been thrown into the cast. Senator Denning is the white hat who has taken it upon himself to protect Clarissa and her family. Alas, he's not without problems of his own; his arise mainly in the form of his spoiled, power-hungry daughter Sloane. Sloane is interested in both Tyler and Trey, especially as long as they are battling for political power.

The character of Trey, as played by Nicholas Walker, seems to be a composite of political ambitions. The push from the Clegg clan to groom him as a

Left: Judge Tyler is played by Rory Calhoun.

Below: Veteran film actor Richard Egan plays Sam Clegg II.

for any TV show set in this country. Indeed, the awesome and beautiful architecture adds such style to "Capitol" that one magazine writer said it could be considered a character in its own right. The show has also been applauded for its use of this gorgeous setting. Outdoor shots are said to be more effective than in many other soaps, and there's a generally slick look to the whole thing that only adds to the excitement.

A Day in DC

While it's still too early in "Capitol's" history to evaluate the kinds of events that take place there, some of the issues touched on are predictable considering the setting.

"Capitol" has shown us corruption in high places. The villains who steal, lie, or otherwise besmirch the scenes they're in are dealt with in two ways: the actual miscreants, the men and women who do the dirty work, are either dispatched or are punished in some other fashion. The power structure behind the scenes,

a significant trend beyond the fact that its stories lie in the Washington theme. There is some talk that as the country approaches the 1984 elections the series will present some exceptionally relevant storylines. There is also talk that as we approach the 1984 Summer Olympics storylines affecting the character of Matt McCandless, an athletic type with ambitions of converting the world to physical health through exercise, will be stressed.

Aside from Julie and Tyler's romance, "Capitol" has focused on Wally's gambling problems, Sloane's romance with a spy, the feud between the Cleggs and the McCandlesses, and Trey Clegg's affair with a former prostitute (who has since left the show).

How well the show continues to handle these DC-related subjects depends on how successful it is in probing beneath the surface. So far, there are signs that "Capitol" will continue to please audiences. In one magazine interview the headwriters said they think of the show in novelistic terms, which allows them to explore their characters and their lives on many levels. They mentioned one story that goes back to the 19th century that makes characters do what they do but doesn't need to be shown on the screen, as in some other film media. Hopefully, the Karpfs' professed love for history will inspire many interesting sidelights in the future.

THE NATIONAL ARCHIVES

Prostitution was introduced to "Capitol" fans as a means of wielding political power. As it turned out, the prostitute fell in love with the upright Sam Clegg III (Trey), and she left town rather than ruin his political career by allowing him to fall too deeply in love with her. Unknown to Trey, however, when the prostitute Kelly left town she was carrying his child.

A lurid, but true, tale of a congressman and his wife, which included her admission that they once made love on the steps of the Capitol building, and a raft of headlines about call boy and call girl rings in Washington again gave "Capitol" vicarious excitement in the imagination of the viewers.

The truly sad aspect of "Capitol" is that its original Myrna Clegg, Carolyn Jones, had to leave because of illness. She was splendid in the role, playing a woman of whom she said: "For all of Myrna's faults, and they are many, remember that she moves out of love. It was her love for Clarissa's husband that drove her to break off their close friendship. It's her love for her

Brian Robert Taylor played Dr. Tom McCandless on the series. The character was sent away but is expected to return. Photo by Ed Geller.

however (the Cleggs, in the person of Myrna, for example), remains very much in command of the next nasty situation set up.

There are tapes that must be found and destroyed; there are papers that can embarrass the wrong people. There's even an ambitious TV newswoman, Sloane, who would do anything to achieve either or both main aims of her life: get a scoop and marry a future president.

Again, the show is still too new to have produced

husband's son, Sam (Trey) that makes her the demanding woman she is. What she needs is to know that she, too, can be loved for her own self."

In an unusual turnabout, "Capitol's" storylines have seemed to improve since its nighttime premiere. Many other shows have boasted an intiguing pilot, only to deliver weaker episodes subsequently. "Capitol," on other shows have boasted an intriguing pilot, only to "Capitol's" regular episodes have toned down the enmity between the entire Clegg and McCandless families and more realistically focused on the hostility between Clarissa and Myrna. Perhaps the producers tried too hard in the pilot to alter their show to fit a nighttime format and audience.

Juliet Reincarnate

Julie Clegg, daughter of Myrna and Sam Clegg, has always been in love with Tyler McCandless, a former war hero. With Tyler returning to Washington in the show's premiere episode, Julie anxiously awaited the renewal of their romance. Myrna totally disapproved of their involvement because she blamed Tyler's mother Clarissa for stealing the only man she had ever loved, the late Baxter McCandless. Using Sloane Denning, who was also in love with Tyler, Myrna managed to make it look like Tyler was having an affair with Sloane behind Julie's back. Upset, Julie broke off her engagement to Tyler. However, when Tyler was finally able to explain his innocence, Julie resumed seeing him.

Not long after Julie and Tyler announced their engagement, Julie was involved in an explosion on a boat. The accident caused her to lose part of her memory. Realizing that Julie no longer had any recollection of making up with Tyler, Myrna plotted to have Lawrence Barrington, a fortune-hunter, pretend to Julie that they were engaged by filling her head with artificial memories.

Although Tyler was very concerned about Julie's condition following the explosion, he was forced to leave the United States for N'shoba on a secret mission. Identifying Tyler as a spy, N'shoba officials had him arrested. With the help of Sloane, who was covering the N'shoba story for her TV station, Tyler was able to escape. Returning to Washington, Tyler was more than a little shocked to discover that Julie was preparing to marry Lawrence. Confronting her, Tyler was able to make her realize they were the ones who were engaged, not she and Lawrence.

Finding out that her mother had set her up, Julie moved into a spare room at the McCandless home. Later, she returned to the Clegg domain when her parents reluctantly accepted her engagement to Tyler.

Just as Julie was about to marry Tyler, Tyler's brother was involved in a serious accident that put him in the hospital. While Wally remained in critical condition, Julie and Tyler once again postponed their marriage. However, with Wally now recovering from a kidney transplant from his brother Thomas, Wally encouraged Tyler and Julie to get married while he was still in the hospital. They were married at the end of July 83.

A Directory of Recent Characters*

Lizbeth Bochman: Student loved by Jordy Clegg and Thomas McCandless. *Tonja Walker*

Brenda Clegg: Myrna's daughter. *Leslie Graves*

Jordy Clegg: Julie's brother; sometimes cruel but growing more sensitive with Lizbeth's help. *Todd Curtis*

Julie Clegg: Trey's assistant; married Tyler; she's the nicest Clegg of all. *Kimberly Beck-Hilton*

Myrna Clegg: The prime mover behind all the problems affecting the Clegg and McCandless relationships; she was in love with Baxter McCandless, whom her once best friend, Clarissa, married. *Marj Dusay*

Sam Clegg II: Myrna's husband. *Richard Egan*

Sam Clegg III (Trey): Myrna's stepson. *Nicholas Walker*

Mark Denning: Sloane's father; unhappily wed; he loves Clarissa. *Ed Nelson*

Sloane Denning: A TV reporter; she'll wed anyone— Trey if possible, Tyler if she could—who might become president. *Deborah Mullowney*

Clarissa McCandless: Mother of Tyler, Matt, Tom, Wally, Gillian; Baxter's widow; Judson's daughter. *Constance Towers*

*The actors/actresses who currently play these major roles are in italics.

Matt McCandless: Athletic and smart; becoming a major McCandless character. *Chris Durham*

Tyler McCandless: Potential presidential candidate; married to Julie Clegg. *David Mason Daniels*

Wally McCandless: In trouble more often than not; secretly in love with Julie. *Bill Beyers*

Judson Tyler: Clarissa's father; a lawyer; his political career was ruined by the Cleggs. *Rory Calhoun*

WHO'S WHO IN WASHINGTON

Original Cast

Actor	*Character*
KIMBERLY BECK-HILTON	**Julie Clegg**
BILL BEYERS	**Wally McCandless**
RORY CALHOUN	**Judson Tyler**
JEFF CHAMBERLAIN	**Lawrence Barrington**
TODD CURTIS	**Jordy Clegg**
JANE DALY GAMBLE	**Shelly/Kelly**
DAVID MASON DANIELS	**Tyler McCandless**
RICHARD EGAN	**Sam Clegg II**
SHEA FARRELL	**Matt McCandless**
DUNCAN GAMBLE	**Frank Burgess**
LESLIE GRAVES	**Brenda Clegg**
CAROLYN JONES	**Myrna Clegg**
DEBORAH MULLOWNEY	**Sloane Denning**
ED NELSON	**Senator Mark Denning**
RODNEY SAULSBERRY	**Jeff Johnson**
BRIAN ROBERT TAYLOR	**Dr. Thomas McCandless**
CONSTANCE TOWERS	**Clarissa McCandless**
NICHOLAS WALKER	**Sam "Trey" Clegg III**
TONJA WALKER	**Lizbeth Bochman**

First Air Date: March 29, 1982

Write to "Capitol" c/o CBS, Television City, 7800 Beverly Blvd., Suite 3365, Los Angeles, CA 90036.

6

Days of Our Lives (NBC)

"Days of Our Lives," which is set in Salem, U.S.A., premiered November 8, 1965, on NBC. NBC introduced three other new serials during that year: "Moment of Truth" (a Canadian-based soap that featured Douglass Watson, now Mac Cory on "Another World"), "Morning Star," and "Paradise Bay." Within a year, "Days of Our Lives" was the only show that had succeeded in avoiding a quick cancellation. Despite not being canceled, "DOOL" wasn't a ratings success during its first year. According to the Nielsens, out of 34 programs on the daytime schedule in 1965 "Days of Our Lives" ranked 32nd.

Until "Days of Our Lives" and "Another World," the networks didn't give a soap much time to catch on with the viewing audience. Hence the speedy dismissals of the three previously mentioned soaps. NBC stuck with "Days of Our Lives" only because of the people associated with the program. Irna Phillips co-created "Days of Our Lives" with Ted Corday (whose past credits included "Guiding Light" and "As the World Turns") and Alan Chase. Screen Gems, a successful Hollywood-based production company, produced the series. Former movie star Macdonald Carey (whose career began on a radio soap Irna Phillips created entitled "Women in White") headed the cast.

In both 1978 and 1979 "DOOL" won the Emmy for best daytime serial, proving that, even after 18 years on the air, good writers, producers, and cast members can keep a serial young and vibrant enough to attract today's audiences.

"Days'" longevity probably is due to its controlling theme: the series describes itself as a show that emphasizes human relationships. Commenting on the inclusion of a robot in the Salem "cast," producer Al Rabin said, "What is exciting is the way human beings' lives will be affected by robots, and we expect to show some of these effects in our stories. But essentially we remain a people show."

Macdonald Carey holds the Emmy he won for his portrayal of Dr. Tom Horton in 1975.

WELCOME TO SALEM, U.S.A.

The Citizens

The Hortons

The core family of "Days of Our Lives" has always been the Horton clan. They include:

Alice: the matriarch of the Horton clan; the character has been played by veteran actress Frances Reid since the beginning.

Tom: Alice's physician husband; Macdonald Carey has always played this role.

Their Children

Addie: A twin who, along with Tommy, is the oldest of the Horton children.

Tommy: The other half of the twins; at the show's

inception, he was listed as MIA from the Korean War (he'd been missing for more than 10 years at that time).

Mickey: The next-oldest Horton offspring, a lawyer; the character has been played by John Clarke since the "DOOL" debut.

Bill: A few years younger than Mickey, Bill has followed in his father's footsteps and is a doctor.

Marie: The baby of the Horton family.

Their Grandchildren

Jessica: Marie's daughter.

Sandy: This granddaughter is the only female physician in the family.

Julie: Considered one of the main characters on the show throughout most of its history; the daughter of Addie and husband Ben Olson, who left Julie to be reared by her grandparents.

The Olsons

One of the original families, but never really a core family, was the Olsons:

Ben: A banker who married Tom and Alice's daughter Addie; father of Julie.

Addie (see the Hortons).

Ben and Addie moved to Europe in "Days' " early years and left Julie in Tom and Alice's custody. Later, Addie, now a widow, returned to Salem, married Doug Williams, and died.

Many other peripheral characters have been introduced over the last 18 years; recently, in fact, characters other than the popular Julie and Doug Williams have taken the fore. (See The Salem Story.)

What Happens in Salem

The original premise of "Days of Our Lives" was medical: Dr. Tom was to be the head of a medical community. However, as the storylines progressed, this emphasis has weakened. The decision to move away from the hospital as the core arena was made to distinguish the soap from other doctor-oriented series, notably "Guiding Light," "General Hospital," and a sister NBC soap, "The Doctors." Although Dr. Tom and his medical offspring continued to claim much of the storyline material, other stories have regularly intruded.

In the beginning "Days of Our Lives" relied heavily on lavish sets and fast-paced stories as a way of grab-

Doug and Julie Williams are in real life played by husband and wife Bill Hayes and Susan Seaforth Hayes. Here they are remarried (on the set).

bing viewers. Realizing the viewers were more interested in the characters and their relationships to one another, the writers quickly slowed the pace and spent more time developing the characters. Within two years "Days of Our Lives" was at the top of the Nielsen ratings.

Like many other soap operas, love is the theme of "Days of Our Lives" which has carried it to the top of the ratings for years. That theme has been reinforced for the viewers in the form of real-life romance. Bill Hayes and Susan Seaforth Hayes, who play Doug and Julie Williams on the show, met on the set, fell in love, and were wed. Nothing sparks the imagination of soap opera viewers more than fictional true love come to life. Those who read soap magazines in the 1970s often were just as anxious (if not more so) to get the scoop on the Hayes as they were to catch up with the Williamses.

THE SALEM STORY

Although both Doug and Julie Williams are still popular characters, there are other characters that receive more attention in today's daytime TV magazines. Two of those characters are Dr. Marlena Evans (played by Diedre Hall) and her husband, macho but sensitive police detective Roman Brady (played by Wayne Northrop). At times Wayne Northrop has succeeded in pulling more votes than the extremely popular Tony Geary (Luke Spencer on "General Hospital") in popularity polls conducted by the soap magazines.

"Days of Our Lives" has had a lot of ups and downs in story quality since William J. Bell stopped writing the program back in the late '70s so that he could concentrate full-time on his own creation, the popular "The Young and the Restless." To this day, loyal

"Days of Our Lives" followers delight in remembering vivid storylines such as that in which Susan Martin (then played by Denise Alexander, now Lesley Webber on "General Hospital") lost her mind and shot her husband David and the time when Mickey Horton lost his memory and thought he was a farm hand named Marty Hansen, who met and fell in love with a shy, crippled woman named Maggie Simmons (still played by Suzanne Rogers). Both were stories penned by the talented Mr. Bell.

Over the last 18 years "Days of Our Lives" has packed a lot of action into the lives of the Horton family and friends. In addition to her love life, Julie, for example, has suffered numerous medical problems, including miscarriage, an accident that made plastic surgery necessary, and other problems. On "Days of Our Lives" there have been murders, attempted murders, amnesia victims, insanity, child custody suits, unwitting bigamy, missing persons, marriage, pregnancy, divorce, and remarriage. What ties it all together? As the producer said, this is a people show, and characters like Julie have provided the common thread. Indeed, a character as well loved as Julie can keep an audience interested for years, as evidenced by the show's popularity. A look at Julie will provide a bit of the flavor of Salem.

Above: Detective Roman Brady, played by Wayne Northrup, married Marlena Evans (Deidre Hall) in the early '80s.

Right: Don Craig (played by Jed Allen) married Marlena Evans (Deidre Hall) in 1979. Hall's twin sister, Andrea Hall-Lovell (right), plays the maid of honor, Samantha.

The History of Julie

One of "DOOL's" most popular characters has always been Julie Olson Banning Anderson Williams. When the show started, she was known simply as Julie Olson, teenage daughter of banker Ben Olson and his wife Addie (both in their early 40s), granddaughter of Dr. Tom Horton and his wife Alice.

When Ben and Addie decided to leave the country to live in Europe, Julie was left in the care of her grandparents. Although Tom and Alice were open in their love for Julie, Julie couldn't help feeling resentment toward her parents for their apparent abandonment. Looking for displays of love and affection wherever she could find it, Julie often exercised poor judgment in her choice of friends and lovers.

Having fallen in love with David Martin, a handsome charmer with the ladies, Julie soon became secretly engaged to him. A crushing blow, however, was delivered to Julie when she discovered that her best friend since high school, Susan, was pregnant with David's baby. Not wanting to see David's baby born illegitimate, Julie graciously stepped aside, leaving the way open for David to marry Susan. Julie even agreed to be Susan's maid of honor. After the baby was born David asked Susan for a divorce, so that he could resume his relationship with Julie, but Susan refused.

Infuriated, Julie began an adulterous affair with David. It wasn't long before she, too, was pregnant by David. Learning of Julie's pregnancy, and convinced that he could still talk Susan into giving him a divorce, David proceeded with plans again to marry Julie. But then fate dealt another crushing blow. One afternoon, while David played with his and Susan's son Richard on a swing, the child accidentally fell off the swing and died. Blaming David for their son's death, Susan lost her mind and shot him. Susan was never convicted of the crime, because her lawyer, Mickey Horton, successfully argued a plea of temporary insanity.

Meanwhile, Julie also gave birth to a baby boy, whom she reluctantly decided to put up for adoption. The baby was adopted by Scott and Janet Banning, who named him Brad Banning. Ironically, Susan Martin became next-door neighbor of the Bannings, unaware that their son was really Julie's. When Scott's wife died suddenly from a brain tumor, Susan began helping Scott take care of the little boy, and the two soon fell in love.

Worried that Susan might marry Scott, and thus become the mother of her child, Julie sued to regain custody of her baby. Since Scott was no longer married, the court awarded Julie custody. Having grown attached to the baby, Scott proposed marriage to Julie so that they could raise the boy together. Knowing that Susan was in love with Scott, Julie said yes, using the opportunity to pay Susan back for refusing to divorce David and for causing his death.

Hearing that Susan had inherited $250,000 after David's death, an enterprising ex-prisoner and con artist named Doug Williams, alias Doug Brent, arrived in Salem. Hoping to swindle Susan out of her money, Doug began romancing her. Seeing through Doug's charms, Susan tried to get him interested in Julie, hoping their romance would end her marriage to Scott. Susan even offered to finance Doug's romance with Julie. Upon meeting Julie, Doug found himself immediately attracted to her. Not long afterward, Julie discovered she was in love with Doug.

An obstacle to their growing love arrived in the form of Julie's mother Addie. Returning to Salem following the death of her husband Ben in Paris, Addie tried to patch up her differences with her daughter. Not wanting to have anything to do with Addie, Julie refused to share any details of her life with her. Hiring a private investigator, Addie learned Julie was seeing Doug behind Scott's back. When she met Doug, Addie found herself attracted to him. It wasn't long before she realized that she, too, was in love with Doug. Having realized her life with Ben had never been a happy one, Addie decided to grab at a second chance for happiness by proposing to Doug. To Addie's surprise, Doug, who had just had a knock-down fight with Julie, impulsively accepted her proposal and eloped with her.

Surprised by her mother's sudden marriage to Doug, Julie immediately began scheming to break them up. Desperate to have Doug for herself, Julie told him she'd do anything to have him back, even if it meant destroying her mother and Scott's happiness. Doug, however, found he was gradually falling in love with Addie. Threatened by Julie's love for Doug, Addie sought to strengthen her hold on him by buying a restaurant for her husband. Later Addie found she was pregnant with Doug's child.

Meanwhile, Julie began making secret arrangements to divorce Scott. She even hired an attractive lawyer named Don Craig to represent her. It wasn't long before Don discovered he was also in love with Julie. Julie, however, was still interested only in Doug.

Susan Seaforth as Julie and Jed Allen as Don Craig.
Photo by Bob Deutsch.

On the day that Julie was going to present Scott with divorce papers a freak accident on a construction site where Scott was working for the prominent architect Bob Anderson killed him. Scott, incidentally, died never knowing his wife was really in love with Doug.

Feeling responsible for Scott's death, Bob Anderson and his wife Phyllis did everything they could to make Julie's life as a widow easier. In a sense, they became Julie's substitute parents. Phyllis developed a particularly close bond with Julie. Julie also grew closer to Don Craig. Deciding she didn't have a chance to make a life with Doug, Julie even accepted Don's marriage proposal.

In the meantime, Doug and Addie's love for one another continued to grow. The only cloud on the horizon appeared when Addie discovered she was suffering from leukemia. Addie tried to keep the news of her disease a secret until after her baby was born, but her family discovered the truth and rushed to her side. The only person Addie succeeded in keeping her secret from was Julie, who still showed signs of hostility toward her mother.

Realizing he was in love with Julie, Bob ended his marriage to Phyllis. At this point Julie wasn't aware of Bob's feelings toward her. Nor was Phyllis. So the two continued to be good friends.

Addie gave birth to a baby girl, whom she named Hope. Discovering her mother had leukemia, Julie quickly reconciled with Addie. Worried about the welfare of her baby and Doug, Addie made Julie promise she'd take care of them after she was gone. Believing she now had a chance for a life with Doug, Julie broke her engagement to Don. Suddenly, Addie's disease went into remission.

Although Julie was happy for her mother, she couldn't help feeling a twinge of regret over losing Doug for a second time. No longer believing in true love, Julie decided to opt for a life of money and accepted Bob's marriage proposal.

Blaming Julie for the disintegration of her marriage to Bob, an emotionally distraught Phyllis made plans to kill her. Buying a gun, Phyllis set out to end Julie's life. After pulling the trigger, however, Phyllis discovered, to her horror, that she had mistakenly shot her own daughter Mary. Fortunately, Mary survived her gunshot wound.

In an attempt to overcome her emotional problems, Phyllis began seeing a psychiatrist.

Not long after Julie's marriage to Bob, Addie lost her life rushing to push baby Hope out of the way of a speeding car. Although Doug was now free to marry Julie, she discovered she was pregnant with Bob's baby. Doug's grief over Addie's death made it impossible for him to consider a life with anyone else, let alone Julie. Unable to deal with his loss, Doug sent Hope to live with Addie's parents. As time passed, however, Doug was finally able to accept Addie's death. Realizing Julie was pregnant with Bob's baby, Doug made a conscious effort to discourage her feelings for him. Bob, on the other hand, aware of Julie's love for Doug, suspected her baby was really Doug's. Despite their problems, Julie and Bob remained married.

Wanting to collect on his inheritance from his deceased grandmother, Julie's son David Banning, Jr., who was now an adult and had developed a reputation for being a ladies' man, returned to Salem with his live-in girlfriend, Brooke Hamilton, a conniving manipulator. Jealous of David's feelings for his mother, Brooke took an immediate dislike to Julie. She even started spreading rumors that Doug was the father of Julie's as yet unborn baby. Accidentally overhearing Julie and Doug discussing their feelings for one another, David immediately assumed Brooke's lie was the truth. Disillusioned with his mother, David stole Doug's car and drove off a bridge. Although David's body hadn't been found, everyone believed he was dead and a funeral service was held for him.

In actuality, David had survived the accident and was living in a nearby town with a middle-class black family known as the Grants. As time went on, David found that he was in love with the Grants' daughter, Valerie.

Respecting the Grants, David accepted their advice

that he return to Salem to patch up his differences with his mother. When a still pregnant Julie discovered David was alive, the excitement caused her to fall down a flight of stairs. At the hospital, Julie learned she had suffered a miscarriage. Deciding there was no longer any reason for her to carry on her charade of a marriage to Bob, Julie made arrangements to divorce him. Once the divorce was finalized, Julie and Doug made plans to marry.

Just as the ceremony was about to take place, Doug's first wife, a Polynesian princess named Kim, arrived in Salem, claiming she was still Doug's wife. According to Doug, they had divorced a long time ago. But Kim said the divorce wasn't legal because she had never signed the divorce papers. What this meant was that Doug's marriage to Addie was invalid. It was soon discovered that Kim had lied. And Julie and Doug once again resumed plans to marry.

Not long after they were married, Julie suffered a terrible accident. While visiting her sister-in-law Maggie Horton on her farm, Julie was trapped in a fire. Although Julie survived the fire, she discovered her face had been horribly scarred. Feeling that she was no longer attractive to Doug, and not wanting him to remain married to her out of a sense of pity, Julie left for Mexico and got a quickie divorce.

At the same time, Doug's ex-sister-in-law Lee Carmichael was growing closer to him. Hurt by Julie's rejection, Doug turned to Lee for affection. It wasn't long before they were making plans to marry.

Meanwhile, Julie heard of a plastic surgeon in San Francisco who had developed a new treatment for patients who were disfigured. Since there was no guarantee the operation would be a success, Julie was reluctant to undergo surgery. Still in love with Julie, despite his involvement with Lee, Doug urged Julie to take her chances with the operation. Flying out to San Francisco, Julie arranged to have the operation, which turned out to be a total success. Her face fully restored, Julie realized how foolish she had been to doubt Doug's love. Heading back to Salem, Julie decided to renew their marriage. To Julie's surprise, however, Doug had already married Lee.

Realizing that Doug still loved Julie, Lee schemed to have Julie killed. When Doug discovered what Lee was up to, he persuaded Lee to have herself committed to a mental institution. While at the institution, Lee agreed to give Doug a divorce, making it possible for him to remarry Julie.

Doug and Julie are still happily married. Their ma-

Julie (Susan Seaforth Hayes) is attracted to and repelled by one of "Days of Our Lives" past characters, played by Alejandro Rey. Photo by Bob Deutsch.

jor problem is Doug's daughter Hope, now an adolescent. Jealous of Doug's love for Julie, Hope feels he takes her side in matters of dispute between them. Julie, on the other hand, feels Doug is too lenient with Hope. With the help of Dr. Marlena Evans, a friend and psychiatrist, Julie and Hope are attempting to work out their problems.

AFFAIRS TO REMEMBER

Besides Julie's loves and the on- and off-screen marriage of the Hayes/Williamses, "Days" has featured many romances, two of which are listed below.

• One of the most important romantic storylines centered on Marie Horton (played originally by Marie Cheatham of "Search for Tomorrow" and more recently by Lanna Saunders). Marie had had a love affair and borne a daughter. She later became a nun. Years afterward she left the convent in search of her child, Jessica. The stormy reconciliation between mother and child provided one of the most dramatic stories on daytime. Jessica had to accept the fact not only that she had a living mother, but that her mother was a nun; and Mom was also the daughter of one of the most important men in town, Dr. Tom Horton. For weeks after the reconciliation, Jessica went through psychological trauma that resulted in split-personality manifestations. Marie eventually left the convent and took up with her former lover, Alex, Jessica's father. Later she fell for Neil. Neil, however, had fallen in love with Liz Chandler, who had become involved with the infamous Stefano Di Mera. Marie finally married Neil although Liz bore his child, only to divorce Neil after he declared his love for Liz. (Liz had accidentally

Lanna Saunders.

shot Marie and was sent to prison for it, causing Neil to admit his true feelings.)
• The marriage between Mickey Horton and Maggie seemed happy enough until Mickey disappeared and was presumed dead. During that period Maggie—who became a surrogate mother for Mr. and Mrs. Evan Wyland, only to ultimately keep the child after Mrs. Wyland's death—was greatly comforted by Don.

MURDER/MAYHEM/MYSTERY

Here, too, Julie has been in the center of the action. A couple of additional mayhem plots are listed below.
• The most dramatic murder story to come out of "Days" in years concerned the Salem Strangler. This madman killed women and very nearly killed two of the show's stars, Jessica and Marlena. Indeed, it was thought that he had strangled Marlena but he'd killed the doctor's twin sister instead. Interestingly, Marlena's twin was played by Deidre Hall's own identical twin, Andrea Hall-Lovell.
• A running murder, mayhem, and mystery story con-

cerned the nefarious Stefano Di Mera. After a year of nearly ruining everyone's life in Salem (and taking several lives as well) Stefano kidnapped a very pregnant Liz and Marlena and was captured; he died in jail of a heart attack.
• A new mystery developed after Liz aimed a gun at Marie and shot her, thinking she was a burglar. She was sent to prison after trying to hide the truth from the law. Meanwhile, Marlena's lovely cousin, Trista, came to Salem and became the target of a new, mysterious "follower."

MILESTONES IN SALEM

Well into the '70s "Days of Our Lives" remained one of daytime TV's most popular soaps. Even today, under the helm of headwriter Maggie dePriest, "Days of Our Lives" is NBC's highest-rated soap. On April 21, 1975, "Days of Our Lives" became the second soap in history to expand to a full hour. It was also the first soap to hold its own in a head-on competition with the then immensely popular "As the World Turns."

During its long run "Days of Our Lives" has initiated a number of innovative and often controversial stories. One of the first involved a nearly incestuous romance between brother and sister Tom and Marie Horton. When Tom returned to Salem his face had been changed by plastic surgery, the result of an accident he experienced during the Korean War. Tom was also an amnesia victim who called himself Dr. Mark Brooks. Meeting Marie, he became inexplicably attracted to her. When they discovered they were actually brother and sister, the shock caused Marie to leave town and become a nun. Years later she returned and is still a major character on the show.

Briefly described in the summary detailing Julie's history, Julie's son David was involved in an interracial romance. The romance came to an end when the actress playing Valerie reportedly pressured the network into letting her character kiss David for the first time on what was to be one of "Days of Our Lives'" highest-rated episodes ever (Doug and Julie were being married for the first time). Due to the extremely negative response from viewers, as indicated by the large volume of mail that poured into NBC's offices, and partly because of the adverse publicity created by the news media, "Days of Our Lives'" then headwriter, Pat Falken Smith, felt she had no choice but to write Valerie and her family out of the show.

Josh Taylor played Jake, the notorious Salem Strangler. Photo by Bob Deutsch.

A number of fans called to protest the death (at the hands of "the Salem Strangler") of Dr. Marlena Evans. Here Deidre Hall responds to a fan.

Richard Guthrie, who played David Banning before Gregg Marx took the part, in a scene with Tina Andrews, who plays Valerie Grant. Photo by Bob Deutsch.

Above: John de Lancie, who plays Eugene Bradford, is shown here displaying the bottles he's received that contain notes from his lady admirers. Photo by Nancy Wilcox.

Below: Bill Hayes, playing Doug Williams, prepares his music for the evening performance at his restaurant, Doug's Place. Hayes began his career as a singer. Photo by Bob Deutsch.

The character of Chris Kositchek is fascinating: a tireless inventor and friend of the psychic, Eugene Bradford. One of his inventions is a robot, which is used in Salem's hospital. The robot is really the creation of a company in New York that manufactures robots for various uses. However, the fame gained by having one of their metal-mental machines, SICO, on a popular soap has led some in the entertainment industry to wonder how soon flesh and blood actors may be replaced by SICO's descendants.

WHO'S WHO IN SALEM

Original Cast

Actor	Character
MACDONALD CAREY	**Dr. Tom Horton**
DICK COLLA	**Tony Merritt**
CHARLA DOUGHERTY	**Julie Olson**
BURT DOUGLAS	**Jim Fisk**
PAT HUSTON	**Addie Olson**
ROBERT KNAPP	**Ben Olson**
FLIP MARK	**Steve Olson**
DICK McLEAN	**Craig Merritt**
FRANCES REID	**Alice Horton**
ROBERT J. STEVENSON	**A detective**

First Air Date: November 8, 1965

Write to "Days of Our Lives" c/o NBC, 3000 West Alameda, Burbank, CA 91505.

A Directory of Recent Characters*

David Banning: Formerly wed to Renee Dumonde; formerly wed to Trish, with whom he had Scotty. *Gregg Marx*

Jessica Blake: Marie's daughter by Alex. *Jean Bruce Scott*

Eugene Bradford: Chris' friend; a psychic; in love with Trista. *John de Lancie.*

Anna Brady: Involved in Di Mera's past; tricked Tony into marriage; once wed to Roman. *Leann Hunley*

Kayla Brady: Roman's sister. *Catherine-Mary Stewart*

Roman Brady: A detective and husband of Marlena; formerly wed to Anna. *Wayne Northrup*

Abe Carver: A detective who helped Roman break the Salem Strangler case. *James Reynolds*

Liz Chandler: Once wed to Tony and Don and later involved with Neil. *Gloria Loring*

*The actors/actresses who currently play these major roles are in italics.

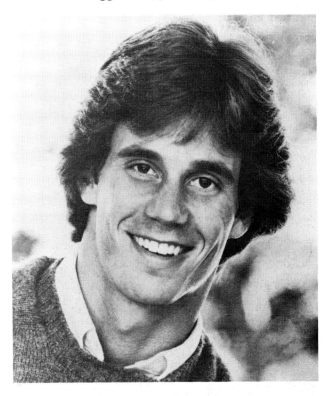

Gregg Marx, presently David Banning.

Thaao Penghlis.

Catherine Mary Stewart.

Don Craig: Ex of Marlena and Liz. *Jed Allen*

Dr. Neil Curtis: Divorced from Marie; was married to Phyllis; in love with Liz. *Joe Gallison*

Tony Di Mera: Married Liz but also loved Renee; his father is the late Stefano. *Thaao Penghlis*

Renee Dumonde: Daughter of Lee Dumonde; was married to Alex days before she was murdered. *Philece Sampler*

Dr. Marlena Evans: Don's ex; now Roman's wife. She was the Salem Strangler's wife's psychiatrist; he killed her twin, Samantha. *Dierdre Hall*

Alice Horton: Wife of Tom; mother of Mickey and Marie; grandmother of Jessica, Julie, and Sandy. *Frances Reid*

Maggie Horton: Mickey's wife; has a child fathered (through artificial insemination) by Evan Wyland. *Suzanne Rogers*

Marie Horton: Tom and Alice's daughter; Jessica's mother by former lover, Alex; Neil's former wife; Mickey's sister; a former nun. *Lanna Saunders*

Mickey Horton: A lawyer; wed to Maggie; Tom and Alice's son; Marie's brother. *John Clarke*

Sandy Horton: Tom and Alice's granddaughter. *Martha Smith*

Chris Kositchek: The brother of the Strangler; he invented the robot. *Josh Taylor*

Robert Leclair: The legal father of his good friend Doug's son. *Robert Clary*

Doug Williams: Wed twice to Julie; wed once to Lee; Owns Doug's Place on the Lake, a restaurant. *Bill Hayes*

Julie Williams: Doug's wife; mother of David Banning; granddaughter of Alice and Tom; grandmother of Scotty. *Susan Seaforth Hayes*

Left: Joe Gallison plays Dr. Neil Curtis. Here he is seen playing a forest ranger in the old series "Empire."

Below: Rosemary Forsythe (left) as Laura Horton and Deidre Hall as Dr. Marlena Evans Craig (now Brady). Photo by Bob Deutsch.

7

Edge of Night (ABC)

"Edge of Night" and "As the World Turns" both made their debuts on CBS on April 2, 1956: sister soaps brought forth by the venerable soap manufacturing company, Procter & Gamble. While "World" was conceived of as a "typical" soap, "Edge" was born and raised as a unique entity in the soap opera world. It was, and remains, the only soap with a murder/mystery/melodrama theme. Indeed, it's the only soap whose longtime writer, Henry Slesar (who recently left the series) was to win an Edgar, the coveted award presented by the prestigious Mystery Writers of America.

"Edge of Night" has had three headwriters during its 27-year run. Irving Vendig, who wrote "Search for Tomorrow" in its first few years, was the show's orig-

Forrest Compton and Ann Flood as Mike and Nancy Karr. Mike Karr is the only character remaining from the original show. In real life, Ann Flood is married to ABC vice-president, Herb Granath. Photo by Ed Geller.

inal writer, staying with it until 1966. Henry Slesar, who has written countless short stories for mystery magazines and scripts for "Alfred Hitchcock Presents," was "Edge of Night's" second headwriter. He was with the show until the middle of 1983, when Procter & Gamble released him, claiming it wanted to take the show in a new direction. "Edge of Night's" current headwriter is Lee Sheldon, who has written scripts for "Charlie's Angels," "Quincy," and "Eight Is Enough." Like Slesar, Lee Sheldon is also a recipient of the Edgar Award for superb suspense writing.

Although "Edge of Night" enjoyed healthy ratings during its first 15 years on the air, things changed when CBS was forced to switch its time slot to early afternoon due to pressure from Procter & Gamble, which decided it wanted all of its CBS soaps to air in a block. At the time, CBS was airing two of its own low-rated soaps, "Love Is a Many Splendored Thing" and "Secret Storm," between Procter & Gamble soaps. The change in scheduling resulted in CBS's two soaps being canceled within a year and a half. As for the "Edge of Night," its ratings continued to slide downhill. Finally, in 1975, "As the World Turns" was expanded to an hour, forcing CBS to cancel "Edge of Night," since the network no longer had any room for it on its schedule. ABC immediately picked up "Edge of Night."

Besides the fact that "Edge of Night" has been a thematic soap in which murder and mystery remain as the basic elements, it has other distinctions: Before the Academy of Television Arts & Sciences created The Daytime Emmy category, "EON" won an Emmy for the 1972–73 series. The honor was presented during the regular nighttime awards ceremony. The first Mike Karr was played by the late John Larkin, who was radio's first Perry Mason, while ex-"Edge" actor Frank Adonis went on to write and star in the thriller-chiller movie, *Ripper*.

"Edge of Night" was not the name the writers originally had in mind for the daytime mystery serial. The original scheme was to produce a TV counterpart for radio's Perry Mason, and the new serial would have carried the same name if a deal could have been negotiated with the original "Perry Mason" show. Curiously, "Edge of Night" proved to be an appropriate title anyway; the show was for years broadcast toward the end of CBS's afternoon schedule, and the phrase also conveyed the feeling of impending darkness that was crucial to the mystery theme. Even the word "edge" implied that, as in the "Perry Mason" episodes, danger would threaten the main characters but never overpower them in the final analysis.

WELCOME TO MONTICELLO

The Citizens

Because "Edge of Night" is a mystery drama, the show hasn't been able to keep the same roster of characters involved in its storylines for the length of time the other soaps do. In fact, characters are killed or sent up the river for life so often that major characters may last for only a year or two. This situation has, however, allowed "Edge" to feature a raft of different well-known actors and actresses over the years. (For more on such "graduates" from "EON," see Chapter 16.)

Like "Perry Mason," "Edge of Night" has often revolved around the Monticello courtrooms. Also like the radio mystery show, "Edge's" original main characters were attorneys, Mike Karr and Adam Drake. Another important figure in Monticello action has always been the local chief of police; in the original show the character was Bill Marceau; in the '70s and '80s the chief was Derek Mallory. To stretch the Perry Mason connection to "EON" even further, the original Mike Karr was actor John Larkin, who once played the analytical Perry on the radio.

Only one character remains from the original cast: that of Mike Karr, played first by Larkin, then by Larry Hugo, and currently by Forrest Compton. While Mike is "Edge's" only link to the 1950s, in its 27-year history the show has picked up some of its ordinarily temporary characters and developed them into fixtures of Monticello. For at least the last five years, for example, the show has featured a cast of characters that more closely resembles the core families of other daytime dramas.

To set the stage for the murderous theme of "Edge of Night," the characters that have endured on the show represent wealth and power; others stay involved in the mysteries that come and go by virtue of their occupations: lawyers, police officers and detectives, reporters, and medical examiners.

Over the last 27 years, some major characters have emerged. Here's a list of the most memorable families that have come and gone:

Joel Crothers (left) and Dennis Parker, playing Miles Cavanaugh and Derek Mallory respectively, have been two of "Edge of Night's" leading lights in the last five years. Crothers is an alumnus of several soaps, including "Dark Shadows." He appeared in the hit, Tony-winning Broadway play, Torch Song Trilogy, before it reached Broadway and still does a great deal of theater. Parker has also done several films. Photo by Bob Deutsch.

The Lanes

Sarah Lane was Mike Karr's first wife, but she was killed, and this founding family was phased out pretty quickly.

The Marceaus

This family lasted until the mid-70s. It consisted of chief of police Bill and wife Martha; Bill's daughter by his first marriage, who left town; the couple's adopted daughter, who was later blown up in a car. Bill was replaced as chief of police and the Marceaus were phased out.

The Whitneys

The Whitneys have been movers and shakers in Monticello for years. The family: Gordon and Geraldine as politician and matriarchal wife; sons Collin (another politician) and Keith (a schizophrenic); Collin's wife Tiffany. All but Geraldine were later killed.

The Hillyers

This family included Rich Orin; daughter Liz; and Liz's husband Dr. Jim Fields. After a divorce, Liz left Monticello to take care of ailing Orin, and Jim crossed the border for a new job in Canada.

The Cavanaughs

Dr. Miles Cavanaugh has remained active on "EON" for years. Frail sister April, who later married Draper Scott, was involved in much mayhem before she and her husband left the country. Miles had two wives: scheming, jealous, and eventually murderous Denise, and Nicole, who finally was able to marry Miles when Denise died. Nicole died mid-1983.

Where the Action Is in Monticello

Monticello isn't much different from any other soap-opera town. There's a rumor that Monticello is really Cincinnati, the home of sponsor Procter & Gamble's empire. Typical of soap cities—and of most American cities of this size—Monticello has suburbs of varying economic levels and varying degrees of elegance within the city. There is the Karr residence, typical of the modest but nice homes many soap characters inhabit; the sophisticated penthouse occupied by the late Nicole and husband Miles Cavanaugh, originally the domicile of April Scott's long-lost mother; and the

Left: Terry Davis played April Cavanaugh Scott.

Below, right: Celebrating the soap's 7,000th segment on April 21, 1983, are (left to right) Sharon Gabet (Raven), Larkin Malloy (Sky), and Lois Kibbee (Geraldine Whitney). Photo by Ed Geller. A former soaper, Sigourney Weaver, appears with Joel Crothers (Miles Cavanaugh). Photo by Bob Deutsch.

Whitney mansion. All of these places have been the scenes of crimes. When it comes time to solve those crimes the action switches to the usual detective-story sites: police headquarters, the courthouse, Dr. Cavanaugh's office (he's also the medical examiner/coroner), Mike Karr's and other lawyers' offices, and the local hospital, where many a death-bed confession has been given and last-gasp clues have been revealed.

In its later years, "Edge of Night" has also taken some of its major characters to farflung lands, where the mystery has continued. Examples include Switzerland, where the Sky Whitney impostor was killed, and the Caribbean, where Raven's marriage of "convenience" was ended when husband Ian Devereaux was caught in the act of espionage.

The Crimes of Monticello

Courtroom dramas remain the most intriguing aspects of "Edge" storylines. Even as the culprits prey on their victims and the forces of good draw closer to capturing or otherwise dispatching the nasties, a veteran viewer conjures up visions of what the most recent courtroom confrontation might be like.

In the past, murderers have been killed on courthouse steps; innocent people have been convicted (but are ultimately freed); and decisions about child custody, money divisions, and so forth have marked some of the Monticello court calendars.

Due to the nature of the show, Monticello's plot has always contained a good deal of contrived and sensational storylines, so perhaps it didn't need to be updated to the same extent as other soaps that have jumped on the "GH" bandwagon. However, with the injection of younger characters over the last several years—such as Mitzi (Lela Ivey), Jody (Lori Laughlin), and others—"Edge of Night's" mysteries are more and more likely to involve the younger set these days, and some of the more recent storylines have reflected this trend.

"EON" mysteries have featured haunted houses, religious cults, black-market babies, and a mythical country where Jody was once held prisoner. But no matter what the circumstances, the storyline of "Edge of Night" adds up to murder, murder, and more murder. As producer Erwin ("Nick") Nicholson says, "No one knows who may become the next victim on this series. Anyone may turn out to be the corpse or the culprit. No one is safe."

Lori Loughlin (Jody Travis) is one of several young stars featured on the "Edge of Night" of the '80s. Loughlin also carries on a modeling career and appeared in the flick Amityville-3D. *Photo by Bob Deutsch.*

MONTICELLO'S POLICE BLOTTER

There's been so much crime in Monticello over the last some 25 years that it's amazing that Mike Karr hasn't retired to some out-of-the-way spot to while away his life uneventfully. Tracing all of the crime he's seen would be a massive task. But we can take a look at the town's crime history by tracing the events of stalwart Nancy Karr's life. Nancy, who married Mike close on the heels of his first wife's death, has always been gracious and graceful, intelligent and insightful, beautiful and usually serene. After a hard day in court, Mike could usually count on coming home to the welcoming arms of his supportive wife, who has seen it all.

*Erwin "Nick" Nicholson, executive producer of "Edge," discusses a scene
with Ann Flood, who has played Nancy Karr for 20 years.*

Monticello through the Eyes of Nancy Karr

One of Nancy's main tasks throughout Monticello history has been to keep her family together—not always an easy task. She was crushed when her sister Cookie was committed to a mental hospital after discovering her husband was fooling around with Tiffany Whitney. Then Nancy's stepdaughter, Laurie, fell for the evil half of schizo Keith Whitney's personality. Laurie was saved from death in the nick of time, and Keith was killed instead.

Nancy, along with Mike, was also responsible for matchmaking outside the family. The memorable wedding of Adam Drake and Nicole Travis was held at the Karr home, and Nancy and Nicole were always close.

Again Nancy's protective instincts came into play when she and Mike suspected Laurie's new love, Johnny Dallas, of being mob-connected. Johnny eventually was led to the path of righteousness, however, and Nancy and Mike gave Laurie their blessings when she married Johnny.

In a subsequent storyline concerning one of several "EON" schizophrenics, Nancy and Mike became the foster parents of Timmy Faraday. When the boy's aunt showed up to claim the child, Nancy was again touched by tragedy. Preying on her attachment to Timmy, the burgeoning Monticello mob kidnapped Timmy and threatened to kill him unless Nancy fed information to them on Mike's investigations of the syndicate. Nancy was thrown into a quandary: she had to save Timmy, but she couldn't bear to do so at the expense of Mike's career. Her solution was to leave him. This, of course, suggested that she had become involved with perpetrator Beau Richardson.

When Richardson was killed the obvious suspect was jealous Mike Karr. The couple rallied together during this time of crisis and Mike was cleared.

After the Beau Richardson incident Nancy's life was relatively calm—until she began investigating a sanitarium run by the diabolical Dr. Kenneth Bryson and his wife Beth. Originally, Dr. Bryson kidnapped Nancy, fearing she'd expose his illegal activities (he was a plastic surgeon who helped give underworld mobsters new identities). However, Dr. Bryson soon discovered he was in love with Nancy. Wanting to leave his wife, Dr. Bryson made plans to give Nancy a new face and run away with her to a foreign country. He even hoped Nancy would one day come to love him as much as he loved her. Fortunately Nancy was rescued before Dr. Bryson had a chance to hoist her onto his operating table.

With the exception of a few close friends being murdered (not an uncommon occurrence in Monticello), Nancy resumed leading a peaceful existence with her husband Mike Karr. Recently, however, Nancy quit her job as a reporter and wrote a play for the Whitney theatre. The endeavor took up a lot of her time, causing Mike to become very jealous. Considering their track record, though, the couple will more than likely be able to work out their differences.

The Constant Victim: Nicole

If Nancy's own life has been relatively calm by Monticello standards, Nicole's has been bizarre at best. Here are a few examples of the strange events to touch Nicole:

1. Nancy's supposed friend Stephanie tried to drive Nicole crazy to avenge the death of her husband and daughter, caused by the mob to which Nicole's father belonged.

2. The new wife of Nicole's ex-husband tried to kill Nicole but murdered Stephanie instead. Nicole was accused of the crime but was acquitted through the skill of attorney Adam Drake, her future husband.

3. Nicole's fiance, Adam, was framed for murder but finally cleared.

4. Nicole was reported killed after a Caribbean cruise

Maeve McGuire was the original Nicole Drake. She returned to soaps as Elena dePoulignac on "Another World." Photo by Bob Deutsch.

ship she and Adam were on was blown up by the mob.

5. Nicole returned to Monticello after having been in a coma for months, and immediately someone started trying to kill her.

6. Adam realized Nicole's peril, and Nicole's doctor suggested using drugs to find out what terrible secret Nicole had learned before her alleged death.

7. Dr. Clay Jordan turned out to be the man who was trying to do away with Nicole. Hired by the mob to find out how much she knew, Dr. Jordan posed as a psychiatrist who would cure Nicole's amnesia, which also made her forget that when she had been rescued from the Caribbean incident she had been to a place called Limbo Island!

8. In the last several years Nicole has had a supposedly terminal disease, has been accused of murder, has been united with her half-sister Jody, and has been killed for good as a result of a change in writing staff and the actress's decision to leave.

Denise Cavanaugh, played by Holland Taylor (standing) tried to keep her husband Miles (Joel Crothers) and Nicole Drake (Jayne Bentzen) apart. She failed dismally.

Donald May played the role of Nicole's ill-fated husband, Adam Drake. Photo by Howard Gray.

Terry Davis (April Cavanaugh) and Tony Craig (Draper Scott) at their nuptials.

AFFAIRS TO REMEMBER

While "Edge of Night" is a mystery show, it is also a soap opera, and as such its storylines have been peppered with a healthy shake of romance. Some affairs that linger in our minds, in addition to those already discussed in this chapter, follow.

Practically every love affair on "Edge of Night" has been marked by melodrama.

- April Scott was deeply in love with her husband, Draper. Draper was falsely accused of killing her mother and was sent to jail. He escaped, and became an amnesiac after a train wreck. A woman named Emily was sure he was her long-missing husband and even insisted, long after Draper remembered who he was and returned to April, that he had fathered her child. It turned out that a guard at Emily's sanitarium was the father.
- The character of Raven, introduced during the '70s, has been involved with several men on the soap.

She was married to Logan Swift with whom she had a child. She later carried on affairs with Sky Whitney and married his lookalike, one of the men whom the evil Dr. Bryson worked on. She dallied with a detective, Derek, in hopes of getting him to testify on her behalf in Logan's custody suit for Jamie. She pursued the real Sky Whitney but, at the instigation of the U.S. government, agreed to marry another admirer, Ian Devereaux, who might be able to slip her some secrets she could then turn over to the Feds. Later the real Sky Whitney admitted he was in love with her and he and Raven were married.

- The teenager, Jody, first fell in love with Nancy's nephew, Kelly. Then she started feeling passionate about a dance instructor, Gavin, especially after there was some suspicion about that Kelly was a killer doing away with some of Monticello's citizenry. Kelly wasn't the murderer, but by that time he'd lost Jody to Gavin and eventually he packed up and went to Italy.
- Another murder got Jody involved in another ro-

Above: A grand wedding for Raven (played by Sharon Gabet) and Schulyer Whitney (Larkin Malloy). In this photo, she's actually marrying Sky's lookalike, Jefferson Brown (also played by Malloy). Photo by Bob Deutsch.

Right: Mark Arnold (Gavin) and Lori Loughlin (Jody). Photo by Bob Deutsch.

Lori Loughlin, as Jody Travis, and Charles Flohe, as Preacher Emerson, were 1983's young lovers. Flohe's character began as a bad guy but caught on quickly with the fans and was thus "redeemed." Photo by Ed Geller.

mance. When her sister, Nicole, and brother-in-law, Miles, became suspects in the death of one Nora Fulton, Jody put on lots of makeup and sashayed to a disco where she met the manager, a James Dean-like man named Preacher. Jody and Preacher developed their relationship beneath the flickering lasers of Monticello's hippest disco and the writers intimate they expect this romance to go at full tilt for a long time.

MURDER/MAYHEM/MYSTERY

These are the bywords of "Edge of Night," and the intricate storylines are too numerous to mention here. But several themes have run through much of Monticello's mystery plot.

Amnesia

Amnesia is one of the most often used techniques on "Edge." Draper Scott suffered from it. Draper was accused of murdering his mother-in-law. On the way to jail he was involved in a train wreck; after his escape, he suffered amnesia for months.

As mentioned earlier, Nicole also suffered from amnesia.

Allen Fawcett, who played the troubled but talented Kelly.

Switzerland, his loyal chauffeur Gunther was done in and another innocent soul—this time Gavin—was indicted. But Mike Karr came up with a solid defense and evidence was presented to prove someone else shot the chauffeur.

By the way, the audience was furious when Gunther—played by the affable part-American Indian David Frohman—was done in. So it was revealed that it wasn't Gunther who died of lead poisoning from a high-caliber gun but his twin brother, Bruno, a real cad. Gunther came back, and the audience reacted with an outpouring of thank-you letters.

In a mystery, again involving Raven, which concerned the theft of industrial secrets, the hapless adventuress proved she had courage when she agreed to marry the mysterious Ian to track down his culprits for the authorities. Marrying Ian produced this polymer of a name for the lady: Raven Alexander Jamison Swift Whitney/Brown Devereaux. Raven has since married the real Sky, so add Whitney to the list.

Rita Jenrette poses with Ray Serra. They played secretary Barbi Kennilworth and gangster boss Eddie Lorimer.

Schizophrenia

The two most notable examples are Keith Whitney, who was killed when his "bad" personality tried to kill his lover, and Serena Faraday, whose alter ego killed her ex-husband.

Paranoia

In fall, 1983, the whole town started going bonkers. The lovely Dr. Corell was called in to help.

Mistaken Identity and Imposture

A big storyline of the last few years centered on the Sky Whitney/Jefferson Brown switch.

The Sky Whitney mixup concerns the aforementioned plastic surgery gambit. A dastard named Jefferson Brown had himself remade to look like Sky so that he could play the rich man-about-Monticello and marry the town's most beautiful woman, Raven.

After Jefferson's comeuppance on a ski slope in

Ernie Townsend plays Cliff, a young lawyer and sleuth. He was one of several soap actors who appeared in the Broadway hit Deathtrap. *Photo by Bob Deutsch.*

The Wrong Victim

Someone's always killing the wrong victim on this show: Pamela Stewart killed Stephanie instead of the intended Nicole. Elly Jo Jamison was killed herself while attempting to murder Liz Hiller and her unborn child. The mob killed Vic Lamont instead of its intended victim, Johnny Dallas. Tiffany was killed when she was mistaken for Nicole.

In the Wrong Place at the Wrong Time

Nicole was accused of killing Stephanie because she left her fingerprints on the knife that killed her when she tried to pull it out of the body.

Adam Drake was set up for the murder of Jake Berman.

Martha Marceau was lured to an apartment where she was set up so that it looked as if she had killed Taffy Simms.

Tracy ran away when she thought she'd be sus-pected of having pushed Geraldine down some stairs, but actually Noel was the guilty party.

Mike was accused of killing Beau Richardson out of jealousy.

Kelly was accused of several murders due to cir-cumstantial evidence.

Nicole was charged with killing Nora because she was at the scene of the crime.

MONTICELLO MILESTONES

"Edge of Night" held out until the very end and was the last show to switch to videotape from live broadcasts.

Another notable moment in the show's history came in 1972, when "EON" became the second to receive the Emmy for best daytime serial.

"Edge of Night" was the first soap to have a resi-dent dance company and a real choreographer, Mich-elle Marceau. The dance storylines began several years ago and were recently phased out.

WHO'S WHO IN MONTICELLO

Original Cast

Actor	Character
TEAL AMES	**Sarah Lane**
SARAH BURTON	**Harry's wife**
BETTY GARDE	**Mattie Lane**
LAUREN GILBERT	**Uncle Harry Lane**
WALTER GREAZA	**Winston Grimsley**
DON HASTINGS	**Jack Lane**
JOHN LARKIN	**Mike Karr**
IAN MARTIN	**A detective Sgt.**
MARY MOOR	**Betty Jean Lane**
MARY ALICE MOORE	**Harry's secretary**

First Air Date: April 2, 1956

Write to "Edge of Night" c/o ABC, 1330 Avenue of the Americas, New York, NY 10019

A Directory of Recent Characters*

Didi Bannister: A lawyer. *Mariann Aalda*

Miles Cavanaugh: A doctor married to the late Nicole; adoptive father of Adam, Jr.; brother of April Scott; formerly married to Denise. *Joel Crothers*

Nicole Cavanaugh: Newswoman first married to Adam Drake, then to Miles; mother of Adam, Jr; half-sister of Jody; killed in 1983. *Lisa Sloan*

Mike Karr: A crusading lawyer, married to Nancy. *Forrest Compton*

Nancy Karr: Investigative reporter, married to Mike Karr. *Ann Flood*

Derek Mallory: Chief of police; widowed; former lover of Raven and Poppy. *Dennis Parker*

Cliff Nelson: A lawyer and associate of Didi; provides comic relief. *Ernie Townsend*

*The actors/actresses who currently play these major roles are in italics.

Geraldine Saxon: The matriarch; Sky Whitney's aunt and owner of WMON; formerly wed to Tony Saxon, a powerful politician. *Lois Kibbee*

Calvin Stoner: A detective. *Irving Lee*

Jody Travis: Nicole's half-sister; once involved with Kelly and Gavin, she's now Preacher's love. *Lori Loughlin*

Gunther Wagner: Sky's chauffeur and twin of Bruno, who died. *David Froman*

Raven Alexander Jamison Swift Whitney/Brown Devereaux Whitney: Daughter of a rich woman who has been married to Kevin, Logan, Jefferson, Ian, and now Sky. *Sharon Gabet*

Schuyler Whitney: Geraldine's kin and Raven's husband; Monticello's richest man. *Larkin Malloy*

Preacher: A hard-on-the-outside-but-sensitive-on-the-inside disco manager involved with Jody. *Charles Flohe*

8

General Hospital (ABC)

"General Hospital" went on the air on April 1, 1963, over the ABC network, the first successful ABC soap. As one of its two remaining cast members, John Beradino (Dr. Steve Hardy), said: "The date is April's Fool and very significant. It would prove either that we were fooling ourselves if we thought we had a chance to succeed or that we would fool those who thought we had no such chance."

The other remaining original cast member, Emily McLaughlin (Nurse Jessie Brewer), recalled: "We were so sure that we had the cast and the stories but that somehow that wouldn't be enough. Fortunately, our most positive feelings proved true."

From its premiere in 1963 until the early '70s, "General Hospital" was ABC's top-rated soap. During the mid-70s, however, "General Hospital's" ratings took a nosedive. Daytime TV fan magazines called the show stale. At one point things got so bad that several cast members actually protested what they felt were horrible scripts.

During the '60s such detriments as dull sets peppered with stiff nurses who seemed anchored in place like mannequins and the predictable organ music were forgivable. After all, that's what all the CBS and NBC soaps were like, too. And up until the mid-70s the show persisted in using its outdated gimmick of calling each of its short segments "acts." The hospital sets were dreary and unimaginative, characters who served no real purpose to the show's story continued to make appearances, and the stories moved at a snail's pace.

For the past five years, however, a modernized "GH" has hovered close to or at the very top of the ratings roster and continues to be the soap most other series feel is their most consistent competitor.

For today's fans, "General Hospital" is the soap that brought the genre to the college campus. Many of the new "GH" viewers expect the heroes and heroines of Port Charles to battle all types of fantastical evil forces—and that's what they usually get.

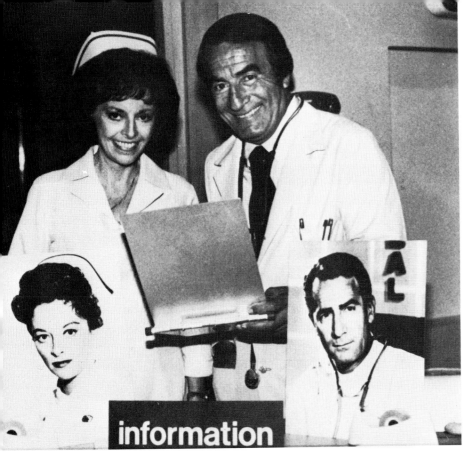

Left: Emily McLaughlin and John Beradino, shown as they appeared in 1978 and 15 years earlier when their characters were first created.

Below: In 1975 the "General Hospital" staff was plagued by this question: Who murdered Dr. Phil Brewer (Martin West, center foreground)? The five prime suspects were portrayed by, from left in background, Judith McConnell, Craig Huebing, James Sikking, Emily McLaughlin, and Valerie Starrett.

WELCOME TO PORT CHARLES

The premise of "General Hospital" originally was to tell the stories of people whose lives moved around the General Hospital of the city of Port Charles, New York. While "GH" has reached far afield of Port Charles and the simplicity of that statement, this was still essentially the case in the early 1980s.

The Citizens

In the case of "General Hospital" the core family is, rather than a normal nuclear family, the staff of the hospital. Over "GH's" 20-plus years many prominent families have been featured in Port Charles doings, but there is no core family *per se* that has been with "GH" for the duration. The staff member characters are, obviously, almost all doctors and nurses. Occasionally a patient has been developed into a long-term character as well. To give an overview of this ever-changing family, the following lists prominent characters of the past and present. Nurse Jessie Brewer and Dr. Steve Hardy are the only characters who remain from the original character list.

(An asterisk denotes those characters who have been seen on the show for at least several years. The names given include only the final or most current surname the characters had.)

The Doctors

Dr. Steve Hardy*
Dr. Prentice*
Dr. Peter Taylor*
Dr. Tom Baldwin*
Dr. Lesley Williams Webber
Dr. James Hobart*
Dr. Howie Dawson*
Dr. Henry Pinkham*
Dr. Alan Quartermaine
Dr. Monica Webber Quartermaine
Dr. Gail Baldwin
Dr. Mark Dante
Dr. Phil Brewer
Dr. Jeff Webber*
Dr. Rick Webber
Dr. Noah Drake
Dr. Grant Putnam

The Nurses

Lucille March*
Audrey Hardy[1]
Diana Taylor[1]
Meg Baldwin*
Jessie Brewer*
Bobbie Spencer

Amy Vining
Ann Logan*

Other Major Characters

Lee Baldwin
Al Weeks*
Eddie Weeks*
Lenore Weeks*
Edward and Lyla Quartermaine
Heather Webber
Alice Grant
Susan Moore
[1]These characters entered the medical profession after being introduced to the show.
Laura Webber
Luke Spencer
Ruby Anderson
Dan Rooney
Tiffany Hill
Robert Scorpio
Jackie Templeton
Rose Kelly
Joe Kelly*
Scott Baldwin
Bryan Phillips
Claudia Phillips

Gerald Gordon recently returned to his role as Dr. Mark Dante. He was also Dr. Bellini on "The Doctors" years ago.

Above: Leslie Charleson plays Dr. Monica Quartermaine, who specializes in a typically male specialty: cardiac surgery.

Rick Springfield was a successful rock star when he joined "General Hospital." He's since left the show but may be returning. Photo by Ed Geller.

David Lewis (Edward Quartermaine) won the Daytime Emmy in 1982. Photo by Ed Geller.

Stuart Damon, the Brooklyn-born Dr. Alan Quartermaine.

Chris Robinson plays Dr. Rick Webber. Photo by Bob Deutsch.

Kin Shriner (Scotty Baldwin) is the son of Herb Shriner. He also has a twin.

Above: Sharon Wyatt plays Tiffany Hill. Photo by Ed Geller.

Right: Rose Kelly is her name, and making the folks of Port Charles feel at home in her pub is her game. Off screen, the lady who plays her is Loanne Bishop. Photo by Ed Geller.

Far from an exhaustive list, the preceding roster should give an idea of the demographics of Port Charles. In the last five years or so, "GH's" main families have been the Hardys, the Webbers, the Baldwins, the Quartermaines (introduced during the late '70s), and a hodgepodge group of waterfront characters led by the lovely Rose Kelly and attorney Joe Kelly, who happens to be her stepson, though they're about the same age.

EVERYDAY PORT CHARLES EVENTS

Most of Port Charles' everyday events would be once-in-a-lifetime events for real people. For the last several years the "GH" writers have given the new youthful audience what they apparently want: adventure and more adventure. This is not to say that love and romance have been neglected, but many critics and viewers feel the show peaked with Luke and Laura and that there will never be a love story to equal that one.

But if "GH" seems to have gone somewhat astray with its way-out plots, as ratings of 1982-83 attest, there is another element that exists on the show that keeps many viewers entranced. It's not altogether unlike the hope that is instilled in "Ryan's Hope;" in the case of "GH," however, even that quality is inflated to heroic proportions. It's not difficult to understand why the audience loves to see the Spencers and company from the wrong side of the tracks not only make good but save the entire world! There is a certain spirit and sense of humor in the caste battles between the legitimate Quartermaines and the less-well-brought-up illegitimate ones, between Luke and the establishment, between Bobbie and the spectre of her past. The camaraderie (of the past) between Luke and Robert Scorpio, the stormy marriage of the doctors Quartermaine, and the indomitable attitude of almost all the characters has a broad appeal.

So, in Port Charles, if you're a tourist, expect to meet a lot of feisty individuals—and don't be surprised to find yourself neck deep in a perilous struggle for no less than world power.

LOOKING BACK AT PORT CHARLES

When "General Hospital" was first broadcast it was 30 minutes long and taped in black and white. This format proved successful until the mid-70s, when the show found itself in serious ratings trouble.

Desperate measures were taken to save the show. In 1976 almost half the cast was written out. New characters were introduced and then, just as suddenly, were written out. Loyal viewers wrote letters complaining about the show's inconsistency.

Despite "General Hospital's" horrendous ratings, Fred Silverman, then in charge of programming at ABC, forged ahead with plans in 1976 to expand the show to 45 minutes, consisting of six "acts." Although the gimmick worked for "One Life to Live," which was flip-flopped with "General Hospital" on the schedule (instead of following "GH," "OLTL" now preceded it), the expanded format did nothing to improve "General Hospital's" ratings. It was even reported that, after viewing the show's 45-minute premiere episode, Silverman ordered the episode canned because it still looked too old-fashioned. Considering the changes that had taken place on other soaps in the mid-70s, "General Hospital" did look pretty dated.

In all fairness, Tom Donovan, the show's producer when it was 45 minutes long, and the Pollocks, "GH's" writers at that time, did make a conscious effort to improve the quality of the program. Unfortunately, the ratings still weren't increasing.

Firing the producer and writers, ABC, which still had faith in "General Hospital," appointed Gloria Monty to be the new producer and went ahead with plans to expand the show to a full hour in 1978. One of Glory Monty's first changes was to make Douglas Marland "General Hospital's" new headwriter.

The changes made by Gloria Monty, with the help of writer Marland and others, revolutionized "General Hospital." Monty revamped all the sets to brighten up Port Charles, she made all the major characters more active by giving every one of them problems and conflicts, and she injected romantic fantasy into the scripts to give "GH" something different to attract viewers and compete with the other "standard" soaps.

Of course, the most well-known romantic fantasy storyline involved the infamous "Luke and Laura." But even before running into Luke, Laura was a controversial character in her own right. Her mother was Dr. Lesley Webber, a woman who had borne her and then given her up for adoption and later reclaimed her. Lesley also went to jail for her, taking the blame when Laura was accused of killing a man she thought loved her.

Luke had come along as part of a criminal subculture in Port Charles. His aunt had been a madam; his sister, Bobbie (later to become a nurse at General

Hospital) was a prostitute.

The Luke and Laura romance, noteworthy also for the controversial "rape" storyline, caught the imagination of younger audiences who immediately adopted "General Hospital" as the "Rocky Horror Show" of soaps.

Unfortunately, "GH's" ratings dropped slightly around the time when Genie Francis (Laura) left the show. At this time the series had gone through a series of different writers, and to viewers it was fairly obvious that the show was floundering frantically in an attempt to hold onto its lofty position. By the middle of 1983, while "GH" still featured adventure plots, it seemed to have been starting to return to some of the more traditional daytime plots—most of them focusing on romance. In contrast with the sensational storylines that rejuvenated the show, "GH" recently began a story in which young bride Claudia was having a hard time adjusting to the lifestyle her husband can provide, which is much more modest than her well-to-do upbringing.

Over the years "General Hospital" has been the scene of numerous romantic entanglements among medical personnel. The love lives of such "GH" women as Lesley, Monica, Audrey, Bobbie, Gail, and others have run the usual course of getting together, breaking up, and getting together again. The only female character who has been with the show since the beginning is Jessie Brewer, and until the Gloria Monty days, Jessie's love life often dominated the "GH" scripts.

Jessie Brewer—Unlucky in Love

It may very well have been the character of Jessie Brewer, played wonderfully throughout "GH" history by Emily McLaughlin, that kept this series near the top of the ratings during the '60s. Jessie is a very sympathetic character: kind and generous, dignified and gracious, Jessie was the ideal to many women—a perfect modern Florence Nightingale. What made the dedicated nurse even more appealing to many fans was the fact that her good heart often got into her sad romantic affairs that left Jessie alone with her medical charts. Over the last 20 years a number of suitors—some almost worthy of her, but most out-and-out cads—have broken Nurse Brewer's heart, and the audience loved sympathizing with Jessie when another louse proceeded to "do her wrong."

Jessie's first tragic romance involved Dr. Phil Brewer, a younger man whose wandering eye was

Nurse Jessie Brewer, played by Emily McLaughlin, as she appeared in the mid-'70s.

often trained on pretty young nurses. The Brewers were divorced after a sickly baby, born to them as a result of a drunken attack on Jessie by Phil, died. Next Jessie turned to Dr. Prentice, who was terminally ill. When Dr. Prentice committed suicide to end his agony, Jessie was charged with murder. Phil proved to be a strong support for Jessie during this ordeal, and when she was cleared they wed again. Through a series of bizarre incidences, Phil disappeared, and eventually Jessie fell for and married a third MD, a psychiatrist by the name of Peter Taylor. As soap-opera luck would have it, Phil then made an untimely reappearance. To avoid being a bigamist, Jessie had her marriage to Peter annulled and tried to make a life with Phil again. Various complications intervened, including Lee Baldwin's falling in love with Jessie and Phil's falling for Diana Maynard. Phil left Jessie again, leaving her vulnerable to the dubious charms of newspaperman Teddy Holmes, who was also younger than Jessie and was seeking a meal ticket. But Jessie was dealt another blow when Holmes ran off with Jessie's niece and ward, Carol, doubling the insult by leaving Jessie to pay off a huge debt he had incurred.

It's not suprising that all of these experiences made Jessie wary of love. During the late '70s, when Dan Rooney became the administrator of General Hospital, it looked as if Jessie's ideal nice guy had finally appeared. Jessie resisted Dan's advances but finally gave in to his suggestion that they go away for a weekend together. Jessie discovered that she just wasn't modern enough to have an affair; nor was she actually in love with Dan. They parted and remain good friends.

During the '80s Jessie Brewer has been seen mainly in the background of "GH," but who knows what future scripts will hold?

AFFAIRS TO REMEMBER

"General Hospital" has featured many torrid romances since 1963. Some of the most memorable ones are described below.

Lucille March: Middle-aged Lucille married Tom Weeks, after a long romance, in 1973. Both characters were part of the show's original roster.

Audrey March: Audrey, introduced to Port Charles during its early years by sister Lucille, has had some rough marriages. Upon her arrival in Port Charles, she fell instantly in love with Steve Hardy, and they were married. But they divorced after Audrey lost a baby and blamed Steve. After leaving Port Charles for a while, she returned, became a nurse, and married Dr. Tom Baldwin. This marriage was an unhappy one as well, and the couple was divorced after Tom raped Audrey, who became pregnant. She left town to have the baby, and when she returned she told everyone that the baby had died. Tom found out that the baby was alive, well, and being hidden out of town, so Audrey agreed to return to him rather than lose her child to him. They were later divorced again, and Audrey married Dr. Jim Hobart, whose hands had been ruined in an accident. Sexual problems arose between them because Audrey didn't really love Jim; she just felt sorry for him. Eventually Audrey remarried Steve, and the happy family was made complete when they were reunited with Audrey and Tom's son Tommy, whom Tom had kidnapped years earlier. *Current name:* Audrey March Hardy Baldwin Hobart Hardy.

Lee Baldwin: Early in "GH" history attorney Lee fell in love with Jessie, who was unavailable. So he married Meg, the mother of Scotty. When Meg died, Scotty was left in Lee's care. (It was around this point in time that Lesley appeared on the "GH" scene; she was Meg's doctor during her illness.)

Lesley Williams: Lesley had an unfortunate affair with former professor Gordon Gray—a notable romance because it produced daughter Laura, whom Lesley gave away and then reclaimed. Lesley married Rick Webber in the mid- to late '70s. They were divorced after Rick had a fleeting affair with Monica, but eventually remarried. *Current name:* Lesley Williams Webber Webber.

Monica: Blonde bombshell doctor Monica first married Jeff Webber on "GH," but she also wanted his brother, Rick. After Monica and Jeff were divorced, Monica met Alan Quartermaine, another doctor whose surgical career had been cut short by an accident that affected his hands. They hated each other at first, and this love-hate relationship has been characteristic of their subsequent marriage. Alan once tried to kill Monica and Rick when he discovered their affair, but Alan and Monica were eventually reconciled. *Current name:* Monica Webber Quartermaine.

Jeff Webber: The younger of the Webber brothers always has had unhappy loves. First he married Monica. He moved from this turbulent marriage to a second one to Heather Grant, whom he married because Heather was pregnant with his child. After a series of transgressions, including stealing their baby and running off to New York to become a star, Heather lost Jeff. Later Jeff fell in love with virginal nurse Ann Logan, who kept waiting for Jeff to free himself from Heather, who was confined to a mental hospital. When Jeff took son Steven Lars out west to get him away from Heather's influence, he fell for a nurse in his new hospital, whom he married, sending Ann a cursory Dear John letter.

Peter and Diana: This couple had a troubled relationship right from the start. Diana married Peter only to give her child by Phil Brewer a name. She found herself falling in love with her husband, but Phil raped her and impregnated her a second time. When Peter found out about the parentage of the child, he divorced Diana, even though they were still in love. After much soul-searching, the two remarried. Both characters were killed off in the early '80s.

Bobbie Spencer: Bobbie may be the only major "GH" character who has never been married on the show. A reformed prostitute, Bobbie has been trying to find her true love for years. When brother Luke was still involved with the mob, Bobbie fell for his partner, Roy. Roy was killed and Bobbie was devastated. Some of Bobbie's later romances were foiled by the skeletons in Bobbie's closet, including a romance with the pretty Dr. Noah Drake, whose blueblood family didn't approve of Bobbie. As of mid-1983 Bobbie was cautiously moving into a romance with Port Charles newcomer D. L. Brock, aggressive land developer who's gone into business with Luke.

Latter-Day Romances:

As most viewers know, the married couple Laura Webber and Scotty Baldwin became a triangle after Luke Spencer "raped" and fell in love with Laura. During the "Summer of Luke and Laura" and the ensuing year, these two had viewers on the edge of their chairs waiting for their love to be consummated in marriage. They had only a few happy months together after the splashiest wedding Port Charles has ever seen. Then Laura mysteriously "died," and Luke was left heartbroken. The Genie Francis void sent "GH" staffers scrambling to find a replacement, but the first one to catch on was Holly Sutton, who originally was part of a scam against Luke. The couple fell madly in love, but the lack of trust Luke felt toward

Above: David Groh plays D. L. Brock. He was formerly Rhoda's husband on the series "Rhoda."

Laura Baldwin (Genie Francis) married Luke Spencer (Tony Geary) in one of the most famous soap weddings ever.

Emma Samms plays Holly Scorpio.

Holly kept coming between them, until Holly married Luke's best friend, Robert Scorpio, because she was pregnant with Luke's child. Everyone thought Luke had died in an avalanche, and Holly was about to be deported. When Luke returned from "the dead" he didn't see Scorpio's marrying Holly as an honorable act, and Holly stayed with Robert when she realized that Luke still didn't trust her.

The most intriguing romances of 1983 were Heather and Scotty and the triangle of Celia, Grant, and Jimmy Lee. Heather and Scotty are deliciously vicious in their plots to get back at all of Port Charles, and they're equally enthusiastic in bed together. Their future seems shaky at best, however, because neither party can quite trust the other (would you?). Celia, a Quartermaine relative, married Grant Putnam, a childhood and college sweetheart she had remet recently, after a lustful affair with Edward Q's recently acknowledged illegitimate son Eric, who grew up with, and goes by,

the name of Jimmy Lee. Jimmy Lee still carries a torch for the aristocratic Celia, and he just may be ready to step in when (or if) Grant is exposed as an impostor and a Communist spy.

MURDER/MAYHEM/MYSTERY

In the good old days, most of "GH's" more violent storylines were closely connected with its romances. Babies were kidnapped, wives were raped by husbands or former lovers, and an occasional accident or suicide was thought to be murder before the facts were exposed.

Recently, however, "GH" became the soap to watch if mayhem was really your cup of tea. The most unusual factor in "GH's" recent mystery plots is their worldwide scope. It's apparently not enough for Luke and Robert to save one person, or even the whole town of Port Charles. They consistently find themselves at odds with international baddies, most of whom are not what they seemed when first introduced to the show. Following is a brief list of mysterious events that have plagued Port Charles since Luke Spencer became a major character.

1. Luke was involved with the syndicate when he was introduced to "GH" during the late 1970s. To prove his loyalty to the mob, he was supposed to kill Mitch Williams, senatorial candidate. When Laura intercepted him on this mission, Roy took over and was killed in the process.

2. After Scotty found out that Luke was Laura's "rapist" and that it wasn't rape after all, Luke and Scotty slugged it out onboard the yacht of Mr. Smith (the mob boss), who had also set up Luke to marry his daughter Jennifer. Luke was knocked into the water and was thought dead at first. When he resurfaced, he and Laura took off for that famous summer, giving themselves the names Lloyd and Lucy and hiding out, among other places, on the upstate Whitaker farm. In the process, they recovered a tremendous cache of mob money, and Luke became something of a hero on their return to Port Charles.

3. With the appearance of cousin Alex Quartermaine came the beginning of the infamous Ice Princess caper. The Ice Princess, a gigantic diamond Alex had stolen and smuggled into the country, actually contained the secret of a science-fictional device that could allow the power-hungry Cassadine family to rule the world. Well, Luke and Robert couldn't allow that, so they smuggled themselves aboard the departing Cas-

Elizabeth Taylor made a "General Hospital" guest appearance as Helena Cassadine; here she is shown negotiating with Robert Scorpio (Tristan Rogers).

sadine yacht, only to find that the enterprising Laura had done the same by disguising herself as a maid. There they fell in with starlet Tiffany Hill, who was just along for the ride and wanted no part of the Cassadines' evil deeds. To make a convoluted story simple, Luke almost singlehandedly saved the world by killing Mikos Cassadine and coming up with the one password that would stop the evil machine from freezing Port Charles solid.

4. Again, Luke and Laura returned home as heroes, but soon the intrigue started up again. In one of the less-well-received plots of recent years, a new black hat arrived in the form of David Gray, who had a nefarious scheme to steal a priceless *objet d'art*. The mysterious Gray also had some pretty hokey hypnotic powers, and after a confusing plot was finally wrapped

up, it was revealed that Gray had used these powers to lure Laura away from Luke and then had killed her.

5. The mystery of 1983 is again an international one. Port Charles has been infiltrated by Communist "moles" who are after a mysterious "Prometheus disc" being developed for an exhibition to be held in Port Charles. Again, Luke and Robert, though now enemies, have become embroiled in the mystery, and viewers are waiting to see if the famous duo will pair up on the same side to save the world one more time.

6. In the middle of the Luke and Laura era, another mystery was featured. This one, however, was simply a murder. Diana Taylor was shot in her apartment, and for a while Heather's rival for Jeff Webber, Ann Logan, was a suspect, because she was spotted near

the scene of the crime. The truth was a long time in unraveling, but it finally came out that Alice, Heather's mother, had done it accidentally.

While still in NYC seeking fame and fortune, Heather had decided that a baby didn't fit into the picture so she sold Steven Lars into adoption and made sure Diana and Peter Taylor became the parents. But after returning to Port Charles, Heather had a change of heart and started conniving to get Steven Lars back from Diana. Trying to drive Diana crazy gradually, to convince her she was an unfit mother, Heather finally slipped Diana a heavy dose of LSD. But fate took over, and the innocent toddler switched two drinks so that Heather got the LSD. She was institutionalized and catatonic for months. When she finally came out of her daze she continued her plot to regain the baby.

After many planning steps and trial runs, Heather escaped from the asylum and went to Diana's apartment to shoot her. Coincidentally, Heather's mother Alice was on the scene, and when she tried to stop Heather, the gun went off and killed Diana. Heather went to jail for the crime until Alice 'fessed up that she was the culprit.

PORT CHARLES MILESTONES

"General Hospital" has been more than the Luke and Laura show or, indeed, the Luke and Holly show.

Several important medical advances, for example, have been dramatized on the soap. One of the most significant was a blood grouping test which definitely affirmed the paternity of the Quartermaine baby. In this storyline the wealthy Dr. Alan Quartermaine believed that his wife, Dr. Monica Quartermaine, bore the child of another doctor, Lesley's husband, Dr. Rick Webber. Lesley, too, believed it because when she assisted at the baby's birth, Monica cried out Rick's name at the moment the child came into the world.

Alan was so sure the baby wasn't his that he was ready to commit murder to avenge his cuckolded ego. As things turned out, the super-sophisticated new test definitely proved he, Alan Quartermaine, had fathered Alan Quartermaine, Jr. Previous paternity tests could only rule out men who were not the fathers. The new test can indicate positive paternity.

"General Hospital," under the direction of Douglas Marland, also began to move out from set and fixed positions. Nurses no longer stood like starched anchors holding up nurses' stations. They moved through hospital wards and, occasionally, into the beds of impatient lovers.

Elizabeth Taylor's jewels, said to be her own, enhanced the Helena Cassadine character.

"General Hospital" made later headlines by introducing the most famous guest star in the world— Elizabeth Taylor, who played the fantastically wealthy Helena Cassadine. It's said the famous actress wore her own fabled jewelry and fantastic sables.

Liz Taylor wasn't the only beautiful screen star to appear as a guest on the soap. In 1975 Mamie Van Doren turned up to play herself in a storyline in which she helped Lesley regain custody of her child, Laura.

A trend toward showing nurses as able professionals, and not just as doctors' lackeys, led to a plot in which the egotistical Dr. Bradshaw began killing people in "General Hospital" itself. Bradshaw was a slick operator: everyone upon whom he operated died because of his sloppy and generally ineffective techniques, but when charged, he implicated a nurse, Ann Logan. In time, Ann was cleared and Bradshaw sent packing.

WHO'S WHO IN PORT CHARLES

Original Cast

Actor	*Character*
JOHN BERADINO	**Dr. Steve Hardy**
TOM BROWN	**Al Weeks**
ROBERT CLARKE	**Roy Lansing**
CAROLYN CRAIG	**Cynthia Allison**
CRAIG CURTIS	**Eddie Weeks**
NEIL HAMILTON	**Philip Mercer**
ALLISON HAYES	**Priscilla Longworth**
LENORE KINGSTON	**Lenore Weeks**
RALPH MANZA	**Mike Costello**
EMILY MCLAUGHLIN	**Jessie Brewer**
HUNT POWERS	**Dr. Ken Martin**
K. T. STEVENS	**Petty Mercer**
ROY THINNES	**Dr. Phil Brewer**

First Air Date: April 1, 1963

Write to "General Hospital" c/o ABC, 1330 Avenue of the Americas, New York, NY 10019.

John Beradino has always played Dr. Steve Hardy.

A Directory of Recent Characters*

Ruby Anderson: Luke and Bobbie's aunt; a former madam, now a nurse's aide. *Norma Connolly*

Dr. Gail Baldwin: Lee Baldwin's wife; Scotty's stepmother. *Susan Brown*

Lee Baldwin: A prominent lawyer; Scotty's stepfather. *Peter Hansen*

Scotty Baldwin: A young lawyer; formerly wed to Laura Vining Webber Baldwin Spencer; currently involved with Heather Webber. *Kin Shriner*

Jessie Brewer: "General Hospital's" head nurse; once involved with Dan Rooney; formerly wed to Dr. Philip Brewer and Dr. Peter Taylor. *Emily McLaughlin*

Mark Dante: A doctor; Rick's longtime rival. *Gerald Gordon*

Natalie Dearborn: Actually Natasha, a Communist agent, friend of Luke. *Melinda Cordell*

Audrey Hardy: Head of the hospital's student nursing service; Steve's wife. *Rachel Ames*

Steve Hardy: Chief of staff at General Hospital; wed to Audrey. *John Beradino*

*The actors/actresses who currently play these major roles are in italics.

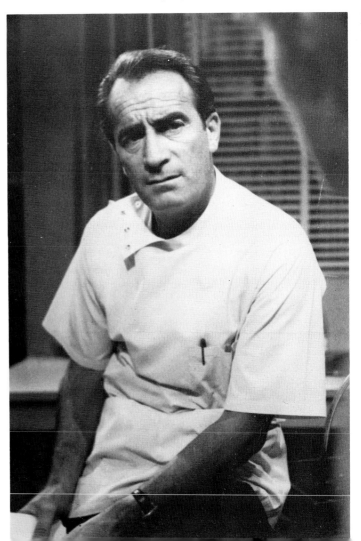

Above: Milton Berle poses with actress Sharon Wyatt (Tiffany Hill).

Right: John Stamos, as Blackie Parrish, has caught the imagination of "General Hospital's" younger fans. Photo by Ed Geller.

Tiffany Hill: Originally Scorpio's love, later involved with Noah Drake, who left town. *Sharon Wyatt*

Jimmy Lee Holt: Edward Quartermaine's long-lost illegitimate son; he's in love with Celia. *Steve Bond*

Blackie Parrish: A once bad kid turning good under the aegis of the Webbers. *John Stamos*

Bryan Philips: A psychologist; wed to Claudia. (Sammy Davis, Jr., played his late father in a guest appearance.) *Todd Davis*

Celia Putnam: Grant Putnam's wife; she had an affair with Jimmy Lee. *Sherilyn Wolter*

Grant Putnam: He is the Port Charles "mole." *Brian Patrick Clarke*

Alan Quartermaine: A doctor; wed to Monica; father of Alan, Jr., and Jason (by former and now late mistress, Susan); Edward and Lyla's son; brother of Tracy. *Stuart Damon*

Edward Quartermaine: Alan's father and the head of ELQ. *David Lewis*

Lyla Quartermaine: The shrewd wife of Edward; mother of Alan and grandmother of Alan, Jr., and Jason. *Anna Lee*

Monica Quartermaine: A respected heart surgeon; wife of Alan; mother of Alan, Jr.; once involved (for one night) with Rick Webber. *Leslie Charleson*

Capt. Bert Ramsey: Port Charles' Chief of Police (his lookalike brother Don Hastings is on "As the World Turns"). *Bob Hastings*

Dan Rooney: The hospital administrator. *Frank Maxwell*

Robert Scorpio: An intelligence agent, once in love with Tiffany, now wed to Holly. *Tristan Rogers*

Bobbie Spencer: Luke's sister, a former lady of the evening who is now a respected nurse. *Jackie Zeman*

Three members of the Kansas City Royals (left to right: Craig Chamberlain, Hal McRae, and Frank White) join Tony Geary (Luke Spencer) and Bianca Ferguson (Claudia Johnson).

Laura Vining Webber Baldwin Spencer: Lesley's daughter; Rick's stepdaughter; former wife of Scotty Baldwin and Luke Spencer; is missing. *Genie Francis*

Luke Spencer: Wed to Laura, once involved with Holly; ex-underworld member currently works with Scorpio. *Tony Geary*

Holly Sutton: Formerly involved in scams; Luke's lover and now Scorpio's wife. *Emma Samms*

Constance Townley: An old lover of Scorpio's now bedding Luke; she's on the trail of the "mole." *Jeanna Michaels*

Jackie Templeton: Involved with Scorpio then with Luke, she's a reporter. *Demi Moore*

Heather Grant Webber: Jeff's former wife; involved with Scotty; Alice Grant's daughter. *Robin Mattson*

Dr. Lesley Webber: Real-life mother of Laura; adoptive mother of Michael and Amy Vining; Rick's wife twice; a doctor at "General Hospital." *Denise Alexander*

Dr. Rick Webber: A member of the Webber family (which includes Jeff Webber) once wed to Heather who left town with his son. *Chris Robinson*

9

Guiding Light (CBS)

Someone once said that on June 30, 1952, the era of radio gave way, finally, to the triumph of television. On that day the millions of soap opera fans who had been devoted to "Guiding Light" since it began on radio in 1937 no longer needed their radios: the adventures, the relationships, the world of the Bauer family could now all be seen and heard, on TV.

"Guiding Light" has been the story of the Bauer clan, who live in the mythical town of Springfield, USA. Indeed, Charita Bauer, who plays the role of the matriarch of the family, Bert Bauer, had been with the show before it went on TV. However, the fact is that when Irna Phillips, the gifted writer who also created "Another World" and "As the World Turns" for TV, first conceived the plotlines of "Guiding Light"

Charita Bauer has been playing Bert Bauer since 1950. Among her radio soaps were "Guiding Light," "Ma Perkins," and "I Remember Mama." Photo by Bob Deutsch.

The Bauer family: Charita Bauer, flanked on the left by Mart Hulswit (Ed) and on the right by Don Stewart (Mike).

for radio in 1937, the main character was a gentle minister named Dr. Rutledge. The title of the soap was a metaphor for this man: the good, kind, and, *guiding light* of his flock. The storylines concerning Dr. Rutledge, his family, and his parishioners were so popular they were incorporated into a book that sold over half a million copies.

The show emanated from Chicago, where other important radio soaps had their headquarters, including "Big Sister," "Pepper Young's Family," and "John's Other Wife."

When "Guiding Light" premiered on radio in 1937 with the main character of Reverend Dr. Rutledge, the show had a distinctly spiritual tone. Dr. Rutledge

preached in a town called Five Points, and the show was accompanied by organ music, which was carried over to TV.

WELCOME TO SPRINGFIELD

The Citizens

In the beginning Papa and Mama Bauer were immigrants with three grown children: Bill, Meta, Trudy. Mama died and Bill married Bert. Trudy, who married Clyde, was phased out soon after the transition to TV. Meta was the colorful member of the family, becoming a model and getting pregnant, then shooting her husband after her son's death by a freak accident was caused by him. Later she married Dr. Bruce Banning, a longstanding character.

Bert and Bill had two sons, Michael and Edward. As she grew older Bert turned from greedy troublemaker to matriarch, and Bill became an alcoholic. He reformed, but later (reportedly) died after falling out of a hotel room window in Chicago.

In spite of the fact that Charita and her character Bert have the same last name (a coincidence), she didn't create the role. The original Bert was Ann Shepherd who played her until 1950. Charita took over then and has been the stalwart Bert throughout the past three decades.

When Bert first appeared it was obvious that she was a woman of high intelligence. Irna Phillips' women always were a cut above the usual caricature that had women depending on their menfolk for intellectual guidance. But soaps never were, and basically still aren't, firebrands of change. So Bert had to operate as a woman whose major role was to push Bill forward through encouragement, patience, and an occasional wise word offered submissively.

Papa Bauer was played by Theo Getz from 1949 until his death 23 years later.

Deaths that affected the show all at once, leaving the cast stunned, included that of Ed Zimmerman (Dr. Joe Werner), Walter Gorman (former director), and Theo Getz.

Current major characters: Millionaire Alan Spaulding, his wife Hope, Dr. Justin Marler and brother Ross; Morgan and Kelly Nelson; Quinton McCord; Henry Chamberlain; Carrie Marler; Nola; and others.

The Third "GL" Town—Springfield

"GL" moved from its Chicago home to Hollywood

Fans and "Guiding Light" personnel were saddened by the sudden death of Ed Zimmerman (Dr. Joe Werner) in 1972. Photo by Howard Gray.

and then to New York in 1949, when the Bauer family replaced Dr. Rutledge as the characters to follow. In keeping with the show's religious theme, the Bauers were a good Christian family who embodied the mores preached earlier by Dr. Rutledge. The emphasis in "GL" has always been togetherness, as manifested by the close-knit Bauers.

With the Bauers came the first "GL" move to a new town. The Bauers lived in Selby Flats, which was supposed to be a suburb of Los Angeles, and the action often turned to Cedars Hospital (based on a real LA hospital). When the show was transplanted to its current locale, Springfield, Cedars Hospital went with it. Essentially, these changes were made to broaden the characters' domain from rural area to larger community.

Despite these moves, "Guiding Light" has retained the moral fiber of the early years, and this is often reflected in its storylines.

Christopher Bernau plays Alan Spaulding.

THE SPRINGFIELD STORY

In 1979 Douglas Marland was lured away from the top-rated "General Hospital" to assume writing chores for "Guiding Light." Marland's previous writing credits included work on "Another World" (he was one of Harding Lemay's subwriters, and a few years later Harding Lemay ended up working as a subwriter for a brief period under Douglas Marland on "GL" and the "Doctors"). Taking over "Guiding Light," Marland immediately instituted a number of changes, such as moving the stories along at a faster pace, emphasizing character over plot, refocusing on the Bauers, and introducing younger characters. It wasn't long before "Guiding Light" became a top-rated soap again for CBS.

In 1982 Douglas Marland quit writing for "Guiding Light" reportedly because of personality conflicts with the then producer Allen Potter (who's currently producing "Another World"). Another factor that influenced Douglas Marland's decision to leave was the abrupt dismissal of Jane Eliot, who played Carrie Marler, in the middle of a story he had spent months developing. Douglas Marland had brought Jane Eliot with him from "General Hospital," where she played Traci Quartermaine. Carrie Marler may return to Springfield; it's unlikely that Jane Eliot will be playing the part.

Following Douglas Marland's departure from "Guiding Light," a number of writers, including Pat Falken-Smith, came and went. Currently, under new producer Gail Kobe, Pam Long (who also wrote and appeared on "Texas") is "Guiding Light's" headwriter. She's also appearing on the soap.

Forty Years with the Bauers

When Mama Bauer died, Papa moved in. Trudy and Meta left town. Bert kept pushing Bill. Papa added an unsettling influence. Bill blamed Bert and Papa for his problems and began to drink a little too much.

Meta, by this time, had become pregnant by a no-good rotter named Ted who wasn't married to her but eventually won partial custody of the son she bore. Ted was a womanizer who also had some doubts about his masculinity, so he subjected his son to rough treatment and insisted on the boy's learning how to box. The child died in the ring. Meta killed Ted but was acquitted on the grounds of temporary insanity.

Michael Bauer was born to Bill and Bert.

Later Billy Bauer was born. (Billy was turned into Ed Bauer.)

In time several babies were born in and out of wedlock.

Hope Bauer was Michael's son by one of his many love affairs. He returned to Springfield to claim his

Jennifer Cooke's departure as Morgan Nelson left John Wesley Shipp's character, Kelly Nelson, ripe and ready for a new romance. A new producer (in 1983) thought it was time to let Shipp sail into new emotional storms. Photo by Bob Deutsch.

Here, Jennifer Cooke (Morgan Nelson) is made up by the "Guiding Light" makeup man. No sooner had she left the series than the offer to do a Warren Beatty movie and a Broadway play opened up. Photo by Bob Deutsch.

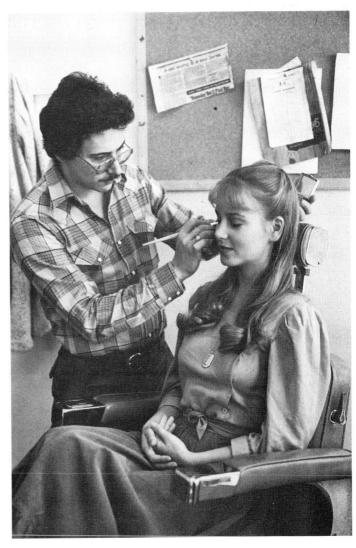

daughter and then left town to set up a law practice in Bay City.

"Another World" fans will recall the character Pat Randolph, one of the most popular soap women. Mike soon became involved in a love affair with the lady. Ms. Phillips had, by now, given the writing reins to Agnes Nixon, who was typing scripts for both "Guiding Light" and "Another World." The typically Nixonian touches began to be seen. Having a character from one soap appear on another is an indication of Agnes Nixon's work.

Another Nixonian touch was the application of current medical procedures to her characters. In this instance, Bill Bauer was given a heart transplant that kept him alive just long enough for the role to have lost its place on the soap. He later died in a fall from a hotel room window in Chicago.

With Mike's having become a lawyer, Ed decided to become a doctor. He also started drinking. He then figured in one of the first daytime wife-beating storylines. (Nixon would pick up on this theme later on, notably in "All My Children.") Brother Mike returned home and, in typical Mike Bauer fashion, fell for his brother's wife.

Things were straightened out between and among the brothers and their ladies. Ed and his wife, Leslie, had a son. It was then that the loyal viewers learned for the first time what Papa Bauer's Christian name was. The baby was named for his great grandfather, Frederick.

Don Stewart as Mike with Cindy Pickett as Jackie Marler (with scarf) and Lezlie Dalton as Elizabeth Spaulding.

A studious moment with Fran Meyers (left), who played "Guiding Light's" Peggy Dillman Fletcher, and Lynn Adams, whose role was Leslie Jackson Norris Bauer. Photo by Howard Gray.

Mike married and divorced Charlotte, a woman who was cruel to his daughter, Hope.

Mike later fell in love again with Leslie. Ed, in a fit of pique at the way his love life was turning out—Leslie had turned him out and so had another one of his loves, Janet—eloped with Holly Norris, who promptly became involved with one of the grandest daytime villains ever, Roger Thorpe.

For a long time Roger would visit his villainy on poor Holly and would die at least twice before fading from the storyline for good.

Meanwhile, Ed and Mike would mature into settled gentlemen, leaving the more passionate ploys and plays to younger entrants into Springfield's environs.

A villain turned sympathetic came along by the name of Alan Spaulding. He married Mike's daughter Hope. He, like his father-in-law, had offspring by previous liaisons, one of whom was Amanda Spaulding, who would become a very good businesswoman.

Papa Bauer is no longer with us. His role was written out following the death of the veteran actor, Theo Goetz. Other once-stalwart members of the cast have also moved on.

The series, which pioneered exotic locations in which Roger Thorpe, for example, plotted his villainy in thick jungles and Alan Spaulding went through a metamorphosis from mean to merely shrewd and expeditious, has had its share of triumphs unequaled by any other soap. It's also had problems. It remains, however, a series whose fans like to remember the past when it literally outshone all other soaps for years and may, again, do so in the future.

Attention gradually drifted away from the Bauers over the years, though Bert was always present, even if in the background.

AFFAIRS TO REMEMBER

- Bill Bauer had many mistresses. While a patient Bert Bauer bore him two sons, Bill sired at least one child who would become a fixture on the series, Hillary.
- Mike Bauer was secretly married to a woman named Julie but was seducing other women, including one who would become the mother of his daughter, Hope.
- Ed Bauer was busy trying to keep Leslie from wandering while he was, in the meantime, bed-hopping himself. Later he married a lovely lady named Rita who, though she doted on Ed Bauer, didn't at all mind sharing her affections with her niece's husband, Alan Spaulding, married to Mike's daughter Hope.
- Alan's former mistress, Jennifer (mother of his daughter, Amanda), later became pregnant by a cad named Mark, a cad who also bedded Ed's daughter, Amanda, between his visits to Jennifer's boudoir.
- A fascinating latter-day romantic romp involved the character of Nola Reardon and the mysterious archeologist, Quint McCord. Nola, who bore a child via a fling with a fellow named Floyd (in real life Nola is Lisa Brown, the star of Broadway's *42nd*

Tom Nielsen plays Floyd Parker, an erstwhile punk rocker, on "Guiding Light." Off-screen, Nielsen has his own music group, Tom Nielsen and the Parker Brothers, named after his on-screen character. Copyright © 1982—KAJ, Inc.

Nola Reardon is played by Lisa Brown. Lisa Brown's real-life husband, Tom Nielson, plays Floyd Parker, her former on-screen lover. Tom is a bandleader whose groups, The Parker Brothers and The Sax Maniacs, appear around the country. Lisa stars in 42nd Street. Photo by Bob Deutsch.

Michael Tylo, who plays Quint McCord, shared the screen with his real-life wife, actress Deborah Eckols, for a few segments early in 1983. McCord was having flashback experiences of an affair with a woman whose face (Eckols' face) haunted him after he saw another woman, the mysterious Rebecca. Rebecca had had her own face altered by plastic surgery. And, yes, she was the woman who haunted McCord's dreams. Detroit-born Tylo wore the western hat at a western-style party, which pleased his Texas-born-and-bred wife.

Street and Floyd is her husband, Tom Nielsen, a musician) came to live in Quint's home and eventually came to share his bed and his heart. Their romance was marked by Nola's penchant for creating fantasies in which she usually figured as the put-upon victim of his passions.

• The theme of brothers vying for the same woman has been repeated several times on this series. Brothers-in-law, mothers and daughters, and best friends (Tim and Kelly were competing for Morgan's virgin body) pit their wits and wiles against one another in an effort to possess bodies in common.

What would poor old Dr. Rutledge have said to all this?

MURDER/MAYHEM/MYSTERY

In May 1983, with the arrival of new executive producer, Gail Kobe, many stars went out on "Guiding Light." In a dramatic conclusion of a storyline, the characters of Mark and Mona killed each other. Other characters were sent into outer reaches. Meanwhile, new mysteries and mayhem storylines were beginning to develop.

Out of the past, some of the more memorable included the following incidents:

- When Michael Bauer grew up he fell in love with a girl who turned out to be his sister Meta's stepdaughter. Meta had already stood trial and been acquitted for the killing of her erstwhile lover, Ted, who was responsible for the death of their son. Like sister, brother got into a passionate situation in which he killed in anger: the first boyfriend of his lady love whom he secretly married. He was aquitted. Bert, however, wanted to make sure that this marriage, which had caused the family so much grief, wouldn't succeed. She achieved her goal, but for a time lost Michael's love. He promptly left home to take a job in South America.

- Amanda Spaulding stood trial for the death of her mother. As it turned out, the woman was not really her mother and the death had simply been an accident. Lucille Wexler, who had raised Amanda as her own child, feared Jennifer Richards would find out that Amanda was her daughter and tell the girl.

- Amanda not only had to deal with having a mother turn up in place of the mother she had been accused of killing; she also learned she was the daughter of one of Springfield's then most notorious nasties, Alan Spaulding, the wealthy head of an industrial empire married to Mike Bauer's daughter, Hope. Amanda was never quite herself after that.

- When Mark Evans turned up, Amanda Spaulding fell! However, she didn't know that Mark and a mysterious stranger named Rebecca (also named Mona) were involved in nefarious doings that would threaten her life. Once again Amanda was plunged into the middle of a murderous situation.

- Meanwhile, Carrie Marler was in a sanitarium, having been placed there after being identified as a killer with a split personality. Will Carrie ever get out?

Two of the soap's most popular characters, Quint McCord and Nola Reardon McCord, are played by Michael Tylo and Lisa Brown. In the early stages of their relationship Nola would have fantasies about herself and the mysterious Quint. In the one pictured here she's caught up in a Jane Eyre situation.

A WORD FROM DOUGLAS MARLAND

Douglas Marland explained the basic premise for the soap's appeal:

"It keeps a central core of stability—the Bauer family, particularly Bert—around whom everyone else moves. Bert is there not as an anchor, necessarily, but as someone whom everyone else can depend on for help and advice when needed."

The series allows for growth. A younger group came in which represents the more youthful aspects of an older group still very much a part of the drama. As Marland explains it: "Each younger person has his or her counterpart in an older one. In this way the audience can see relationships and identify with certain characters whose experiences they feel most sympathetic with."

Leslie O'Hara arrived as the mystery woman, Rebecca, a.k.a. Mona Cartwright. Photo by Ed Geller.

WHO'S WHO IN SPRINGFIELD

Original Cast (Radio)

Actor	Character
MERCEDES McCAMBRIDGE	**Mary Rutledge**
JOHN HODIAK	**Ned Holden**
RAYMOND EDWARD JOHNSON	**Mr. Nobody from Nowhere**
ARTHUR PETERSON	**The Reverend Dr. Rutledge**
RUTH BAILEY	**Rose Kransky**
SARAJANE WELLS	**Also Played Mary Rutledge**
ED PRENTISS	**Also Played Ned Holden**
GLADYS HEEN	**Torchy**
JONE ALLISON	**Meta Bauer (she brought the role to TV)**

First Air Date: January 25, 1937

Original Cast (Television)

Actor	*Character*
JONE ALLISON	**Meta Banning**
CHARITA BAUER	**Bertha (Bert) Bauer**
SUSAN DOUGLAS	**Kathy Grant**
THEO GOETZ	**Papa Bauer**
JAMES LIPTON	**Dr. Richard Grant**
HERB NELSON	**Joe Roberts**
LYLE SUDRO	**Bill Bauer**
ALICE YOURMAN	**Laura Grant**

First Air Date: June 30, 1952

Write to "Guiding Light" c/o CBS, 51 W. 52nd St., New York, NY 10019

A Directory of Recent Characters*

Bertha (Bert) Bauer: Mike and Ed's mother; Hillary's stepmother; Hope's grandmother; Alan, Jr.'s great grandmother; widow of Bill Bauer. *Charita Bauer*

Ed Bauer: A doctor; Freddie's father; Bert's son; Mike's brother, Hillary's half-brother; Hope's uncle. *Peter Simon*

Hillary Bauer: Mike and Ed's half-sister; daughter of the late Bill Bauer and his mistress, Simone; she's a nurse at Cedars. *Marsha Clark*

Mike Bauer: Bert's son; Ed's brother; Hope's father; Alan, Jr.'s grandfather; Hillary's half-brother; he's a lawyer. *Don Stewart*

Henry Chamberlain: Vanessa's and Quinton Mc Cord's father; Bea's lover; an important businessman. *William Roerick*

Vanessa Chamberlain: Henry's daughter; businesswoman once in love with Ross Marler. *Maeve Kinkead*

Trish Lewis: Owned business with Vanessa. *Rebecca Hollen*

Helena Manzini: A beautiful adventuress whose place in Quint's past may influence his place in Nola's future. *Rose Alaio*

Justin Marler: Jackie's husband; Philip Spaulding's real father; a doctor. *Tom O'Rourke*

*The actors/actresses who currently play these major roles are in italics.

Two members of the "new" "Guiding Light": Scott Aleksander (Philip) and Krista Tesreau (Mindy). These young folks are recreating one of the most successful "Guiding Light" themes under new headwriter Pam Long and producer Gail Kobe. Photo by Ed Geller.

Mart Hulswit, who once played Ed Bauer, was released from "Guiding Light" because the show wanted a younger and more romantic actor to play the part. Photo by Howard Gray.

Michael Tylo.

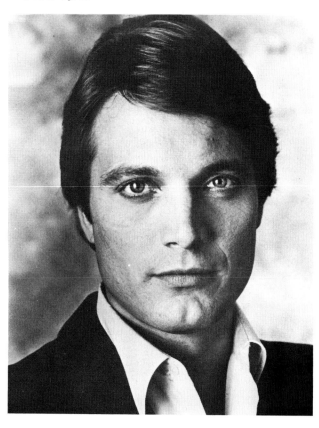

Two of the lovely Lewis ladies: Trish (played by Rebecca Hollen) and her kin, Mindy (played by Krista Tesreau). The Lewis clan look to be the next big family unit on the show after the Bauers. Photo by Ed Geller.

Above: Don Stewart was once a Strategic Air Command B47 bomber pilot.

Left: Warren Burton, who won an Emmy when he worked in "All My Children," turned up in "Guiding Light" playing the head of a hospital. His character's name: Warren Andrews. Burton has written comedy for Lily Tomlin and is an accomplished song and dance man. Photo by Bob Deutsch.

Beulah Garrick plays the mysterious Mrs. Renfield. Her husband, Bernard Pollock, is a stage manager and actor.

Denise Pence (Katie) is the mother of two daughters, Jonal and baby Brett. Her husband is Steve Broockvor, a choreographer (A Chorus Line). Photo by Ed Geller.

Rose Alaio (Helena Manzini) is another one of those soap actors who keeps a busy outside acting schedule. Here she poses with the photographer's cat, Clarence. Photo by Bob Deutsch.

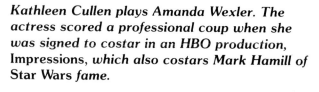

Kathleen Cullen plays Amanda Wexler. The actress scored a professional coup when she was signed to costar in an HBO production, Impressions, which also costars Mark Hamill of Star Wars fame.

Rebecca Hollen plays Trish Lewis.

John Wesley Shipp.

Ross Marler: Husband of the institutionalized Carrie; Justin's brother; ex-lover of Vanessa; a DA. *Jerry ver Dorn*

Quint McCord: An archaeologist; Nola's husband; Henry's long-lost son. *Mike Tylo*

Kelly Nelson: A young doctor who'd been wed to Morgan, Jennifer's daughter. *John Wesley Shipp*

Floyd Parker: A singer; the real father of Nola's baby, Kelly Louise; Katie's brother. *Tom Nielsen*

Katie Parker: A nurse; Floyd's sister. *Denise Pence*

Maureen Reardon: Mother of Nola, Tony, and Maureen; in love with Henry. *Ellen Dolan*

Nola Reardon: Quint's wife; mother of Floyd's baby, Kelly Louise; once in love with Kelly Nelson. *Lisa Brown*

Mrs. Renfield: The mysterious housekeeper at Quint McCord's home; now in Europe. *Beulah Garrick*

Jennifer Richards: Alan's former lover with whom she had Amanda; later bore Morgan; her father was Logan Stafford. *Geraldine Court*

Alan Spaulding: Father of Amanda and Alan, Jr; adoptive father of Philip; married to Hope Bauer; formerly wed to Elizabeth and Jackie. *Chris Bernau*

Amanda Spaulding: Jennifer's daughter by Alan Spaulding; Morgan's half-sister; Ben's ex-wife; head of L.T.A.; formerly Mark's lover. *Kathleen Cullen*

Hope Spaulding: Alan's wife; Mike's daughter; Bert's granddaughter; Alan, Jr.'s mother; Philip's stepmother. *Elvera Roussell*

10

One Life to Live (ABC)

"One Life to Live" made its debut on the American Broadcasting Company network on July 15, 1968. Cocreated by Agnes Nixon, it dealt with a theme that had become very important to Nixon: the struggles of class in a typical American community and the aspirations of those who tried to move upward and those who often stood as a bulwark determined that their less economically assured neighbors should not pass.

The series also brought the concept of ethnic struggle to the daytime medium. Obviously "preferred" families bore the name of Lord and Vernon, for example, while other folks who lived on the other side of the tracks were Woleks and Rileys. "OLTL's" working title was "Between Heaven and Hell," but was changed because the network wouldn't approve it; they thought it was too racy.

Mike Storm plays the good doctor, Larry Wolek. Photo by Howard Gray.

Victoria Lord Riley Buchanan, as played by Erika Slezak, represents all that is good, true, and classy on "One Life to Live." Photo by Howard Gray.

Cathy Craig, now a newspaper reporter, wrote a feature story detailing the horrors of venereal disease. At the episode's conclusion viewers were given an address to write if they were interested in obtaining a copy of Cathy's story. More than 9,000 requests reached ABC's executive offices.

In its 15 years on the air, "OLTL" has had three different producers. Doris Quinlin, the show's original producer, left shortly after Agnes Nixon sold the show to ABC-TV. Joseph Stuart, "OLTL's" next producer, started in 1977 and left in early 1983 to produce ABC's latest soap "Loving." Jean Arley is "OLTL's" current producer. Besides having worked on "Ryan's Hope" and "Love of Life," Jean Arley was also ABC's executive producer in charge of daytime programs.

"OLTL" premiered as a half-hour serial, expanded to 45 minutes in 1976, and went to a full hour in 1978.

Like all new producers, Arley decided to make some changes to improve the overall tenor of the show. Like Agnes Nixon, Arley believes that soap operas should be entertainment first and foremost; while educational and social issues, as well as adventure and exotica, will be woven into the storylines, neither will be added gratuitously. "One Life to Live" has occasionally tortured viewers with long, drawn-out plots with long, drawn-out conclusions, and Arley's aim is to speed things up a bit to retain viewer interest. Finally, Arley believes that for every great character that is written there is a great actor or actress to bring that person to the audience. "One Life to Live" has noticeably held on to actors and actresses who play major roles and with whom the fans identify.

WELCOME TO LLANVIEW

The Citizens

As mentioned previously, class struggle is what the core families of "OLTL" are really all about. On opposite ends of the economic scale are the wealthy Lords and the upwardly striving Woleks. Somewhere in the middle were the Rileys. Viewers of today will note that Larry and Danny Wolek are really the only active Woleks left (and ever since Karen Wolek took off with Steve Piermont, even Larry's role has been peripheral), and the Rileys have long since departed Llanview. The rich scions of Llanfair, however, are still "lording" it over the rest of the town.

Here's a brief rundown of the core families:

"One Life to Live" premiered before "All My Children" on the same network, but Agnes Nixon had written the story for "All My Children" first. Perhaps it was her fondness for the "AMC" proposal that led her to create Llanview and its characters as neighbors of Pine Valley.

Agnes Nixon, "OLTL's" creator, introduced the program with a desire to educate, as well as entertain, her audience. When character Cathy Craig developed an addiction to drugs, "OLTL" took its cameras to New York's Odyssey House Drug Rehabilitation Center and showed Cathy with ex-drug addicts in actual group therapy sessions. A few years later, in 1972,

For years Nat Polen played patriarch Jim Craig. After the actor's death the Craig family all but disappeared from Llanview. Photo by Howard Gray.

miered, but their three children made good on their own. Anna, the oldest, served as substitute mother for her two brothers, Vince and Larry. Larry was the baby, and while Vince put him through medical school, Anna provided moral support and sage advice. After running a trucking company, Vinny became a cop, who was killed several years ago by the evil Ted Clayton and his poisonous ring. Anna married Dr. Jim Craig and thus moved into the circle of high society (but she always retained her unpretentious personality). After veteran actor Nat Polen died, Jim Craig was written out, and Anna's part faded into the woodwork.

The Rileys

This family consisted of newspaperman Joe and his sister Eileen. Eileen married Dave Siegel and they had two children, Timmy and Julie. In separate incidents,

The role of Julie Siegel was originated by Lee Warrick, who has also appeared on "General Hospital." Photo by Howard Gray.

The Lords

Victor Lord, wealthy tycoon and founder of the Llanview newspaper *The Banner*, had two daughters, Victoria and Meredith. The younger daughter, Meredith, died after being assaulted by burglars, but not until after she had married Larry Wolek and borne a son, Danny. Victor treated his older daughter like the son he never had, grooming her to take over *The Banner* after his death. Viki, after suffering emotional problems due to her upbringing, blossomed into Llanview's quintessential lady.

Characters later introduced into the Lord family include Dorian Cramer, who married Victor, and Tony Lord, who was revealed to be the illegitimate son of Victor. Dorian, who wanted Victor and his money all to herself, spent years trying to keep Victor and Tony apart and competing with Viki on every little thing as if her life depended on it.

The Woleks

The Wolek parents were dead when this show pre-

both Dave and Timmy later died. Eileen and Julie later left town and were never heard from again, even when Joe died! Joe had managed to get "killed" and come back from the dead, father an illegitimate child, and fall in love with and marry Viki, who was pregnant with their second son when Joe died a final death.

The Buchanans

During the last several years a new family has caught on big in Llanview, the Buchanans:

Patriarch Asa Buchanan has two sons, Bo and Clint, and he's been at odds with them on and off since the family's arrival in Llanview. Asa hit town ostensibly to look after his ownership of the mythical football team the Philadelphia Cougars, while Clint simultaneously showed up to take over the editorship of *The Banner* after Joe's death. Clint had left home in his teens, and he and Asa were on the outs. Bo, on the other hand, was warm and trusting of Asa and just about everyone else, and he embodied the qualities of "good ole boy" and sharp businessman who managed much of the Buchanan empire.

In one of "OLTL's" characteristically long storylines, Olympia Buchanan, Asa's wife, was introduced to the show as a French woman named Nicole, and her appearance, after she had supposedly been dead for years, wreaked all types of havoc in Llanview.

Other characters who had major roles over the years included the cousins of the Woleks, Jenny and Karen; Marco Dane and brothers Mario Corelli and Gary Corelli; Dr. and Mrs. Will Vernon and their children Samantha and Brad; Cathy Craig, Jim Craig's disturbed daughter, who became a well-known author; Steve Burke, once married to Viki; Ed Hall and ex-wife Carla; Wanda Wolek, the late Vinny's wife; Pat Ashley (the role was written expressly for Jacquie Courtney when

Judith Light (Karen Wolek) with Phil Carey (Asa Buchanan, center) and Joe Stewart, producer of "One Life to Live."

Jacqueline Courtney, along with George Reinholt, switched networks and soaps when she was released by "Another World." Her "One Life to Live" character, Pat Ashley, remained in the limelight throughout the late '70s and early '80s. Photo by Ed Geller.

she left "Another World"); Becky Lee Hunt Abbott Buchanan; and many others.

A Day in the Lives of Llanview

Again, much of Llanview activity is spawned by class struggles among the Lords, Buchanans, and others. The Tylers of "AMC" have their counterparts in the Lords of "OLTL." More specifically, Phoebe Tyler Wallingford shares with Dorian Lord Callison a distinct aversion to having to be too close to lesser folk. Both ladies have a sense of *noblesse oblige* which obliges them to be as kind as possible to the non-aristocratic families into which they, themselves once married. But

they don't feel they have to like the *hoi polloi*.

Marriage is one way the residents of Llanview have of crossing class lines. Another is by means of introducing wealth from outside the community.

This show has always liked to show young mothers raising their kids on their own. It also emphasizes independent women, such as Viki (publisher/editor), Edwina (reporter, editor), the new Carla (lawyer), Pat (reporter turned TV talk show star), etc.

Another recurrent theme has been the kidnapping of women. Examples: Pat and then Sam were kidnapped by Dick Grant (who has since reappeared after escaping from prison during a flood disaster). Pat was held captive by her crazed twin sister Maggie, who had been brought up in England. Viki was kidnapped by but rescued from Ted Clayton.

THE LLANVIEW ARCHIVES

"One Life to Live" seems to have been consistent over the years in one way that makes it different from other soap operas of today: the audience it aims for. "OLTL," perhaps connected with its afternoon time slot, always seems to have written its scripts to appeal to women in their 20s and 30s. Though it has introduced young characters over the last few years—Cusi Cram as Dorian's long-lost daughter Cassie, for example—the main characters and the main love stories are usually not teens.

The Many Faces of Llanview's Citizens

"OLTL" is one of the soaps that consistently manages to recast roles successfully. Often, the succeeding actor becomes more popular than the one that originated the part. A good example of this took place in 1977 when Judith Light, who won two Emmys for Best Actress while on "OLTL" replaced Kathy Breech as Karen Wolek.

Another example is the character Dorian Kramer Lord Callison. In all, four actresses have played the part. Nancy Pinkerton originated the role in 1973. She left the show temporarily in 1974 due to illness and was replaced by Dixie Carter. Returning to "OLTL" a few months later, Nancy Pinkerton stayed with the show until 1977, when she left for good because she was unhappy with the terms of her new contract. Claire Malis took over the part, bringing new vulnerability to Dorian. Claire Malis left in 1979

Cusi Cram was the original Cassie, Dorian's daughter. She left the show to concentrate on her education. Here she is shown with her mother, Lady Jean Campbell. Photo by Ed Geller.

holt, who were now playing Pat Ashley and Tony Lord on "OLTL." Since the three actors had helped "Another World" become a top-rated soap with their Alice/Steve/Rachel love triangle, it was obvious the powers that be at ABC wanted to create the same kind of love triangle on "OLTL." However, by the time Robin Strasser finally did decide to join "OLTL," George Reinholt had long departed.

When Allan Miller, who played the very popular character Dave Siegal, left the series in 1972 to accept a position teaching drama at Yale University, it was decided that, rather than recast the role, Dave Siegal would die suddenly from a heart attack. Not long after the character's death, thousands of letters poured into the network's executive offices wanting to know why the actor had left the series. Not wanting to alienate their viewers, ABC printed a form letter explaining Allan Miller's reasons for leaving "OLTL."

Finding a Daytime Slot

When "OLTL" and "General Hospital" expanded to 45 minutes in 1976, a number of daytime TV fan magazines accused ABC of trying to be different because NBC and CBS were expanding their popular

Allan Miller played the popular Dave Siegel on "One Life to Live." Photo by Howard Gray.

to pursue a career in Hollywood and was replaced by Robin Strasser, who is still with the show today.

Back in 1976, Robin Strasser was offered the role of Cathy Craig Lord, but she turned it down because she didn't want to play an already existing character. Instead, she accepted a part on "All My Children," playing a new character, Dr. Chris Karras. After two years, Robin Strasser, who had created the role of super-bitch Rachel Davis on "Another World," grew bored playing a good character. Having a change of heart about stepping into another actor's shoes, Robin Strasser accepted the role of Dorian on "OLTL."

Interestingly enough, if Robin Strasser had accepted the part of Cathy Craig Lord back in 1976, she would've been reunited with former cast member from "Another World," Jacquie Courtney and George Rein-

soaps to a full hour. There was, in fact, more to ABC's decision than just trying to be different. For one thing, "General Hospital's" ratings weren't even good at the time. "OLTL," on the other hand, managed to hold its own against the second half hour of NBC's then high-rated soap, "Another World." This was partly because, months earlier, "OLTL" hired two actors who were extemely popular on "Another World," Jacquie Courtney and George Reinholt. When the decision was made to expand "OLTL" and "General Hospital" to 45 minutes, the shows were flip-flopped on the schedule. That way, "OLTL" would be starting a full half hour before "Another World." Also, NBC's the "Doctors," which "OLTL" would be now competing against, was beginning to suffer in the ratings. ABC's strategy was that viewers who wanted to watch Jacquie Courtney and George Reinholt, but didn't want to miss "Another World," could do so without missing a sizable portion of "Another World." It was also ABC's hope that viewers from "Another World" would stay tuned for "OLTL's" additional 15 minutes. There was also a possibility that there'd be a spillover to "General Hospital" because viewers tended to watch their soaps in chunks, usually on the same network. Although "General Hospital's" ratings remained as low as ever, "OLTL's" did rise. But it wasn't because viewers were tuning out "Another World." Its high ratings remained the same. What "OLTL" had succeeded in doing was attracting millions more new viewers to daytime TV, thus reversing a tune-out trend that had started in the mid '70s.

The daytime viewing audience was changing. No longer was it made up of just housewives. A whole new audience was emerging, one that consisted of housewives, college students, high school students, and men who were home during the day because they were either unemployed, or worked at night. You could say this was also the beginning of the ratings war among the three networks. Half-hour soaps that were popular were expanded to an hour. Soaps that did poorly in the ratings were cancelled. Within a year, ABC was number one in daytime as well as in prime time. It's currently still holding on to its number one position, though the second half hour of "Price Is Right" has currently replaced "General Hospital" as the number one show in daytime.

Featured Stories

Some of the storylines and thematic conflicts that

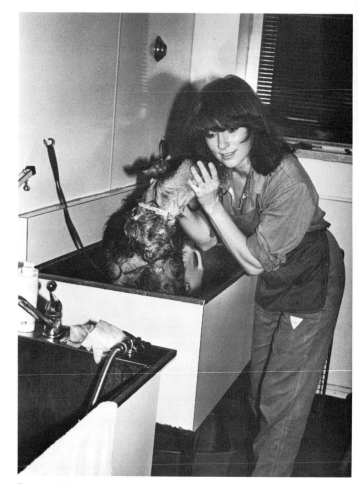

Brynn Thayer plays Jenny, a former nun who has since become involved with several of the series' men. In real life, Brynn is a former teacher from Texas who married her "One Life to Live" costar, Gerald Anthony (Marco/Mario) with whom she had only a fleeting on-screen affair. Photo by Ed Geller.

have been featured over the last 10 years are described below.

One favorite theme on this show involves hookers with hearts of gold who go straight after being moved by true love. In instances in which the hooker occasionally slipped up, as in the case of "OLTL's" Karen Wolek, it's only because of some greater need, such as saving her husband's life or finding the identity of a dastard threatening the security of the town of Llanview.

There was also, as there was on "AMC," a rapist. But unlike the monster who was finally blown up on "AMC" (Ray Gardner), Brad Vernon is redeemable if not yet thoroughly redeemed. His saving grace has been his patient father, Dr. Will Vernon, and his sister, Samantha. However, while they love him, they have never blindly tolerated any of his misdeeds in the past.

For years a baby-mixup story was the underlying

Robin Strasser (left), who plays Dorian, poses with Brynn Thayer (Jenny). Strasser injected a quality of vulnerability into the nasty character of Dorian.

Gerald Anthony plays the conniving but often lovable Marco Dane. The actor admits that he frequently got mixed up when discussing Marco and Mario during the period when he played twins. Photo by Ed Geller.

plotline that tied together several of the characters. Jenny Janssen, a former nun, bore a child who died soon after birth. Her sister, Karen, a former hooker who married Dr. Larry Wolek (the son of a blue-collar family who made good by improving his occupational standing) substituted the child of Katrina, another former hooker. Baby Mary was raised by Jenny until relatively recently when the identity of her real mother became known. The identity of the baby's real father was never in doubt. Brad Vernon was assumed to have sired the child, as he had Jenny's dead infant.

The character of Marco Dane/Mario Corelli moved from being a pimp to a somewhat more respectable position, but he is still opportunistic. Marco is always looking for the easy way to make a big score. He even pretended to be a doctor at one time, taking the place of his twin brother, Mario.

He represents the person who has to go his own way even if it's strewn with rubble. He's too impatient to wait and, in many ways, is the correlative of the wealthy Asa who "lucked out" with oil and cattle while Marco still looks for his gimmick.

The imperious Dorian Lord, a doctor, moved into high society by marrying Victor Lord, the most powerful and wealthy man of Llanview. Upon his death, she became the town's *grande dame*. Dorian is not above doing the wrong thing for whatever reason she thinks is right, *for her*. She groomed a lawyer, Herb

Erica Slezak plays Victoria Lord Riley Buchanan. Photo by Bob Deutsch.

admires.

Victor Lord, Viki's father, totally disapproved of Viki's romance with tough newspaperman Joe Riley. Although she had spent her entire life trying to please her father, Viki found she loved Joe too much to give him up. The conflict caused Viki to develop a split personality.

Viki's alter-ego, Nicki Smith, did whatever she damn well pleased. Frequenting bars in search of fun and excitement (something the very upper-class Viki would never do), Nicki met Joe's best friend Vinnie Wolek (who didn't realize she was really Viki). Soon, a romance developed between them. When it was finally discovered that Viki suffered from schizophrenia psychiatrist Dr. Marcus Polk was brought in to treat Viki (Dr. Polk, a fictional character, also made several appearances on "OLTL's" sister soap, "All My Children"). Before long, Viki was able to overcome her emotional problems.

Viki and Joe were finally married, but their conjugal bliss ended abruptly when Joe was in a car accident and believed dead. Consequently, Viki turned to staid

Lee Paterson (Joe Riley) and Erika Slezak (Vicky) in a clinch.

Callison, for the governor's mansion, married him, and had visions of ruling the State House through him. Herb resigned the day after he won the election, which threw Dorian for a loss, but not enough for her to leave Herb.

The dark-haired, dark-eyed Dorian is often posed against the blonde, blue-eyed Pat Ashley, also a Lord widow (she was married to Victor's son, Tony, who was finally killed off early in 1983).

The Life of an Heiress: Victoria Lord

Silver spoon notwithstanding, the life of an heiress is not always a charmed existence. Let's take a look at Victoria Lord to get a fuller picture of Llanview.

The character of Viki was first played by Gillian Spencer (now Daisy/Monique on "AMC"), and Erika Slezak took over the role in the 70's. Slezak has received numerous kudos for turning Viki from a dominated poor little rich girl into the lady that everyone

Al Freeman, Jr., plays detective Lieutenant Ed Hall, who was assigned to investigate Marcie Wade's death.

Steve Burke, who also worked for *The Banner*.

Steve Burke's secretary, Marcie Wade, who was secretly in love with Steve, became very jealous of Viki's romance with her boss and set out to make Viki think her mental illness had returned.

Steve found out and confronted Marcie. A fight sued between them, and Marcie's gun accidentally went off, killing her. Steve was charged with Marcie's murder. While Steve was on trial, Joe Riley, now an amnesia victim, returned to Llanview and managed to find the clue that would ultimately clear Steve of Marcie's murder.

When, as inevitably happens in daytime drama, Joe Riley was discovered as among the living, Viki had to choose between the two men. She finally opted for Joe. Unfortunately, in the interim, Joe had impregnated hopeful writer, Cathy Craig. When Joe found out, he did the noble thing and proposed. Cathy, who didn't want a loveless marriage in spite of the baby, said no. She changed her mind, it was too late; Joe and Viki had eloped.

Cathy's baby was born very ill. The doctors at Llanview hospital told Viki privately that the problem was an inherited one and would be passed to any child of Joe's. Viki kept the truth from Joe and told him that she couldn't have children. (An offshoot of this secret led to Viki's being blackmailed. When the blackmailer was killed, Viki was among those suspected of the crime, but cleared.) Cathy's baby, Megan, died as a result of an accident while Viki was frantically driving her to the hospital. Cathy, of course, blamed Viki even though Viki was in the hospital in a coma, near death, as a result of the accident. When Viki recuperated she and Joe conceived a child, and Viki decided to go ahead with the pregnancy despite the risks. Dorian, who at this point hated Viki because Viki had tried to protect her dying father from Dorian's clutches, took the chance to get back at Victor's daughter by telling Joe the truth about Megan. This caused a major rift between the Rileys until Joe realized that Viki's actions had never been malicious.

Cathy Craig, who had since married Tony Lord, began to crack under the pressure of all that had happened between her and Joe and because of Megan's death. When Viki's son Kevin was born Cathy flipped completely and kidnapped the baby to make him her own. Eventually the child was returned to the loving arms of Joe and Viki's.

Joe and Viki's marriage was never dull, but at this point it seemed that they were beginning to settle down to a happy life. A year or two later, however, not long after Viki became pregnant again, Joe came down with some form of terminal illness. But Viki remained strong throughout the ordeal. Joe died with dignity in his own bed and the heartbroken widow went on bravely with the help of her friends, especially Larry Wolek, who served as Viki's lamaze coach. A few months later Joey was born. Viki went back to *The Banner* and decided she could handle both the publisher's job she had been handling and the editor's job Joe had left vacant. She poured all her energy into her work and the care of her two sons and was beginning to run herself ragged when help arrived in the form of Clint Buchanan, who became the new editor of *The Banner*. It didn't take Clint long to fall in love with Viki, but Ms. Riley wasn't ready to fall in love again.

Enter suitor number two: ex-con Ted Clayton, who presented himself to Llanview as an art dealer. Ted was after Viki's money, and he made some pretty desperate moves to tie Viki to him, including drugging her. Clint and company finally rescued Viki, and Ted was killed.

Gradually, Viki began to realize that she loved Clint, and after a couple of close calls that threatened to keep them apart the couple was blissfully wed—but

Above: Clint Buchanan is played by Clint Ritchie. Photo by Bob Deutsch.

Below: Echo, the mysterious woman from Clint Buchanan's past, is played by Kim Zimmer, who previously starred on "The Doctors." Photo by Ed Geller.

trouble was imminent for Clint and Viki once more, in the form of new characters Echo and Giles.

AFFAIRS TO REMEMBER

- Meredith Lord and Larry Wolek: rich girl meets poor boy.
- Ed Hall and Carla Gray: they were Llanview's premier black couple.
- Cathy Craig and Joe Riley: Their love was never mutual.
- Dorian and Victor Lord: Was she after his money alone or did she really love him? Was she responsible for his death?
- Tony and Cathy: A stormy romance if there ever was one.
- Jenny and Tim Siegel: She, a former nun, married him on his death bed.
- Pat and Tony: She bore his son and married another man.
- Jenny and Brad: The saint and the sinner.
- Karen and Larry: They just weren't compatible.
- Bo and Pat, Bo and Georgina, Bo and Becky, Bo and Delilah: This guy just isn't very lucky.
- Asa and his loves: Ever trying to prove his youth and his manhood by wooing younger women.
- Edwina and her loves: Originally a social climber shooting for Richard Abbott, Edwina has mellowed, especially after being humbled by her affairs with Clint, Mario/Marco, and Marco's brother Gary. Everyone knows Edwina and Marco really love each other.

MURDER/MAYHEM/MYSTERY

To supplement the mayhem discussed so far in this chapter, here's a list of notable criminal storylines:

- Viki Riley was involved in a murder trial as a defendant. No less an important lawyer than Paul Martin came from Pine Valley (the locale of "All My Children") to Llanview to defend Ms. Viki and, of course, win her case for her.
- Marco, Karen's pimp, thwarted her attempts to escape from him by taking revenge against Viki Riley, who was helping Karen. He took a photo of Viki's ward, Tina, and created a composite using Tina's face and someone else's nude body. He hoped, in this way, to blackmail Viki. Marco was later murdered. It turned out that it was really Mario, Marco's twin brother, who died.

Robert Woods (Bo Buchanan) and Steve Fletcher (Brad Vernon) play two of Llanview's eligible young men. Photo by Ed Geller.

Above: Mary Gordon Murray plays Becky Abbott, the hapless singer. Miss Murray is a Broadway star who has appeared in Little Me. Photo by Ed Geller.

Left: Shelly Burch plays Delila Ralston Buchanan, who has been married to both Asa Buchanan and son Bo. Photo by Ed Geller.

- Brad Vernon caused his wife Jenny heartbreak by raping her sister Karen.

- Samantha, in a fit of anger over being rebuffed by Tony Lord, drove off in her father's car with her father's fiancee as a passenger. The car crashed, the fiancee died, and Samantha was left horribly scarred. In time, of course, the scars were removed by cosmetic surgery (which almost always happens on a soap after a character has had time to repent).

- Pat Ashley's long-lost identical twin Maggie turned up in Llanview, tied Pat up, and kept her in the basement after assuming her identity. Every now and then she came down to see her sibling to berate her and chortle about her success in fooling everyone. Of course, Pat was saved just before her evil twin could do her in.

- Where Pat had sinister sister problems, so did Dorian. Her sister, Melinda, was released from a mental hospital and immediately started making problems for all concerned. She shot Peter Janssen (whom Jenny was to marry after being divorced from Brad) and tried to kill Dorian. Melinda was finally undone but not until a thoroughly shaken Dorian nearly collapsed in an emotional breakdown.

- Katrina, Mary's real mother, was later indicted for murder but was saved when the true identity of the murderer was revealed.

IT HAPPENED HERE FIRST

During the early '70s Dr. Joyce Brothers made several appearances on the soap. Playing herself, Dr. Brothers counseled Viki's sister Meredith, who was suffering from depression following the birth of her son Danny. This was the first time a psychologist appeared on a soap as herself. Years later, Dr. Brothers made a few appearances on "As The World Turns," once again playing herself. This time Dr. Brothers was counseling a young girl who had started experimenting with drugs. In 1979 "General Hospital" hired Dr. Irene Kassorla to counsel Lesley Williams Webber, who was having problems in her marriage with Rick.

WHO'S WHO IN LLANVIEW

Original Cast

Actor	Character
DORIS BELACK	**Anna Wolek**
LYNN BENISH	**Meredith Lord**
PETER DEANDA	**Dr. Price Trainor**
NIKI FLACKS	**Karen Martin**
JOE GALLISON	**Tom Edwards**
ERNEST GRAVES	**Victor Lord**
ELLEN HOLLY	**Carla Gray**
ALLAN MILLER	**Dave Siegel**
LEE PATTERSON	**Joe Riley**

First air date: July 15, 1968

A Word From Judith Light (ex-Karen Wolek)

"I feel that I've been lucky in that I've been able to play a character like Karen on a soap like 'One Life to Live.' There's a great deal of heavy emotion, of course. But a lot of humor as well. Karen has a sense of humor. So do Dorian (Robin Strasser) and Jenny (Brynn Thayer) and the other women—and, of course, the men, too. Humor is part of the human condition. To leave it out is to leave out something that makes us unique; that makes us human. This show never forgets who we are."

"One Life to Live" cast members enjoy an evening with guest star Sammy Davis, Jr., who has played the recurring role of Chip, a hood. Other "One Life to Live-ers" in this photo include (top row from left to right) Michael Storm (Dr. Larry Wolek), Robin Strasser (Dorian Lord Callison), and Gerald Anthony (Marco Dane); on either end of bottom row are Judith Light (Karen Wolek) and Steve Fletcher (Brad Vernon). Photo by Bob Deutsch.

A Directory of Recent Characters*

Becky Lee Abbott: Ex-wife of Richard Abbott; involved with Bo and then married to Asa; a C & W singer. *Mary Gordon Murray*

Pat Ashley: Ex-wife of Tony Lord, Paul Kendall; ex-lover of Bo Buchanan; a TV reporter. *Jacqueline Courtney*

Asa Buchanan: Texas millionaire who moved to Llanview; he's a distant relative of the Woleks: Anna, Larry, Jenny, and Karen; dad of Clint and Bo; ex-husband of Olympia, Sam, and Delilah; now married to Becky. *Philip Carey*

Bo Buchanan: Asa's son; Clint's brother; married his father's ex, Delila; also was involved with Pat, Mimi, and Becky. *Robert Woods*

*The actors/actresses who currently play these major roles are in italics.

Clint Buchanan: Asa's son; Bo's brother; wed to Viki; he publishes *The Banner* and *The Chronicle* with Viki. *Clint Ritchie*

Viki Lord Riley Buchanan: Wed to Clint; widow of Joe Riley; Victor Lord's daughter; Tony Lord's half-sister; mother of Joey and Kevin Riley. *Erika Slezak*

Dorian Lord Callison: The leader of Llanview society; a doctor whose license was restricted; wed to former District Attorney Herb Callison; mother of Cassie; widow of Victor; stepmother of Viki. *Robin Strasser*

Herb Callison: A lawyer; he resigned the governorship; loves Dorian, his wife. *Anthony Call*

Anna Craig: Dr. Jim Craig's widow; Larry's sister; Karen, Jenny, and Asa's cousin. *Phyllis Behar*

Emma Samms with Matthew Ashford, who played Drew Ralston, Delila's intern cousin.

Marco Dane: Posed as his dead brother, Dr. Mario Corelli (caught by Dorian) he aided Karen's baby switch scheme; he's in love with ex-wife Edwina. *Gerald Anthony*

Rafe Garretson: Asa's nephew; he loves Katrina; a policeman. *Ken Meeker*

Ed Hall: Carla's ex-husband; a police detective; Karen's friend. *Al Freeman, Jr.*

Ina Hopkins: Runs a boarding house where ex-prostitutes Karen and Katrina had lived. *Sally Gracie*

Jenny Vernon Janssen: A former nun once wed to Brad Vernon; Karen's sister; Peter Janssen's widow; engaged again to Brad. *Brynn Thayer*

Katrina Karr: Mary's mother; former prostitute involved with Brad; runs restaurant with Ina. *Regan McManus*

Edwina Lewis: A reporter; once wed to Marco and still in love with him. *Margaret Klenck*

Delila Ralston: Wed Asa; had an affair with Bo; when Asa returned from the "dead," she divorced him to marry Bo. *Shelly Burch*

Brad Vernon: Will's son; Samantha's brother; Jenny's ex; Mary's father with Katrina; a not-too-well-reformed scoundrel. *Steve Fletcher*

Samantha Vernon: Will's daughter; Brad's sister; married Asa but was nearly killed by Nicole, Asa's still (then) living wife. *Dorian Lopinto*

Will Vernon: A psychiatrist; dad of Brad and Samantha; grandfather of Mary. *Anthony George*

Larry Wolek: A doctor; wed to Karen; Anna's brother; kin to the Buchanans and Jenny; Danny's father. *Michael Storm*

Wanda Wolek: Vinnie's widow; owns a C & W club. *Marilyn Chris*

11

Ryan's Hope (ABC)

Ryan's Hope first aired over ABC on July 7, 1975. From the beginning, the show was on a "prove it" course. Today, much of the credit for "RH's" success lies with its writers and creators Claire Labine and Paul Avila Mayer. The seeds for the show were sown while the talented duo was still writing for "Love of Life" during the '70s. While they were fulfilling their chores with CBS, ABC approached Labine and Mayer about creating a new serial tentatively titled "City Hospital." The idea didn't appeal much to the writers, who countered with a suggestion that the story center around an Irish-American family who owned a bar across the street from a hospital. ABC agreed to let them give it a try, but they suggested that the new title for the show be "A Rage to Love."

The fact that the title "Ryan's Hope" was eventually accepted expresses the writers' feelings toward

Kate Mulgrew was the first Mary, the eldest daughter of Maeve and Johnny. Photo courtesy of Daytime TV *magazine.*

Some of the Ryans and friends in 1978 (left to right): Bernard Barrow as Johnnie Ryan, Helen Gallagher as Maeve Ryan, John Gabriel as Seneca Beaulac, Nancy Addison as Jillian Coleridge, and Michael Levin as Jack Fenelli.

the show. Both writers have said that they want "Ryan's Hope" to fulfill all their own personal fantasies. It's important to note, however, that "fantasies" here don't necessarily consist of the exotic stories that have marked many daytime dramas of the '80s. Both Labine and Mayer, from small families, like to fantasize about the type of large, close-knit family that the Ryans represent, and hope—for the future, for happiness for the whole clan, for family warmth, and for spirit and independence—is what this series is all about.

Several factors mitigated against "Ryan's Hope's" success as a soap opera. The writers themselves were aware of the tough odds against a new daytime drama succeeding, but they forged ahead with plans to make "Ryan's Hope" unique despite the prevailing tendency toward imitation among daytime series. Even after "Ryan's Hope" was put on the air, the writers

were sure it would be a temporary thing, but the unique mix of ethnic diversity, real-life location, and "realistic" characters proved to be a winner for all involved. Perhaps the fact that "Ryan's Hope" characters seem more realistic is due to the fact that much of the story *does* come from real life.

HOW "RYAN'S HOPE" WAS BORN

All literary creations, including the scripts of soap operas, are said to contain seeds of the writers' own experiences which, when planted in soap opera soil, blossom into a different flower but are still related to its genetic genie.

"Ryan's Hope" was drawn from characters both writers have known in real life. Labine, however, drew upon more familiar sources in shaping her soap.

The family that first appeared concurrently with the

Ryans, the Beaulacs, represented a French Canadian clan Labine and her husband, Clem Labine (publisher of *The Old House Journal*) knew very well.

One of Labine's favorite early characters on the soap was Mary Ryan; later Mary Ryan Fenelli. She was the strong-willed, courageous elder daughter of Maeve and Johnny; the loving sister of Siobhan, Frank, and Pat Ryan; and the mother of little Ryan Fennelli. She would die in a mob vendetta.

The real Mary was based on a real Mary Ryan, later Mary Ryan Munistieri, with whom Claire Labine had worked as cowriter on several soaps. Ms. Munistieri continues as a writer on "Ryan's Hope." Her fictional alter-ego was "killed off" after the last actress to play the role left the show. It was decided then not to continue the character with another actress. Actually, the first woman to play Mary Ryan, Kate Mulgrew, stamped an indelible impression of her own personality into the role, making it difficult for anyone else to portray Mary. Mulgrew herself said that when she first read for the role, the writers felt they had found their soap opera "Mary" and immediately began to fit the character around her. The tailoring was so well-fitted that another actress, Nicolette Goulet (Robert Goulet's daughter), was never able to wear it so well when she inherited the role. The strong presence of Kate Mulgrew seemed to hover, like an aura, around Goulet's Mary Ryan.

It was as if the writers had repeated a Frankenstein-like act; taking two flesh and blood women, the real Mary Ryan and Kate Mulgrew, to create their living, breathing *person*. No wonder then that no one else but Kate could be what they had so artfully and so uniquely made.

Even parts of the "Ryan's Hope" setting have their foundations in fact. Besides being set in what many would call the "most real" city in the nation, New York, the sets on "Ryan's Hope" really look like places you'd find in New York. In one photo of Claire Labine in the dining room of her New York brownstone, the setting is remarkably similar to the look contrived for the Coleridge brownstone.

WELCOME TO RIVERSIDE

The Citizens

When "Ryan's Hope" debuted in the mid-'70s there were essentially three major families—the Ryans, of course; the Beaulacs; and the Coleridges. The Ryans are not poor; nor are they wealthy. In a way, they represent the traditional American dream family: hopeful immigrant couple moves to New York and there rears a batch of healthy American children who take advantage of all the educational and other privileges and go on to make good—though they never *ever* lose track of their roots. The Coleridge family members, in contrast, were born with silver spoons in their mouths, but as it goes in the American dream, the Coleridge offspring end up mingling with the less-well-born Ryans via Riverside Hospital, where all the poor-kid-made-good and rich-kid-stayed-good characters work, mostly in harmony. The Beaulacs represented another immigrant faction, these from French Canada. The Beaulacs quickly dwindled to a single family member in "Ryan's Hope's" storylines.

A rundown of the major "Ryan's Hope" characters:

The Ryans

Maeve and Johnny (matriarch and patriarch): Irish immigrants who own an Irish bar in New York across the street from a hospital.

Frank: eldest son, John Kennedy-like, NYC cop eventually turned lawyer-politician.

Pat: second son, intern and then doctor.

Malcolm Groome has portrayed Pat Ryan (now Dr.) since the show's inception. Photo by Diana Church.

Mary: 2nd daughter—feisty and smart, etc., became a journalist.

Siobhan: didn't appear at the beginning of the show but has since become a major character; the youngest Ryan, a rebel who became a police officer.

Cathleen: oldest daughter; rarely appears—is married with children and living in another state.

Delia: Family friend of the Ryans since childhood, she thinks of herself as a Ryan and as Maeve's daughter, always seeking approval from Maeve and Johnny.

Little John: Delia and Frank's son; has lived with Maeve and Johnny most of his life.

The Coleridges

The wealthy friends of the Ryans, also live in Riverside, in a classic NYC brownstone.

Jill: Lawyer, married to Frank.

Faith: intern with Pat and then pediatrician at Riv-

Ron Hale plays the sometimes errant Dr. Coleridge. Photo by Bob Deutsch.

Currently, Faith is played by Karen Morris-Gowdy. Photo courtesy of Daytime TV magazine.

erside Hospital; on-again, off-again lover of Pat.

Roger: the black sheep of the family; brilliant surgeon.

Ed Coleridge: father of family, who has died.

The Beaulacs

A French-Canadian couple, connected with Ryans through hospital.

Seneca: head of neurosurgery at Riverside Hospital; has always been unlucky in love, especially due to his own arrogance and desire to manipulate.

Nell Beaulac: Seneca's late wife, died at the very beginning of the show.

Peripheral Major/Supporting Characters

Jack Fenelli: Investigative journalist, columnist, and recently TV newsman—provides counterpoint to the Ryans because he was an orphan and represented in the beginning (and sometimes still) the antithesis of the Ryan family closeness.

Nancy Addison plays Jillian Coleridge. Photo by Bob Deutsch.

Bob Reid: Delia's long-suffering, always-loyal brother, the common sense factor, formerly a cop with Frank, always Frank's friend.

The factor that ties all three families, and the other periperhal characters, together on "Ryan's Hope" is mother Maeve Ryan. There is no doubt in viewers' minds that the Ryans are a matriarchal society. Certainly, Johnny Ryan plays a strong father role, but it is to Maeve that all the soap's characters turn—for advice, for a shoulder to cry on, for the best corned beef and cabbage in town, for spiritual guidance, and for the cozy warmth that she has instilled both in Ryan's Bar and in the upstairs apartment in which the family has always lived.

"Ryan's Hope," which started as essentially a matriarch-dominated but male-oriented series, has always done a good job of reflecting the times. That is, where

Left: John Gabriel plays the arrogant Seneca Beaulac.

Maeve Ryan was, still is, the mother figure around whom the family revolved, she was fixed in place. Like the Queen Bee of a hive, she was a necessary part of the family but was not expected to move far from where she exercised her authority—the home. Meanwhile, her children might move around. Occasionally, they could come home for a lavish dollop of wise, Celtic matriarch advice, but they rarely stayed too long.

There is no argument above Maeve and Johnny's maintaining their traditional values on this soap. The idea is to present a strong core family structure, which acts as a mooring place for the rest of the clan.

In essence, the Ryan father and mother figures maintain the stability that allows their young ones and their children's peers to rush into their futures, jump at opportunities, and (quite often) pounce into bed with partners new and renewed.

Maeve and Johnny are there to tsk-tsk but never to turn away from their brood regardless of how much they may disapprove. They're also there to show pride in their accomplishments and give support when courage lags behind ambition.

A Tour of Riverside

When "Ryan's Hope" debuted in 1975, Riverside was a unique setting for a daytime drama, and possibly a risky one.

First, there was the fact of its being set in a real city, New York. No Oakdale, Bay City, Salem, Springfield, USA. (The attraction of the mythical sites was that they could be anywhere in the country, including *your* hometown.)

The fact that New York was chosen was unusual. Much of the country really believed it when they said it was all right to visit the Big Apple, but not to live there. Polls also indicated that many thought New York had a population that was a cross section between "Moscow-led 'liberals'" and "Sodom and Gomorrah sex maniacs."

Riverside bears a close resemblance to the real NYC neighborhood Riverdale (or, it might be theorized, it could be based on NYC's Riverside Drive). A guess would place the neighborhood on Manhattan's middle-class west side, and all the usual city neighborhood landmarks are there: hospital, Chinese restaurant, park, and so on.

The hub of the series is, obviously, Ryan's Bar. The fact that this pub is conveniently located directly across the street from Riverside Hospital has made for some easily interwoven medical plots; in fact, in the show's early days, Riverside Hospital and medical storylines were much in the forefront of "Ryan's Hope" episodes. "Ryan's Hope" has, since the show's first five years, drifted further and further from the Riverside Hospital influence, but the medical theme has been maintained through the new setting of a clinic set up by Faith and Pat.

What's Going On in Riverside?

If ratings really reflect success, then it's fairly clear that "Ryan's Hope" has succeeded where other soaps have failed due to its strong sense of family—and hope. At its peak, "Ryan's Hope" was notable for avoiding some of the more outlandish themes and plots that were sweeping the other dramas. In fact, it was during the infamous King Kong and King Tut storylines that RH's ratings dropped notably. The widely acclaimed series had lost critical credibility, and it took some time for the show to recover in the ratings game after that.

For the most part, since its inception, typical events in Riverside have been similar to those of other series: love, marriage, and divorce; birth, death; deception and confession, and so on. What often made "Ryan's Hope" different was the multidimensional characters who underwent all this trauma. The Ryan and Coleridge children in this soap were and are modern people who realistically agonize over the conflicts brought upon them by the demands of work as opposed to those of family, the importance of God versus the importance of various sociological issues, loyalty to family as well as the need to become independent, contributing members of society.

In addition, the things that happen to members of the Ryan clan and their friends are often influenced by their setting. On "Ryan's Hope" it is rare that a female character who happens to be pregnant marries merely in the name of propriety. The Ryans are also a religious bunch, but the children don't necessarily follow the teachings of the church as strictly as do their parents. At one point during the '70s Siobhan worked for Planned Parenthood while Maeve staunchly opposed birth control. And many of "Ryan's Hope's" plots have focused on the disputes among family members who will support their kin to the death but will also fight for their right to "do their own thing," despite family opposition. The Ryans are so inextricably entwined, in fact, that what one Ryan does *always* affects the others. Some examples:

In 1978 Frank Ryan was played by Daniel Hugh-Kelly.

- Mary Ryan died trying to prove that Siobhan's intended, Joe Novak, wasn't as clean as he seemed.
- Maeve's attempt to spread her wings beyond Riverside through a dance contest she entered with another man caused a rift between Maeve and Johnny that made the entire family crabby.
- Frank's loves have affected everyone: he married Delia and their son has remained in the custody of Maeve and Johnny ever since the divorce; nearly all the Ryans have made some sort of move to get Jill and Frank together over the years; his brief affair with Faith before returning to Jill split the sisters apart for what seemed like for good, etc.
- After a brush with death during 1983, Pat has been able to foresee the future—albeit foggily—for his siblings (a gift that Maeve is also said to have in the form of "feelings").

Other plots have made the family believable because they interact with the city they live in. When "Ryan's Hope" decides to inject itself with some excitement, it usually bears some connection to typical NYC problems: politics, organized crime, scandals, and journalism. And when "Ryan's Hope" discusses religion, it's not talking WASP. One of Pat's former loves, for instance, was a girl named Nancy, and their romance provoked a memorable scene in which Maeve and Nancy's mother talked about the problems inherent in a marriage between the Irish Catholic boy and a Jewish girl.

THE RIVERSIDE ARCHIVES

One of the most interesting changes that came about in "Ryan's Hope" took place at the very beginning of the show. A la Jack Kennedy, son Frank was slated for an early exit via death from the Ryan clan, but the character was so instantly popular that writers Labine and Mayer were forced to rewrite frantically to keep him on. Since then, Frank's escapades—romantic and otherwise—have served as a fulcrum for the soap's storylines. Again, Frank represents the American dream. Son of modest immigrants, he started out as a New York cop, went to law school, ran for Congress, became a senator and then had to resign, started to run for Congress again and had to withdraw because of a second scandal. Along the way he has wooed and been wooed by just about all the prominent "RH" ladies, many of whom were attracted to his success as well as his cocky Irish good looks. During its most successful years, "RH" plots revolved around Frank's and the rest of the Ryan's trying to deal with

Geoffrey Pierson, the latest Frank Ryan.

everyday problems as well as some more unusual ones relating to their various civic activities.

In 1980, however, ABC purchased "Ryan's Hope" from its creators, and the whole tenor of the show began to change. ABC apparently decided that what was working for "General Hospital" could work for "Ryan's Hope." Unfortunately, this proved not to be the case, as "RH" flitted from one outrageous storyline to the next in pursuit of the elusive viewer. It was during this time that the middle-class homey atmosphere of "Ryan's Hope" gave way to a more glamorous view of New York life. Suddenly Delia was the owner of a fabulous restaurant in Central Park, which attracted all the Manhattan celebrities. The show also introduced the fabulously well-to-do Kirklands, who drank champagne in chauffeur-driven limousines on the way home from the ballet and were perfectly capable of coming up with $10 million in cash to get Joe Novak out of a lethal bind.

As of early 1983 Labine and Mayer returned to their writing duties at "RH," and the Kirklands were summarily written out. And in an attempt to regain what had been lost, the writers brought back some of the orginial "RH'ers," including casting director Shirley Rich, Malcolm Groome as Pat, and Ilene Kristen as Delia. "Ryan's Hope" is beginning to look the old Riverside that viewers knew and loved, but only time will tell whether or not the viewers' interest will be renewed.

If there is a "Ryan's Hope" foil to Frank Ryan, the boy who almost always makes good, it is probably Delia. The thorn in everyone's side, Delia has been trying to become a Ryan—one way or another—since she was a child. And Delia's manipulations have affected the cast's lives through stealth as much as Frank's above-board actions have through ambition.

The History of Delia

Essential to the character of Delia, and underlying most of her actions, is the fact that she grew up without a mother. Befriended, along with brother Bobby, as a child by her compassionate neighbor Maeve, Delia has never stopped seeking for approval of Maeve. Above all, she wants to be accepted as a member of the Ryan family. To this end, she has wreaked havoc in the family for nearly ten years.

First Delia fell for Frank Ryan. (What better entree to the family than through marriage to its oldest son?) They were married and divorced, but Delia kept the ties to the Ryans tight indirectly by proving to be an

Above: Ilene Kristen portrays the hypersensitive and hyperkinetic Delia.

Below: Young Jadrien Steele, who plays Frank and Delia's son, John.

unfit mother for Frank and Dee's son little John. Visiting him at Maeve and Johnny's apartment has often been the excuse Delia has used to show up at Ryan's Bar.

After the failure of her first Ryan marriage, Dee decided to go after second son Pat. Luring him away from fellow intern and lover Faith, Dee made sure she became pregnant, and of course she received the support of the Ryan family when she made it clear that she expected Pat to marry her. The fact that she had a miscarriage before the nuptials didn't stop her from going on with the farce, however; soon after their marriage, Dee faked a miscarriage so that Maeve would not take away that all-important approval of her. Dee now had everything she wanted, but the life with an intern didn't suit her fantasies of life with up-and-coming Dr. Pat Ryan. Again she was divorced.

Finally it seemed that Dee had met her match—and her true love—in one Dr. Roger Coleridge, himself a black sheep in the family who, like Dee, had often had to grovel for forgiveness from his family for his many transgressions. Roger truly loved Dee exactly as she was, but still Dee was not satisfied. Her penchant for lying to protect herself at all costs finally split them up, and Dee somehow dug up another Ryan to focus on. This one was Barry, a playboy-promoter from the Chicago branch of the family. Unfortunately for Dee, he proved to be even more adept at conjuring up his own version of the truth than she was, and this romance never blossomed into marriage. Since those days, Delia has occasionally used Roger's lasting love for her to trick him into doing something for her, and by 1983 it seemed that Roger had finally given up on poor Dee.

Along the way, Dee has also caused trouble by making some unholy alliances—among them Tiso Novotni and Joe Novak, who helped her set up and then "keep" the Crystal Palace; her stockbroker, who wanted her to trade her body for funds to make up her investment losses; and just about anyone else who could further the cause of Delia Reid Ryan Ryan Coleridge. At this juncture, Delia is once again the humble waif seeking for approval. She's lost the Crystal Palace and her entire glamorous life she built around it and is probably plotting a new and devious way to insinuate herself into the Ryan fold.

AFFAIRS TO REMEMBER

- Frank and Jill: Though all the "RHers" agree they've always been made for each other, Frank and Jill

Two of "Ryan's Hope's" former stars, Randall Edwards and Michael Corbett. Edwards played the role of Delia Coleridge after the character's original interpreter, Ilene Kristen, left for California and before Ilene returned. Corbett played bedhopping Michael; when the character was written out he resurfaced as Warren Carter, another sly, slick type on "Search for Tomorrow." Photo by Bob Deutsch.

didn't marry until the summer of 1983. Frank had been married to Delia and involved with Rae Woodard and Jill's sister, Faith. Jill's attention was once diverted by a dying rock star, and she was married to Seneca, but she's always loved Frank.

- Jack and Mary: In one of "RH's" most poignant romances, Jack Fenelli and Mary Ryan were just beginning to settle down with daughter Ryan when Mary was wasted by the mob. In 1983 Jack was introduced to his new love, Leigh.

- Siobhan and Joe: The youngest Ryan loved Joe Novak dearly, but his constant lies about his criminal life kept a rift between them. After their last reconciliation, Joe left NYC to protect Siobhan from mobsters who wanted to kill him.
- Kim and Rae and Michael and Seneca: This triangle-plus evolved when powermonger Rae and flighty daughter Kim began sleeping with the same young stud, Michael. To complicate matters, Kim was already married to much-older Seneca. The upshot: Michael was killed and Kim and Seneca divorced.

AFFAIRS TO FORGET

- Delia and Prince Albert: In this incredible storyline Dee was kidnapped and taken to the top of Belvedere Tower by a love-crazed gorilla she'd befriended at the zoo.
- Faith and Ari: In this misbegotten plot Faith was thought to be the reincarnation of a mummified Egyptian princess with whom archaeologist Ari was obsessed.

MURDER/MAYHEM/MYSTERY

Among others, these storylines wreaked havoc on the Ryan family and friends:

- Desperate for funds of her own, Kim paired up with baddie Orson to fake the kidnapping of her own daughter, Arley. The plan backfired, however, and she was lucky to get out of this one alive.
- Siobhan posed as a hooker in the early '80s in a police scheme intended to stop a mad killer of prostitutes. The plan succeeded, but it cost Faith's lover and Siobhan's boss, Mitch Bronski, his life.
- Joe Novak was constantly running from "the family" of mobsters from whom he wanted to split, and various Ryans happened into the crossfire.
- Long ago Jill married Seneca instead of Frank because Seneca tricked her into believing baby Edmund was his child, not Frank's. When the truth about the blood test was finally revealed, Jill and Seneca went through a somewhat violent divorce.

The Evolution of a Character

Said John Gabriel (Seneca Beaulac):

"In the beginning, Seneca Beaulac was a proud,

Gordon Thompson, who played Ari and is now on "Dynasty," with Ron Hale (Roger Coleridge). Photo by Ed Geller.

manipulative, and possessive man. He hadn't intended to come to New York but he did when his first wife, Nell, left him and came to the city to get away from him.

"He followed her and then decided to stay. Later on Nell became very ill. She was dying; the cause was an aneurysm.

"Nell's death changed Seneca. He was still possessive, still jealous. But he also learned to be more tender, more yielding and vulnerable. The brilliant man of science was hurt in his relationship with Jillian when he learned she still loved Frank Ryan. He tried to hold onto her. But then he became involved with a young woman named Kimberly.

"Seneca has grown in his pain. I think—and I believe the audiences also think—that he's a far more feeling—more accessible—man than he was when he first came to New York. . . . Change is growth and growth is change and Seneca seems to embody those principles very well. . . ."

WHO'S WHO IN RIVERSIDE

Original Cast

Actor	*Character*
NANCY ADDISON	**Jill Coleridge**
BERNARD BARROW	**Johnny Ryan**
FAITH CATLIN	**Faith Coleridge**
JUSTIN DEAS	**Bucky Carter**
MICHAEL FARIMAN	**Nick Szabo**
JOHN GABRIEL	**Seneca Beaulac**
HELEN GALLAGHER	**Maeve Ryan**
MALCOLM GROOME	**Patrick Ryan**
ROSALINDA GUERRA	**Ramona Gonzalez**
RON HALE	**Roger Coleridge**
MICHAEL HAWKINS	**Frank Ryan**
EARL HINDMAN	**Bob Reid**
ILENE KRISTEN	**Delia Reid Ryan**
FRANK LATIMORE	**Ed Coleridge**
MICHAEL LEVIN	**Jack Fenelli**
KATHERINE (KATE) MULGREW	**Mary Ryan**
HANNIBAL PENNEY, JR.	**Clem Moultrie**
DIANA VAN DER VLIS	**Nell Beaulac**

First Air Date: July 7, 1975

Write to "Ryan's Hope" c/o ABC, 1330 Avenue of the Americas, New York, NY 10019.

A Directory of Recent Characters*

Seneca Beaulac: Once wed to Kim and Jillian; he's the father of Kim's child, Arley. *John Gabriel*

Jillian Beaulac: A lawyer; one of Seneca's ex-wives; she's the half-sister of Faith and Roger; married to Frank. *Nancy Addison*

Delia Coleridge: Formerly wed to Frank and Pat Ryan and Dr. Roger Coleridge; she's mother of Frank's son, little Johnny Ryan; she owned a nightclub. *Ilene Kristen*

Faith Coleridge: A doctor; Jill and Roger's sister; in love with Pat. *Karen Morris-Gowdy*

Roger Coleridge: A doctor; Jill and Faith's brother; formerly wed to Delia. *Ron Hale*

Jack Fenelli: Father of Ryan, born to his late wife, Mary Ryan; close to his in-laws. *Michael Levin*

*The actors/actresses who currently play these major roles are in italics.

Kimberly Harris Beaulac: Rae Woodard's daughter; wed to Seneca mother of their daughter. *Kelli Maroney*

Joe Novak: Siobhan Ryan's husband; erstwhile mobster, out of town. *Roscoe Born*

Bob Reid: A former detective; Delia's brother. *Earl Hindman*

Frank Ryan: A lawyer; once involved with Rae, formerly married to Delia; married to Jill; father of little Johnny Ryan; Maeve and John Ryan's son; brother to Pat, Cathleen, Siobhan, and the late Mary. *Geoffrey Pierson*

Johnny Ryan: Maeve's husband; father of Frank, Siobhan, Pat, and the late Mary; grandfather to little Johnny and Ryan Fenelli. *Bernard Barrow*

Maeve Ryan: Johnny's wife; the matriarch of the family; mother of Frank, Pat, Siobhan, Cathleen, and the late Mary; grandmother of little Johnny Ryan and Ryan Fenelli. *Helen Gallagher*

Pat Ryan: A doctor; son of Maeve and Johnny; brother

Kelli Maroney played precocious Kim Beaulac, whose role has been cut out, at least temporarily. Photo by Bob Deutsch.

of Frank, Siobhan, Cathleen, and the late Mary; once in love with Faith. *Malcolm Groome*

Siobhan Ryan (Novak): Daughter of Maeve and Johnny; sister of Frank, Pat and the late Mary; wife of Joe Novak; a policewoman. *Marg Helkenberger*

Rae Woodard: A powerful media person; Kim's mother; once involved with Frank; once in love with Hollis Kirkland. *Louise Shaffer*

Louise Shaffer (Rae Woodard) won a supporting actress Emmy for the 1982-83 season. However, nothing pleased her more than to assist a local chapter of the ASPCA in raising funds. Photo by Ed Geller.

12

Search for Tomorrow (NBC)

"Search for Tomorrow" is television's oldest soap opera. It made its debut over the CBS network on September 3, 1951. It began as a live, 15-minute-a-day show. Its principal character was a young widow named Joanne Barron, played by a former movie actress, Mary Stuart.

Even before reaching the airwaves, daytime TV's longest-running network soap underwent a significant change. Its title was changed from "Search for Happiness" to "Search for Tomorrow." Owned by Procter & Gamble, the program was created by Roy Winsor, whose past credits included a writing stint on one of network radio's first successful soaps "Vic & Sade." Winsor also wrote and directed episodes for another famous radio soap, "Ma Perkins."

A few weeks after "Search" debuted, CBS unveiled "Love of Life." A press release described the sister CBS soapers as "... concerned with private emotional conflict ... its characters show the ability to survive." According to an early network press release, "CBS-TV's "Search for Tomorrow" is the compelling story of the Barron family—Father, Mother, daughter-in-law, and grandchild. It is the story of an American family dominated by the 'old-fashioned' elders, successful and secure. It is the story of a young widow and her child, and their pathetic struggle to voice the ideas of the young. It is the story of the folks next door, and the misunderstandings and heartbreaks that mar their lives."

"Search for Tomorrow's" premiere episode introduced two new products to the American housewife, Joy and Spic & Span. Since the program's commercials were often televised in the same studio, it was not uncommon for the camera to cut from a closeup of the young, suffering Joanne Barron to a perky model, standing just a few feet away, mop and pail in hand, happily extolling the virtues of using Spic & Span.

Cast and crew of "Search for Tomorrow" on the set in the early days (left to right): Robert Mandan, Melba Rae, Larry Haines, Ann Williams, Ken Harvey, Mary Stuart, and Carl Lowe (with a crew member). Photo by Howard Gray.

In the beginning, sets weren't even sets. They were just pieces of sets. Doors and window frames were hung on piano wire from the grid to indicate walls. Furniture was grouped together in an imaginary space. The home viewing audience saw black walls in every room because the walls of the studio were covered with a black velour cyclorama to absorb light and give the illusion of enclosed areas.

"Search for Tomorrow's" production budget for one week in 1951 was $8,025.75. Compared to the more than $250,000 spent on a week's worth of episodes for daytime TV's latest soap offering, "Loving," $8,025.75 seems pretty skimpy.

For the first 13 weeks "Search for Tomorrow" was written by Agnes Nixon. Assuming the writing chores after Agnes Nixon was Irving Vendig, who lived in Sarasota, Florida, and was never able to watch the program because the one local station in his town didn't carry it.

A 15-minute serial until 1968, when it expanded to a full 30 minutes, "Search for Tomorrow" was followed for many years by "Guiding Light," another 15-minute serial. Irna Phillips, "Guiding Light's" creator, hated her show's 15-minute format and once suggested to Mary Stuart that they combine the two soaps and make a single new 30-minute serial. Being the star of "Search for Tomorrow," Mary Stuart was totally against the idea.

During the last two years "Search for Tomorrow" has had at least five different teams of writers churning out its scripts. Longstanding characters, such as Kathy Taper, a character who had been featured on the program since 1971, and Janet Collins, Stu Bergman's daughter, were written off, and new, younger characters were added to the cast. The focus has shifted from Joanne Barron Tate Vincente Tourneur to Liza and Travis Sentell, a wealthy, attractive couple in their late 20s. In 1979 Rod Arrants, who plays Travis Sentell, was the first soap opera actor to be featured alone on the cover of "TV Guide."

Rod Arrants and Sherry Matthias play Travis and Liza Sentell, "Search for Tomorrow's" hot young lovers/adventurers.

WELCOME TO HENDERSON

The Citizens

Joanne Barron was a young widow; she also had a daughter, Patti. They lived in Henderson, a small town located somewhere in the Midwest. Penniless after her husband Keith's death, Joanne, for the first time in her life, was forced to go out and look for work.

It's impossible to trace the history of this series without coming back, from time to time, on the character Mary Stuart created. In 1954 an article in "TV Guide" suggested that Stuart's role epitomized the theme of the soap ". . . Frankly, tomorrow had better come for (them) soon on this show . . . (they) keep searching for happiness (but) keep winding up in a hospital or a lawyer's office."

Indeed, poor Joanne was forever finding her periods

of happiness shattered by death, divorce, desertion, and drinking (one of her latter-day husband's problems, not hers). Still she hangs in there, forever hoping that one day—tomorrow—it will all come out right for once and forever.

Joanne came into television soaps fresh from the model soap heroine of radio. She was expected to endure (villainesses suffer, heroines endure) and was expected to be hopeful that her rewards will come.

Mary Stuart continued to play Joanne through the years and through Joanne's different surnames courtesy of her several marriages (most of them relatively unhappy).

When "Search for Tomorrow" premiered it had a unique single-family cast. Other soaps that have endured have normally begun with at least two major families to create ready-made conflict. Most soaps also changed or added families as time moved on, and "SFT" was similar in this respect. Mary Stuart, as courageous Joanne, was always a popular character in this progenitor of TV soaps, but not even this veteran series could ignore the signs of the times, and the Barrons, including the ever-present Joanne, have in the '80s been replaced as the show's stars by other, younger characters.

For more information on the past and present population of Henderson, see the end of the section, "Who's Who in Henderson."

Henderson: Midwest, U.S.A.

Henderson is a typical Midwestern soap opera concoction. It has the usual mix of rich and not-so-rich citizens, and there are suitable milieus for the individuals in all economic strata.

What to Expect in Henderson

What you could expect to witness in the town of Henderson depends to a great extent on when you arrived in town. Considering that it has been on TV continuously since 1951, it's no surprise that its look has changed. Besides the fact that modern mores allow "SFT" to deal with many more topics today than 30 years ago, technical advances of the last three decades have given "Search," among other soaps, a radical facelift.

Being aired live during its first few years presented a number of problems. If an episode ran short, Mary Stuart and Larry Haines, two actors still with the show in 1983, were often asked by the director to improvise phone conversations to fill the time. Once, during a big love scene between two characters, played in a park on a moonlit night, there was suddenly a very loud crash. Realizing the sound had been heard by the viewing audience, one of the actors felt compelled to acknowledge the noise. Looking over his shoulder he commented, "Those darn squirrels!"

When "SFT" debuted it was centered on the more traditional topics concerning familial love and duty and honor and all the other acceptable subjects and values of the day. But in the '80s this show has made a real effort to modernize. It's taken the obvious route of emphasizing younger romances and adventure plots, but it's kept its overhaul well-rounded by also depicting the life of a middle-aged professional woman, showing how she combines her professional and personal life. As several series have discovered, however, it was the latter that viewers found more interesting than the former. Some of Travis and Liza Sentell's wilder adventures apparently didn't have the intended effect on the audience. Ratings nosedives during these storylines proved once again that the new adventure theme cannot just be plunked into the mainstream of the traditional daytime TV town without loss of credibility.

The fact that Henderson is chock full of wealthy types makes for the usual complications that lots of money brings in soap operas.

THIRTY YEARS IN HENDERSON

According to the Nielsen report issued in June 1975, "Search for Tomorrow" was daytime TV's second-highest-rated soap, with a 9.4 rating, and it commanded the largest share of any soap at that time, with 37 percent of the viewing audience tuned in to follow the trials and tribulations of Henderson's somewhat confused citizens. By 1983 "Search for Tomorrow's" ratings had fallen considerably from its initially high post, but some positive movements have been noted of late. One reason for "Search for Tomorrow's" recent low ratings is that a number of NBC affiliates across the country don't carry the program.

In 1982 "Search for Tomorrow" switched networks, from CBS to NBC. It was the second soap to make such a change. Although low ratings were the main reason CBS decided to drop the show, there was another reason. Wanting to attract a younger, more urban audience (which is more appealing to sponsors), CBS felt its chances would be better if it opted for a new soap rather than give "Search for Tomorrow" yet another facelift.

The Trials of Joanne Barron

Until recently, when Joanne took a back seat to some younger characters, she, along with actress Mary Stuart, remained a constant in Henderson. The best way to find out what's gone on there in the last 30 years is to ask Joanne. In lieu of that, we can review Joanne's history to see Henderson through her eyes.

Finding a job at Henderson Hospital, Joanne met and fell in love with Arthur Tate, who also worked at the hospital. Despite a number of obstacles, such as a woman's pretending to be Arthur's first wife, who was presumed dead, and the mob's obsession with wanting to own Joanne's Motor Haven (a roadside diner Joanne acquired after leaving her job at the hospital) so they could traffic illegal drugs, Joanne and Arthur were finally married. A few years later, Arthur suffered a fatal heart attack and Joanne became a widow for the second time in her young life. But she didn't remain alone for long.

Joanne soon fell in love with Sam Reynolds, a former business associate of Arthur's. Unfortunately, Joanne was not able to marry Sam because he already had a wife, Andrea Whiting Reynolds. Although Sam and Andrea hadn't lived together in years, Andrea refused to give Sam a divorce. Incensed by Sam's love for Joanne, Andrea tried to kill him. Slipping what was supposed to be a lethal dose of a drug called Hemador into Sam's drink, Andrea accidentally got the glasses confused and ended up taking the drink herself. Although Andrea didn't die, Sam was charged with attempted murder (while Andrea was rushed off to the hospital, the police mistakenly assumed Sam had tried to kill her). Not wanting to see Sam sent away to prison, Andrea confessed that she was the one who spiked the drink. After seeking psychiatric help, Andrea agreed to give Sam a divorce. But before Sam and Joanne could be married, Sam suddenly left town for a business trip in Africa.

While Sam was away, Joanne was involved in a very serious automobile accident that cost her her eyesight. Recovering in the hospital, Joanne was struck another blow when friends informed her that Sam had been killed in Africa. Joanne soon fell in love with the handsome doctor who had saved her life after the automobile accident, Dr. Tony Vincente.

As fate would have it, Tony was already married to a rich, conniving woman named Marcy, who pretended to be crippled so that her husband wouldn't leave her. When Tony finally discovered that Marcy was just faking her paralysis, he divorced her. While all this was going on, Joanne managed to regain her

Larry Haines (Stu) and Mary Stuart (Joanne) cut the cake for "Search for Tomorrow's" 30th anniversary in 1981. Photo by Bob Deutsch.

eyesight. With Tony free, Joanne made plans to marry him.

But just as the ceremony was about to take place, Sam Reynolds returned to town. It turned out that Sam hadn't died after all; he was just suffering from a bad case of amnesia. Resuming her relationship with Sam, Joanne decided to marry him. Just as the marriage was about to take place, Joanne came down with another case of blindness. It was soon determined that Joanne's blindness was caused by the emotional stress because, as it turned out, Joanne really loved Tony, not Sam. Not wanting to lose Joanne, Sam, who had undergone a complete personality change while in Africa, kidnapped her. Taking Joanne to a hide-away cabin deep in the woods, Sam tried to keep her there but was shot and killed by two lowlifes who stumbled upon the cabin in search of food. The shock of Sam's death caused Joanne's eyesight to return once again. Returning to Henderson, Joanne was now free to marry Tony.

Shortly after Joanne and Tony were married, an attractive nurse named Stephanie Wilkins arrived in Henderson and accused Tony of being the father of her young daughter Wendy. Stephanie's deception was soon exposed, though, when Wendy's real father came to town and publicly claimed her as his child. Not long afterward, Tony suffered a fatal heart attack while attempting to save a patient who was being beaten up in the hospital's stairwell.

After the proper mourning period Joanne met and fell in love with a wealthy businessman, Martin Tourneur. Despite some serious character flaws on Martin's part, such as drinking and gambling problems, Joanne married him. There was, however, one character flaw Joanne couldn't abide. Catching Martin in bed with her arch rival Stephanie, Joanne asked for a legal separation. As things stand, Joanne and Martin are still separated. But Joanne is starting to show signs of warming up once again to Martin, who really does love her.

Since the show has changed significantly over the last few years, it seems only fair to review a few of the more recent storylines to complete the "SFT" picture.

Wealthy Martin Tourneur is played by John Aniston.

became the individual's search for the promise of tomorrow.

- When Wyatt died he left the care of his daughter, Suzi, to Joanne. This created still another sharp division between Stephanie and Joanne.

  In later years, Suzi and Brian, Stefanie's ward, would fall in love. They wouldn't marry, but for a while, Joanne and Stefanie wondered if they would eventually wind up in the same family anyway.

- A rather bizarre storyline involved the rape of a nun. The character of David Sutton fell in love with a beautiful and mysterious woman named Renatta. She had been a nun who left the convent to see if she really had a vocation or if her life belonged in the outside world. When she left the convent, she

Val Dufour has always been popular with soap fans. He has played John Wyatt on "Search for Tomorrow," Walter Curtin on "Another World," and Andre Lazar on "Edge of Night." Photo by Howard Gray.

Since the show has changed significantly over the last few years, it seems only fair to review a few of the more recent storylines to complete the "SFT" picture.

- The character of Rusty was just no good. He wanted Travis and Liza to divorce so that Travis could marry a woman who could bear an heir to the fortune left by a Sentell progenitor. Rusty also did some other nasty things besides arranging for Liza and Travis to separate. By the time Rusty was done in, Liza was pregnant with Travis' child and the Sentells reconciled.

- In the latter half of 1983 Joanna Lee became the newest executive producer. Changes were made. Stephanie became the owner of a television station that would wield a great deal of influence in Henderson.

- A storyline about juvenile diabetes was introduced with a youngster named Andrea (who had been living with Stephanie) as a court-awarded foster child, developing the condition. Andrea learned how to live with diabetes. A man named Michael Kendall helped Andrea learn about disabilities and how to overcome them. He was played by blind actor/singer/composer, Tom Sullivan. Sullivan brought an added dimension to a series whose basic premise once again

stayed with Prince Anthony, where she expected to be safe while sampling the world slowly after her experience in the cloisters. The Prince, however, assumed that the lady was a courtesan, and when she resisted his advances, he raped her.

David, who had fallen in love with her when she first came out into the world, flew to Italy to find her and when he did, he realized that she was pregnant with her rapist's child. He married her and brought her back to America. But things didn't work out for them. Renatta died of smoke inhalation in a burning house while giving birth. Just before her death, David found her and saved the child. He then left Henderson.

- Over the years Joanne and her longtime friend, Stu Bergman (played by former radio actor Larry Haines, who joined the series in 1952), have remained a core family unit though they never married and were never romantically involved.

The Stuart-Haines (or, rather, the Joanne Barron Vincente Tourneur-Stu Bergman) nexus have all had storylines somehow leading to and from them. Examples:

- The Sentell family has become the dominant one over the years. The character of Travis Sentell is involved in business with Mary's most recent husband, Martin Tourneur (played by "Love of Life" veteran, John Aniston).
- The character of Stephanie Wyatt has become an increasingly important one over the years. Stephanie, brilliantly played by Marie Cheatham (who originated the role of Marie Horton on "Days of our Lives") has moved from prime bitch to sharp, shrewd businesswoman. At one time Stephanie believed that her husband, John Wyatt, loved Joanne. She never forgave Joanne for that. In later years Joanne and Stephanie's paths crossed frequently, not the least important crossing being the romance between Martin and Stephanie, a sort of latter-day act of revenge, perhaps. The difference is that Joanne didn't encourage the late John Wyatt's affection, while Stephanie certainly went to all lengths to seduce Tourneur who was getting upset with Joanne's admonishments about his drinking.
- Stu Bergman's son, Tom, remains an important character. As a lawyer, he is involved in some way

Marie Cheatham, who plays the plotting, scheming Stefanie, originated the role of Marie Horton on "Days of Our Lives." Texas-born, Oklahoma-raised Marie, who is part American Indian, is working on a film on the life of Quanah Parker, an Indian chief whose mother was a white farm girl. Marie's Manhattan apartment is filled with exotic orchids she raises herself. Photo by Bob Deutsch.

Peter Ratray (far right), as Scott Phillips, joins Christopher Lowe and infant Carinda Mazzo, who play his sons Eric and Doug.

with just about *everyone* who comes to Henderson, USA.

Stu became Jo's friend and father confessor. He was there when the world closed in on her. He was also there when the good things happened. The two went into business together several times.

Why didn't they ever marry?

A former cast member of the series suggested "... they didn't have to marry. They already had what *every* good marriage needs: love, warmth, mutual respect, and maybe, who knows, an occasional sexual encounter."

A Look at the Future

"Search for Tomorrow's" current producer is Joanna Lee. In 1974 Lee was awarded an Emmy for an episode of the "Waltons" she wrote. Lee feels the program could pick up more viewers if the network would just expand the show to an hour. As Lee sees it, a longer format would give her more time to explore and develop the characters. Ms. Lee has also asked NBC and Procter & Gamble for more money to promote the show. In the meantime, Lee is concentrating on storylines that deal with "human emotions, romance, and the family," in the hopes that viewers have tired of the bigger-than-life stories currently employed on other soaps.

AFFAIRS TO REMEMBER

Most of the memorable affairs in Henderson have concerned Joanne in one way or another. A few more recent romances included these:
- Liza Kazlo and Travis Sentell fell in love, married, and then their adventures began.
- A cad named Chance Halliday came to Henderson. For a while he wooed Janet Collins. When he was about to marry Janet (who owned the Collins Corporation) his former wife turned up and tried to kill herself. Chance did nothing to help the lady. Instead, he made plans to kill David Sutton, and failed.

Rod Arrants (Travis Sentell) and wife Patricia Estrin once shared working space on "Search for Tomorrow," but a new producer and writer sent Pat packing.

Marcia McCabe (investigative reporter Sunny Adamson), as she appeared in 1981.

- As mentioned earlier, Travis and Liza Sentell are forever getting involved in all sorts of mysteries and shady dealings with dangerous characters. For a while, they were the targets of the infamous Ninja, the Japanese equivalent of the Mafia.
- Martin somewhat redeemed himself in a mayhem-directed storyline. A compulsive gambler as well as a drunkard, he lost a fortune to several crooked card players. With the help of Stephanie and the intrepid "girl reporter" Sunny (Ted's lovely daughter), Martin risked the rest of his money (and, perhaps his life, as well) setting up a crooked game in reverse. With the money he won back, he helped Stu Bergman finance the reconstruction of a riverboat into the restaurant Stu was hoping to own.
- Eunice, Joanne's sister, was murdered during the late '70s.

Marie Cheatham (Stefanie) and Morgan Fairchild, who played Jennifer before moving on to other endeavors. Photo by Bob Deutsch.

- The character of Kathy Phillips was forever in a bind. A brilliant lawyer, Kathy had problems juggling a marriage, a lover, a jealous husband, and a child conceived via dubious paternity. (When her husband, Scott, started drinking, Kathy sought comfort from a friend, David. Soothing words soon led to bed and Kathy's pregnancy resulted from that encounter.)

  When Scott learned David was the father he nearly killed him, but in time Scott and Kathy reconciled and left town.

  When Kathy returned, Dr. Max Taper's brother, Garth, caught her eye. The two sparred emotionally until they made love on the sands of a beach in Jamaica and were married. Fate, however, was not to be kind to Kathy. Garth was killed, and once more Kathy left town.

MURDER/MAYHEM/MYSTERY

A few of the most intriguing plots in this category are listed.

- Eunice's ex-husband, Doug Phillips, had been murdered just the night before.
- Jennifer Pace Phillips (Morgan Fairchild) went on trial for murder in the mid-70s.

MILESTONES FOR "SFT"

"Search for Tomorrow" was the first TV soap to incorporate comedy into its format. Stu and Marge Bergman, played by Larry Haines and Melba Rae, two veterans of radio shows, provided the soap with its comic relief. The Bergmans were working-class neighbors of Joanne Barron, the program's young heroine. Originally intended to be used for just a few episodes, the couple became so popular they were soon made permanent cast members. In 1971 Melba Rae died suddenly from a cerebral hemorrhage. A few months later her character quietly died off camera.

"Search for Tomorrow" was also the first TV soap to feature a pregnancy in its storyline. Following closely on the heels of Lucy Riccardo's famous pregnancy in the mid-50s, Joanne Barron, now Joanne Tate, became pregnant and bore a son to her husband Arthur Tate. A few years later, much to the chagrin of Mary Stuart, who had a son in real life, the child was hit by a speeding car and died.

"Search for Tomorrow" also pioneered location shooting. When the series first began, Mary Stuart recalls, the characters sat around kitchen tables. In the 1970s the "Searchers" were already moving out into the world. In the 1980s they had been to the Orient, the Caribbean, and across the country.

Another first was for "SFT" having its heroine as a working woman. When Joanne Barron's husband died she had to get out and support her family. Together with neighbor, Stu Bergman, Joanne Barron bought and ran a successful motel (then called a motor haven). That small business grew into Henderson's most important hotel and restaurant.

Once more citing Mary Stuart: " 'Search for Tomorrow' not only showed women that they could work—women have always known that and women have always had to support their families . . . (it) also showed them that they could be businesswomen and own and manage property. . . ."

WHO'S WHO IN HENDERSON

Original Cast

Character	Actor
IRENE BARRON	Bess Johnson
KEITH BARRON	John Sylvester
JOANNE BARRON	Mary Stuart
PATTI BARRON	Lyn Loring (Later on she added an "n" to her name: Lynn)
VICTOR BARRON	Cliff Hall

First Air Date: September 3, 1951

Write to "Search for Tomorrow" c/o NBC, 30 Rockefeller Plaza, New York, NY 10020.

A Directory of Recent Characters*

Ted Adamson: Sunny's father; always in pursuit of an affair with someone. *Wayne Tippit*

Tom Bergman: A lawyer; Stu's son. *Robert Lupone*

Warren Carter: Kristen's quasi-racketeering brother; unhappily wed to Suzi. *Michael Corbett*

*The actors/actresses who currently play these major roles are in italics.

Warren Carter: Kristen's quasi-racketeering brother, unhappily wed to Suzi. *Michael Corbett*

Jenny Deacon: Andrea's real mother; Michael loves her. *Linda Gibboney*

Brian Emerson: Was in love with Suzi but married Kristen. *Jay Acovone*

Rhonda Sue Huckaby: A singer who works at Stephanie's TV station. *Tina Johnson*

Above: Peter Haskell has to stay in shape just to keep up with his changing roles and storylines. Back in the late '60s he starred on "Bracken's World," and he made his soap debut via "Ryan's Hope" as Hollis Kirkland in the '80s. From there he took a role as villainous Lloyd Kendall on "Search for Tomorrow." Photo by Bob Deutsch.

Below: Chris Atkins and Cyndy Gibb. Photo by Ed Geller.

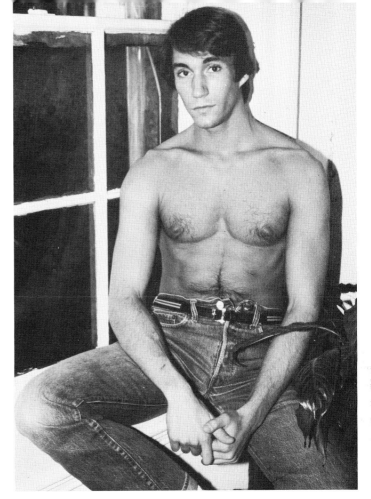

Michael Corbett. Photo by Bob Deutsch.

Tina Johnson.

Harry Goz.

Timothy Patrick Murphy.

Michael Kendall: A blind singer and composer, in love with Jenny; friend of little Andrea. *Tom Sullivan*

Steve Kendall: Michael's macho brother; in love with Stephanie; sports announcer at Stephanie's TV station. *Phillip Brown*

Sunny McClure: Ted's daughter; loves Dane Taylor. *Marcia McCabe*

Andrea McNeil: Keith's younger sister; lives with Stephanie; claimed by Jenny, her real mother. *Stacy Glich*

Keith McNeil: Was married to Wendy. *Craig Augustine*

Lee Sentell: Travis's cousin; the father of Roger Lee, whom Travis and Liza had hoped to adopt. *Doug Stevenson*

Liza Sentell: The widow of a composer, she married Travis, and has been the subject of many an adventure; mother of Turner. *Sherry Mathis*

Travis Sentell: Martin Tourneur's nephew; a brilliant businessman; wed to Liza; father of Turner. *Rod Arrants*

Dane Taylor: Friend of Travis and Liza; involved with security matters; involved with Sunny. *Marcus Smythe*

Joanne Barron Vincente Tourneur: A businesswoman; guardian of Suzi Wyatt, Stephanie's stepdaughter; separated from Martin. *Mary Stuart*

Martin Tourneur: A wealthy alcoholic gambler; he's Travis' uncle and a good friend to Liza; separated from Joanne. *John Aniston*

Stephanie Wyatt: The widow of John Wyatt; she's had affairs with Ted Adamson and Martin Tourneur, as well as several other Henderson men; owns a TV station; long-time adversary of Joanne's; mother of Brian and Wendy; stepmother of Suzi. *Marie Cheatham*

Suzi Wyatt (McNeil): Wed to Warren although she loves Brian; her late father, John Wyatt, asked Joanne to raise her if he should die. *Cynthia Gibb*

Wendy Wilkins: Stephanie's daughter; once wed (unhappily) to Keith. *Lisa Peluso*

Millie Taggart, who played the role of Janet on "Search for Tomorrow," has also written for that soap and for "As the World Turns." Photo by Howard Gray.

13

The Young and the Restless (CBS)

"The Young and the Restless" made its debut over CBS on March 26, 1973. Its storylines dealt openly with problems in marriages, with the challenges facing the younger generation coming to maturity in the difficult '70s, and with the older generation facing changes in a world that has suddenly left them behind.

There are strong relationships within this soap opera. Never has a subject in which the parties are involved been handled cavalierly or superficially. Everything that goes into a storyline is deeply and thoroughly explored.

When "The Young and the Restless" premiered in 1973 the younger, more urban women were switching away from the older soaps to game shows. Placing a strong emphasis on younger characters, who were played by very attractive, sexy actors and actresses, "The Young and the Restless" succeeded in hooking these women, just as "As the World Turns" had hooked their mothers back in the '50s. Although "The Young and the Restless" was innovative in regard to focusing

Melody Thomas as Nikki.

on younger characters, the stories were told in a forth-right, traditional manner. Examining the family unit has always been a strong point. Unlike most soaps, "The Young and the Restless" doesn't manipulate its characters to fit a proposed storyline. Instead, the plots spring out of the characters interactions with one another.

Following "The Young and the Restless's" success, one short year after its premier, a number of older soaps began trying to imitate the program, in hopes that some of the ratings magic would rub off on them as well. Some, such as "General Hospital" and "As the World Turns" managed to catch up with the times, while also increasing their ratings. Others, such as "Love of Life" failed, and were subsequently canceled.

Owned by Screen Gems, now Columbia Pictures, and taped in Hollywood, "The Young and the Restless" was created by William Bell and his wife Lee Phillip Bell. Besides cocreating "Another World" back in the '60s, William Bell also wrote for "As the World Turns" and the "Guiding Light." Based on William Bell's success with "Days of Our Lives," a show that suffered from low ratings when it premiered, all three networks, as well as Procter & Gamble, were after him to create a new soap. Originally titled "The Innocent Years," it was changed to the "Young and the Restless" just before the series premiered.

William Bell is also co-executive producer of "The Young and the Restless," along with H. Wesley Kenney, who has worked on "Days of Our Lives" and has also directed several episodes of "All in the Family." John Conboy was the program's first executive producer.

As headwriter of "The Young and the Restless," William Bell exercises more control over his program than any other writer working in soaps today, including Agnes Nixon. Unlike most soap writers, William Bell doesn't like to plot his show too far in advance. Sometimes the direction of a story will change if a certain chemistry takes place between the actors. A good example of this took place in 1982 when the very wealthy and reserved Victor Newman found himself falling in love with his beautiful young protege Nikki Reed, who was a professional stripper. Worried that Nikki might grow too attached to him, Victor arranged for architect Kevin Bancroft, who was closer to Nikki's age, to begin dating her. Although the actor playing Kevin, Chris Holder, was hired for only a few ap-

Jeanne Cooper plays Kay Chancellor and gets some of the sexiest storylines, though she plays a mature woman.

pearances, William Bell found himself so impressed with his work that he decided to make Kevin Bancroft a major character.

In April 1973, *Variety* praised "The Young and the Restless" in its review, calling it one of the more "sophisticated serials to come down the pike." In 1973 a TV critic for the *Chicago Daily News* spent a week watching the soaps for a series he was writing on daytime TV. In his series he cited "The Young and the Restless" as being the best of the crop because its characters obviously cared for one another. In 1983 "The Young and the Restless" was awarded an Emmy for best daytime drama.

WELCOME TO GENOA CITY

The Citizens

"The Young and the Restless" set the trend that "General Hospital" and other soaps subsequently aped: it featured mainly young characters. Not only were the featured residents of Genoa City young; they were also beautiful. These slick creations of "Y&R" writers still manage to carry out storylines concerning modern and sensitive issues. This is not to say that "Y&R" has nothing to offer the mature viewer. On the contrary, it has some fine actors and actresses playing interesting and significant roles, such as Kay Chancellor, played beautifully by Jeanne Cooper.

In the early days "The Young and the Restless" focused on the upper-middle-class Brooks and the lower-class Fosters. In 1982, following the departure of several key actors, the emphasis was shifted to the wealthy Abbotts and the middle-class Williams family. Normally, when a show changes that drastically, there's a dip in the ratings. "The Young and the Restless," however, has continued to be a top-rated soap.

Current Events in Genoa City

According to an early Screen Gems press release, " 'The Young and the Restless' combines 'man-woman' chemistry, young people, and music." Music has always been a big part of "The Young and the Restless." Since the beginning, "The Young and the Restless" has always featured at least one character who sings. Music was emphasized, rather than kept in the background, to bridge in and out of scenes, because William Bell felt it would be more effective to try incorporating it dramatically into the show's format. Since then, preachers, businessmen, and other unlikely figures have uncharacteristically broken into song on the show—and even danced.

"The Young and the Restless" is notable for the fact that most of what happens on the show concerns current events.

During its more-than-10-year run, "Y&R" has tackled a number of controversial subjects intelligently. In the mid-70s the program featured a lesbian attraction between two women. On prime-time shows in the '70s characters, such as Edith on "All in the Family," worried about having breast cancer. On "Y&R" a popular middle-aged character discovered that she did, in fact, have breast cancer and had to have a mastectomy.

Another major character was raped in a park by an unknown assailant. Rather than have the character become pregnant, and then discover the rapist was her second-cousin, "Y&R" showed the humiliation many women have to go through after such an ordeal. The rapist was apprehended. But after a lengthy trial he was released because the court felt there wasn't sufficient evidence to substantiate the victim's accusation. The rapist, by the way, was played by Tony Geary.

"Y&R" has also featured strippers and gigolos. On the more serious side, it's tackled the subject of obesity and the common problem of bulimia among young women. While "Y&R's" main goal is to entertain, it presents the viewers with a wide enough variety of current issues to be somewhat informative as well.

Genoa City History

Suffice it to say that Genoa City history is convoluted; and with the breadth of subjects covered and the variety of characters, it's no wonder. To get an exemplary picture of what's gone on here for the last 10 years, let's take a look at Jill's history.

The Life of Jill Foster

The odds were against Jill Foster when she was introduced to America. While her brothers were busy going to law and medical school, Jill and her mother were working hard to support the family, which had been deserted by the father years ago. Jill worked as a lowly beautician but dreamed of more glamorous worlds. And she thought those dreams had come true when wealthy alcoholic client Kay Chancellor offered her a job as a personal secretary. Jill was enamored of her ritzy new surroundings and soon also fell for Kay's neglected husband Phillip. Jill insisted that their love not be consummated until she could make sure that Kay would kick the habit. Kay finally sobered up when she discovered their love, and her new clear-headedness allowed her to initiate some devilish plans to get her husband back.

Her most powerful weapon came in the form of Brock Reynolds, a righteous man who had recently been reborn and wanted to help his mother Kay beat the bottle. Kay talked him into marrying Jill to keep her from Phillip. Jill accepted Brock to get out of what she felt was a no-win situation with Phillip. She and Brock were married by Brock himself and never made

Brenda Dixon, who originated the part of Jill Foster in 1973, returned to the role in 1983 after a 4-year absence.

Deborah Adair portrayed Jill Foster from 1980 through 1983. Photo courtesy of Daytime TV *magazine.*

love. Then Jill found out she was carrying Phillip's child from a single instance of passion, and Phillip finally divorced Kay. Driven mad with jealousy, Kay tried to kill Phillip, and he married Jill on his deathbed so that she would get his fortune, but Jill didn't know he was so close to death.

Jill and her whole family moved into the Chancellor mansion, which now belonged to Jill, and Kay initiated a suit to prove that Phillip had never legally married her because he had forced Kay to sign divorce papers when she was under the influence and didn't know what she was doing. She won the case and the Fosters moved back to their humble abode. Kay became obsessed with the child that would be Phillip's and offered Jill $1 million for custody of the baby. Jill agreed but backed out when the baby was born, deciding to sue for part of the Chancellor estate. She lost when it was claimed that she had slept with Brock and the baby could be his.

Now Jill was really out for vengeance. She started trying to drive Kay crazy so she'd take to the bottle again but was talked out of the scheme by her mother. Unfortunately, Kay had already gone on a binge again.

Still hungry for money, Jill set her sights on the widower Stuart Brooks, even though he was also seeing her mother Liz. Fearing that Stuart and Liz were growing too close, Jill seduced Stuart. Not long after, Jill announced that she was pregnant. Although Stuart was now in love with Liz, he felt marrying Jill would be the right thing to do.

Once they were married Stuart discovered Jill wasn't pregnant. Although Stuart wanted a divorce, Jill was unwilling to grant it. Finally, one night Stuart almost choked to death on a chicken bone. Having been trained in the Heimlich maneuver, Jill managed to save his life. Needless to say, Stuart was very grateful to Jill for saving his life. Gaining a new respect for Stuart, Jill agreed to divorce him. A short time later, Stuart married Jill's mother Liz.

It wasn't long after Jill met and fell in love with wealthy businessman John Abbott. While working at John's business, Jabot cosmetics, Jill began dating him. John's grown-up son Jack was also attracted to Jill, who was closer to his age. Nevertheless, Jill continued dating the senior Abbott. Jill even wanted to marry John, but he felt there was too big a difference in their ages.

One night Jack finally managed to seduce a drunken Jill. John arrived home and discovered them making love. Earlier, John had written Jill a letter declaring

Steven Ford, former President Ford's son, (Andy) and Melody Thomas (Nikki).

his love for her. However, after seeing Jill in bed with his son, John decided to leave the country. It wasn't until later that Jill received his letter, and by then it was too late for her to explain herself.

Having given up on John's ever returning to Genoa City, Jill became involved with Andy Richards, a physical education instructor (played by former president Gerald Ford's son Steven). Although Jill thought she loved Andy, there were problems from the start. The main problem was that Jill didn't think Andy was ambitious enough. Second, to save on expenses, he wanted them to live in Jill's mother's old house after they were married. What finally broke up their relationship was John Abbott's sudden return to town.

Concerned about the way Jack was running Jabot, John decided it would be best if he came to town to see what was happening with the business. Realizing John was in town, Jill made it a point finally to explain to John what had happened the night he found her in bed with Jack. After a while, John found it in his heart to forgive Jill and resumed dating her.

Sensing that John was falling in love with Jill again, Jack tried to break up their relationship. While John was out of town, Jack fired Jill from Jabot. In retaliation, Jill accused Jack of sexual harassment on the job. Not wanting to face a public court trial, Jack agreed to give Jill a large financial settlement out of court. Despite Jack's efforts to end his father's relationship with Jill, they ended up married.

Not long ago, John underwent open-heart surgery. Recently, his first wife, Dina, has come back to town and is very interested in Jill's past. As Jill sees it, Dina poses a very definite threat to her marriage.

AFFAIRS TO REMEMBER

- Kay Thurston is an older woman with a weakness for charming men. At one time she fell for the wiles of Derek Thurston. Derek immediately set himself up as her secretary's lover. Kay and Derek argued over his two-timing; they reconciled and during a cruise, they argued again. This time Kay jumped overboard in an attempt to kill herself.

    The character of Kay Chancellor Thurston remained off camera for a while during actress Jeanne Cooper's temporary absence from the series. When Jeanne returned, Kay came back to Genoa City as well and revealed that she had been saved and nursed back to health by a Cuban refugee named Felipe.

- Another older couple, Stuart Brooks and Liz Foster, married after a stormy romance and went on to share a stormy marriage.

- Among the younger set, the Foster brothers—Greg and Snapper—have their shares of woes with the women in their lives. Greg is bewitched, bothered, and bewildered by his young wife, Nikki, while Snapper's wife, Chris, unprepared to deal with the demands of marriage to a doctor, feels neglected.

    Greg begins an affair with April, who accepts his advances now that she is reconciled to the fact that she'll never be able to marry Paul, the father of her baby.

- April and Paul were thrown together originally when they were both victims of the drug cult, the New World Commune.

- Meanwhile, the mysterious, wealthy Victor Newman, one of the largest shareholders in Prentiss Industries, fell in love with Lauralee (or Lori) Prentiss.

From left to right: Jaime Lyn Bauer, Julianna McCarthy, Robert Colbert, Victoria Mallory, and Dennis Cole.

Beth Maitlan as Tracy Abbott.

Lauralee, however, was busy with her own affairs, including trying to keep custody of her sister Leslie's child. Leslie had left the boy with Lori while she recuperated from a nervous condition. Lauralee used seduction as a weapon trying to woo Lucas, the boy's legal father, into her bed and, thus, on her side of the looming custody battle.

• While this was going on Victor's wife, Julia, went to bed with her young lover, Michael. She became pregnant. But Victor was far from delighted to learn that a new Newman was on the way. Victor, Julia learned, had had a vasectomy.

Victor went through a good deal of bother to punish the errant lovers. He had a special room built in his basement where he kept Michael prisoner and tormented him with images of Julia being made love to by her own husband.

Eventually, Julia and Michael left town. Julia re-

The royal wedding festivities.

During the royal wedding festivities in 1981, Leslie Brooks (Victoria Mallory) was invited to perform for the royal family. Here she arrives at the palace with her escort, Lance Prentiss (Dennis Cole).

turned later on, but to a much changed situation.

• A tender romance developed between Danny Romalotti, a singer in a local night club, and Tracy Abbott, Jack Abbot's sister. In the evolution of this romantic storyline Tracy, an overweight, shy girl, is determined to lose excess poundage and become the "dream girl" Danny desires.

As Tracy learns that love must be self-centered as well as outreaching, she becomes a more assured, healthier person—and the opposite sex finally begins to notice.

• An interesting storyline involving Kay Chancellor Thurston after her return to Genoa City developed out of the older woman's attraction to the young, muscular owner of a local beauty shop. In time, Kay began to lean on Cash for everything—from advice about business and through her entire life. In time the relationship ended.

• Years earlier Lori had been involved with Lance Prentiss and married him. After they separated Lance left town. The original cause for their breakup was instigated by his mother, Vanessa, who hated Lori. She told Lance that Lori had written a book

about her sister Leslie's earlier nervous breakdown. Leslie, shaken by the book, was unable to go through with a concert tour. Lance helped her and spent a night with her. Leslie became pregnant with Lance's child. Lucas, Lance's brother, married her to give the baby its name and to raise it as a Prentiss.

When Lance finally returned to Genoa City, Lori was overjoyed and hoped to rekindle their old love. Lance, however, was engaged to a French girl. Lori, nonetheless, persisted, and eventually broke through to Lance, who started to fall in love with her again.

The Lance-Lori love story didn't end happily. Once more Lance left. Lori later used Victor's lingering love for her to investigate a mysterious business deal in which Victor is involved.

- Meanwhile, Julia returned to Genoa City and eventually saved Victor's life after he succumbed to a long, careful plan devised by Eve to poison him. Julia and Victor, no longer husband and wife, and not at all passionate lovers, developed a new friendship. Where it may lead? Only the writers know for sure—and one of the writers working under headwriter William Bell—is Meg Bennett, the actress who plays Julia.

MURDER/MAYHEM/MYSTERY

There have been several terrifying incidents in Genoa City, all of which have chilled and thrilled the viewers. Among them were a drug/occult commune and Victor's descent toward death by poison. Others include the stalking of Nikki by a mad killer, and Lauralee's indictment for Vanessa Prentiss' murder.

Vanessa, who had hated Lori from the day she married her son, Lance, began to hate Lance as well when he decided to reconcile with Lori against his mother's wishes.

Several years earlier Vanessa was badly burned and her face left scarred after she was involved in an accident she helped to cause. With Lauralee's encouragement she underwent surgery and her skin was restored. But her hate for Lori seethed nonetheless.

Later, when she learned she had only two months to live, she decided to destroy both Lori and Lance. In her diary she confided her anger and her hate and her plans. In public she seemed the picture of reconciliation. She poured sweetness and affection upon her son and once and future daughter-in-law. She insisted on helping Lori with her plans for her second marriage to Lance.

One afternoon, while Lucas was playing with Brooks (the child Lance fathered with Leslie and whom Lori was caring for), he heard his mother scream out "Lori, keep away; don't touch me." He rushed upstairs to find a shocked Lori looking through an opened window. Vanessa had jumped to her death, but the circumstantial evidence pointed to Lori as her killer.

- In time the diaries were discovered and Lori was cleared.

GENOA CITY MILESTONES

"The Young and the Restless" fans were shocked when one of the characters developed breast cancer and had to undergo a mastectomy. John Conboy, the producer of the show at that time, explained: "We knew we were entering a difficult area here. But we also knew that there were many women who had to face this situation every day in real life and many people who were either related to these women or their friends who would also experience pain on their behalf. While it's true we are an entertainment medium, we also recognized the fact that our audiences were becoming more sophisticated and wanted stories of substance. . . ."

The woman (Jennifer Brooks, played by Dorothy Green) who underwent the mastectomy learned, through counseling (shown in sensitively produced scenes) how to regain her self-esteem and how not to think of herself as any less a woman or a person.

The series also dealt with an important subject in the late '60s and through the '70s: drug abuse among the young. "Y&R" picked up, as well, on the mushrooming drug and occult cultures. A young woman on the series, April Stevens, was a victim of one of these groups, and the audience was shown how easily anyone—even a bright, positive young girl—can fall under the spell of a compelling figure.

The series also has explored the relationship between an older woman and a much younger man.

Rape, suicide, marital neglect, marital infidelities, and sibling rivalries have all figured in strong, hardhitting storylines.

Tracy's story went beyond the mere development of a diet and exercise storyline. Instead, the girl developed the first-ever case of bulimia on daytime television.

A Word from David Hasselhoff (ex-Snapper)

"Soap operas are supposed to be—or were originally considered—made mainly for women viewers. But (while he was on "The Young and the Restless") I realized that men are also watching and I think it's because they were responding to honest storylines. We never put the men down. They are every bit as strong as the women. Our series also gives strong storylines to characters who are young, a littler older, and those more mature. . . . As I say, the stories never play down to any segment of the audience or play up any one segment in order to ignore the importance of any other group. . . ."

David Hasselhoff, as Snapper Foster, left "The Young and the Restless" a few times to try his luck at a nighttime career. In 1982 he scored with the series, "Knight Rider." Photo by Tony Rizzo.

WHO'S WHO IN GENOA CITY

Original Cast

Actor	*Character*
ROBERT CLARY	**Pierre Roulland**
ROBERT COLBERT	**Stuart Brooks**
LEE CRAWFORD	**Sally McGuire**
WILLIAM GRAY ESPY	**Snapper Foster**
DOROTHY GREEN	**Jennifer Brooks**
JANICE LYNDE	**Leslie Brooks**
TOM HALLICK	**Brad Eliot**
JAMES HOUGHTON	**Greg Foster**
JULIANNA MCCARTHY	**Liz Foster**
PAMELA PETERS	**Peggy Brooks**
TRISH STEWART	**Chris Brooks**

First Air Date: March 26, 1973

Write to "The Young and the Restless" c/o CBS, 7800 Beverly Blvd., Los Angeles, CA 90036.

Robert Lupone and Janet Eilber rehearse for Swing, *a Broadway musical.*

A Directory of Recent Characters*

Ashley Abbott: Jack and Tracy's sister; worries about Jack's womanizing and Tracy's health. *Eileen Davidson*

Jack Abbott: Patty's husband; son of John Abbott; Ashley and Tracy's brother; a womanizer. *Terry Lester*

Jill Abbott: Liz's daughter; John's wife. *Deborah Adair*

John Abbott: Father of Jack, Ashley, and Tracy. *Jerry Douglas*

Patty Abbott: Jack's young wife; she's Paul's sister and daughter of Carl and Mary Williams; she's unhappy in her marriage. *Andrea Evans-Massey*

Tracy Abbott: Once unattractive, she's learning to like herself; loves Danny Romalotti. *Beth Maitland*

Alison Bancroft: Earl's wife; Kevin's mother; hates Nikki; has plans for her grandchild. *Lynn Wood*

Earl Bancroft: A wealthy man; Kevin's father; once had an affair with Kay. *Mark Tapscott*

*The actors/actresses who currently play these major roles are in italics.

Kevin Bancroft: Wealthy former husband of Nikki; Alison and Earl's son. *Christopher Holder*

Nikki Reed Foster Bancroft: Sister to Dr. Casey Reed; ex of Greg Foster and Kevin Bancroft; once in love with Victor; married Kevin; former honky-tonk dancer; mother of Victoria by Victor. *Melody Thomas*

Liz Brooks: Mother of Jill, Greg, and Snapper; estranged wife of Stuart. *Julianna McCarthy*

Stu Brooks: Father of Leslie, Peggy, Lori, and Chris. *Robert Colbert*

Chris Foster: Separated from Snapper; a model, mother of Jennifer, sister of Leslie, Peggy, and Lori; Stuart's daughter. *Lynn Topping*

Julia Newman: Victor's ex-wife; she's involved with Jabot Cosmetics. *Meg Bennett*

Victor Newman: Julia's ex; once in love with Lori; nearly killed by Eve Howard. *Eric Braedon*

Lauralee Prentiss: She left town shortly after investigat-

Michael Damian.
Photo by Ed Geller.

ing a business matter involving Victor; twice wed to Lance; sister of Leslie, Peggy, and Chris; daughter of Stuart. *Jamie Lyn Bauer*

Leslie Prentiss: Ex-wife of Lucas; mother of son, Brooks, by Lucas's brother, Lance; sister of Peggy, Lori, and Chris; daughter of Stu; a pianist, who's suffered several serious nervous declines. *Victoria Mallory*

Lucas Prentiss: Lance's brother; legal father of Brooks; ex-husband of Leslie. *Tom Ligon*

Andy Richards: Once in love with Jill; in love with Jabot model Diane Jenkins. *Steve Ford*

Danny Romalotti: A rock singer; brother of Gina; Tracy Abbott worships him. *Michael Damian*

Gina Romalotti: Danny's ex-convict sister. *Patty Weaver*

Kay Chancellor Thurston: A wealthy woman who wants to rekindle her affair with Earl. *Jeanne Cooper*

Carl Williams: An honest, recently retired police lieutenant who had to deal with problems in his department; Mary's husband; father of Paul and Patty. *Brett Hadley*

Mary Williams: Carl's wife; Paul and Patty's mother. *Carolyn Conwell*

Paul Williams: Once in love with April Stevens, with whom he shared weird experiences in the cult; he has since been an undercover agent on the side of the good guys; in love with ex-prostitute Cindy Lake. *Doug Davidson*

14

The Newest Soap, Loving (ABC)

On June 26, 1983, nighttime television was enlivened with the presentation of a two-hour "movie" called *Loving*, starring Lloyd Bridges, Geraldine Page, and several other actors who would never again be seen in the daytime serial of the same name that would make its debut the next morning.

In the two-hour prime time feature, Bridges and others set up the storylines that would later be carried through on this, the first new ABC soap in eight years. Bridges was shot and killed in the movie. On the soap he would be referred to as the late Johnny Forbes, a self-made millionaire who fathered one of the serial's most important characters, Roger Forbes, a former United States ambassador and an ambitious university president.

Geraldine Page, with whom Bridges has worked in the theater in the past, played the role of Amelia Whitley, a woman from Forbes' past.

Many of the members of the daytime soap also appeared in the special, which was directed by Michael Lindsay-Hogg.

It appears to be the "thing," these days, to introduce daytime soaps with a nighttime presentation the evening before the matinee debut. "Capitol" did it with excellent results.

So far as the daytime show is concerned, it has the expected Agnes Nixon and Douglas Marland touches: there are references to social issues and an awareness of "generations" (the latter is particularly Marlandian).

The heroine of the piece is Merrill Vochek (played by Patricia Kalemenber), who is an ambitious (but not ruthless; although the two are usually synonymous in soaps) television reporter/anchorwoman. She will be the center around whom much of the action will move.

Roger Forbes (played by John Shearin) is attracted to her and, in spite of the fact that he has a devoted wife, Ann Alden Forbes (Shannon Eubanks), Merrill finds herself drawn to him as well.

Ann Williams, now appearing as alcoholic June Slater on "Loving," is a veteran soap actress. Former credits include the role of Eunice Riley on "One Life to Live" and parts on "Search for Tomorrow" and "Edge of Night." Photo by Howard Gray.

Nixon has always liked the idea of crossing the railroad tracks, as it were, in a social setting. In "Loving," the people who live in the university town of Corinth (in the northeast — possibly close to Philadelphia) come from several economic and social backgrounds. But there is mobility. The Vocheks are moving up (at least Merrill has). Their next-door neighbors, the Donovans, are mobile. One son, Douglas, is a playwright and drama professor at the university. His younger brother, Mike, elected to go into police work after Vietnam. The Vocheks and the Donovans will move within and throughout the more rarefied atmosphere of the Forbes and the even more remote atmosphere of the fabulously wealthy Aldens. (Roger Forbes' wife is an Alden.)

The university dean, Garth Slater, played by veteran actor John Cunningham, is an envious man who begrudges Forbes his wealth, his position, and his rich wife.

Cast Members:

Among the actors who are in the daytime serial (at least through the rest of 1983, before people start being written out for one reason or another) are:

Bryan Cranston plays **Douglas Donovan**.

Patricia Kalemenber plays **Merrill Vochek**.

John Cunningham plays **Garth Slater**.

Susan Walters plays **Lorna Forbes**.

Marilyn McIntyre plays **Noreen Vochek Donovan**, a nurse at Corinth Memorial Hospital. (McIntyre's last soap outing was in "Search for Tomorrow.")

Terri Keane plays **Rose Donovan**, Noreen's mother-in-law. Terri is a soap veteran from "Edge of Night," "One Life to Live," etc.

Wesley Addy plays **Cabot Alden**.

John Shearin plays **Roger Forbes**.

Shannon Eubanks plays **Ann Alden Forbes**.

James Kiberd plays **Mike Donovan**, policeman, Noreen's husband.

Perry Stephens plays **Jack Forbes**, Roger and Ann's son.

Susan Walters plays **Lorna Forbes**, Roger and Ann's daughter.

The series is projected towards highlighting the

Geraldine Page and Lloyd Bridges appeared on the nighttime premiere of "Loving."

professional and personal ambitions, including the conflicts between and among the various families whose different backgrounds make up a brilliant pattern of social "patches" that sometimes clash but always seem to work out.

It's interesting to note that one of Agnes Nixon's early "causes," the anti-Vietnam campaign (which first surfaced in her then brand-new series, "All My Children," in 1970), continues to remind her viewers of its long and lingering effects upon the American psyche. Her character, Mike Donovan, bears his Vietnam scars—both physical and emotional, in his relationships with other people.

"Loving" is the newest soap on the block and, as such, has been updated. Vochek is a television reporter; but the same sense of quest for truth, justice, and the American way (via Agnes Nixon's direction) continues.

Part II:
The Inside Story

15

Behind the Scenes

What do the cast members of soap operas think and feel about those characters with which they're so intimately involved? Who are the movers and shakers in soapville? What causes some of the crazy twists and turns that many soap plots take? Why do soap operas use certain transparently unbelievable gimmicks to make their soap characters do what they want them to do? And what's it like to work on a soap opera? You will find the answers to these and many other questions in this glance behind the soaps' doors

A FEW WORDS ON THE MOVERS AND SHAKERS

Thousands of individuals are involved in the on-air and behind-the-scenes work that is necessary to produce today's soaps. While they all deserve praise for the jobs they perform, a few names come to mind when it comes to assigning credit for making soap

operas what they are today.

Irna Phillips

Few would argue with the fact that the late Irna Phillips should be called the Mother of Soap Operas. Indeed, Phillips' vaunted soap opera career went as far back as 1930, when she began writing and developing some of the earliest radio soaps, in Chicago. She gave both radio and TV soaps their early midwestern flavor and imbued them with the strong family values she knew her audience would insist on. In fact, one of her most remarkable achievements probably was the fact that she made "Another World" a hit, despite predictions to the contrary.

That Phillips was a genius in her genre is undisputed. And to attest to that fact are the hugely successful careers of two of her protégés: William Bell and Agnes Nixon, both of whom have taken Phillips' teachings and run to the top of the ratings with them.

Agnes Nixon, the reigning queen of soap operas, talks into a dictophone machine while working on a script.

Agnes Nixon

Agnes Nixon—known affectionately as "Aggie" to the scores of actors with whom she's worked over the years, may be the most prolific writer for television in the entire history of the medium.

In 1983 her newest production, "Loving," made its debut over the ABC network. Cowritten with Emmy Award winning writer, Douglas Marland, the series is set in a small town near Philadelphia. At its center is a university and around this school are the characters who set the series in motion. Among some of the graduates of other soaps who appear are Meg Mundy (of "The Doctors") and Marilyn McIntyre (ex-"Search for Tomorrow"). Also returning to soaps are two favorites who haven't been on daytime series in several years: Ann Williams (formerly on "Search") and Teri Keane, from "Edge of Night."

With "Loving," the remarkable Ms. Nixon achieves a notable record; she has created four soaps—"All My Children," "Search for Tomorrow," "One Life to Live," and "Loving." No one else since Irna Phillips has done this for daytime television. In addition, she co-created "As the World Turns" and served as headwriter for "Guiding Light" and "Another World."

Previous to her daytime work, Nixon wrote for such classic television series as "Studio One," "Philco Play-house," "Robert Montgomery Presents," " Somerset Maugham Theater," "Armstrong Circle Theater," "Hallmark Hall of Fame," "Cameo Theater," and "My True Story."

Nixon has had a serial on the air five days a week—52 weeks a year—for more than 20 years.

What, she was asked, is the secret of her success as a dramatist?

"I remember to entertain my audiences," she's said.

A Nashville, Tennessee, native who now lives in a suburb near Philadelphia, Agnes Nixon enjoys being steeped in the pre-Revolutionary atmosphere of her area. (Her home was once an inn in Colonial times.) Her love for history helped her write and produce a remarkably sensitive and accurate series, "The Mansions of America," based on a family's life in Ireland and, later, in the United States.

According to Agnes Nixon, a soap writer should be able to judge the wider aspects of what appears to be a major social movement. She has carefully avoided jumping onto fad-wagons.

Some of her "AMC" actors offer their own assessments of Agnes Nixon:

Eileen Herlie, the Scottish-born stage veteran who plays Myrtle: "Aggie understands the importance of writing good comedy scenes. That's the mark of a superb dramatist: someone who can tell a highly dramatic, highly charged story and yet know how to insert comic relief at the right moment. Also, she understands that women are excellent comic actors and do not have to be turned into caricatures either. . . .''

Kim Delaney (Jenny): ''I'm always amazed at how sensitive the scripts are to the problems of young people. Not that they shouldn't be, of course. But young people don't always find such awareness of their problems among older people. . . .''

James Mitchell (Palmer): ''She respects actors and provides intelligent roles one can feel very good about playing. . . .''

Lisa Wilkinson (Nancy): ''When Agnes learned about my off-camera singing career she decided to incorporate my singing on camera as well. She knows how much I love to sing. I believe she created a story line in which Nancy gets to do a few songs as much to make me feel good about my singing as to add a dimension to Nancy Grant's character.''

And a last word from Agnes Nixon: ''When you write about people you have only one basic theme—everything else is subordinate to it. That theme is: relationships. We don't live in a vacuum; we live with and among other human beings. What we do or don't do affects them as well.''

In 1981 Agnes Nixon received a special award from the Television Academy of Arts & Sciences to honor her for her long and noteworthy contribution to the medium.

William Bell

While Agnes Nixon took her career and her creations to New York and the East Coast, William Bell stayed in Chicago with the same success. Bell has written for numerous soaps during his remarkable career, but his greatest success probably is the soap he created and still owns, ''The Young and the Restless.'' Loyal to his home grounds, Bell set ''Y&R'' in Wisconsin, and the glamorous, racy, and daring series has garnered much praise from critics and viewers alike. For more on William Bell and ''The Young and the Restless,'' see Chapter 13.

MOTIVATION AND MANIPULATION

Many behind-the-scenes factors have led to surprising plot twists and cast changes. Here's a review of some of the most intriguing incidents.

William J. Bell.

Nothing motivates soap writers and producers as much as ratings. When "General Hospital" skyrocketed to the top via Tony Geary (left) and Genie Francis, other soaps tried to capture the same success by introducing "Luke-alikes" to their casts. Actors who have been said to have the Luke look include Christopher Rich (middle), who plays Sandy Cory on "Another World," and Rod Arrants (right), who plays Travis Sentell on "Search for Tomorrow." Though fans persist in comparing Arrants with Geary, the "Search for Tomorrow" actor was actually in the cast of "Search" before Tony Geary ever arrived in Port Charles. Photo of Tony Geary and Chris Rich by Ed Geller.

Cast Changes

Nothing distresses soap opera viewers more than tuning in to their favorite show to find their favorite character or cast member in absentia. Gasps of dismay have been known to ring throughout the nation following the dreaded words "The part of _____ will now be played by. . . ." Sometimes, in fact, regardless of how attached they are to a character, the disappearance of that character from the show is sometimes more easily accepted than the appearance of a new face speaking the character's lines.

The following are some of more notable examples of cast changes and how they came about.

• Soap magazines fairly screamed the news when George Reinholt and Jacqueline Courtney were dismissed from the set of "Another World," and fans rushed to their newsstands to find out why such popular cast members had been dumped.

The real-life *contretemps* between "AW" director, Harding Lemay, and two of its most popular stars, Jacqueline Courtney and George Reinholt, who created the role of Steve Frame, was big news. As Alice and Steve, Courtney and Reinholt were America's most popular daytime couple.

Reinholt, however, was a difficult—although brilliant—actor. Paul Rauch, the producer of "Another World" at the time, is quoted in Lemay's book, *Eight Years on Another World*: "George was becoming impossible to work with. . . . His performances were becoming highly unreliable. . . . It wasn't only his interrupting of our schedules and his refusal to take direction. . . .It was also his treatment of directors and fellow actors which was intolerable."

Reinholt was fired. He joined "One Life to Live" as Tony Lord. Also joining him was the usually affable Jacqueline Courtney, who may have left the series because of the way the role of Alice Frame would be written with Steve Frame's departure. Soon Jacquie and George were attracting the audiences again. But George and the "Life" authorities would come to more disagreements than concurrences and once again Reinholt was released from a soap, never to reappear on one (at least up to this writing).

- In the same way, Dorothy Penberthy of "Another World" (Pat Randolph) was summarily fired one day. The actress and her fans were so distressed that Penberthy held a press conference to explain what she knew of what had happened. Apparently, regardless of her popularity, it was decided that Penberthy and character Randolph did not fit with the new young look of "AW." Ironically, Dorothy Penberthy was asked by the producers to return to "Another World" to recreate the role of Pat Randolph, for Pat's departure had left a noticeable void in the show. Ms. Penberthy turned down the offer, and decided not to return to the show.

- Sometimes it's not so easy to find a reason for the elimination of a character or an actor. In the case of Courtney and Reinholt, new actors were brought on to replace the former Alice and Steve. In other cases, both the character and the actor are bid farewell. When Rosemary Prinz left "As the World Turns," for example, the show was forced to send the character off to England, which infuriated the viewers, but not so much as it did when the producers tried to hire a Prinz lookalike to take her place. Penny Hughes may not have been ready to be put out to pasture, but Prinz was impossible to replace.

- In "Search for Tomorrow," the character of John Wyatt, played to great applause by Val Dufour, was suddenly killed to the surprise of "SFT" fans.

  Why was John Wyatt removed from the story by having him suffer a heart attack when he could just as well have left his bitchy wife to marry Joanne? Some suggest it was because Val Dufour overshadowed his role. Others imply that it was because John Wyatt had been written into a corner and there was no easy way to get him out. Whatever the reason, Val Dufour's leaving left a gap in the show-press linkage for a long time.

- One of the most sought-after and written-about characters to bewitch audiences at the ripe old age of 18 was Genie Francis, who played Laura on "General Hospital." When she decided to leave the show at the peak of her popularity, it appeared that "GH" might never recover. (Talented Genie left the show to try her luck on nighttime television.) ABC took the unusual tactic of trying to replace her by injecting a bevy of young blondes into the script (and writing them out just as quickly), most of them named Laura.

  "GH" writers really looked like they'd been caught unawares by Francis's departure when subsequent episodes floundered around in an attempt to justify Laura's sudden disappearance.

Plot Manipulations

This brings us to one of the other frustrating tactics soap producers use: manipulating plots to account for cast changes or to lay the groundwork for future storylines. Here are some examples:

The Fantastic Soap Time Machine

One of the most laughable, but widely accepted, techniques soap operas use to put or keep characters in the middle of the action is to play fast and loose with their age. One has to laugh (or grimace) when a 12-year-old character leaves the show for a few months and returns in full bloom as a nubile 18-year-old. Some examples:

When Laura of "GH" really came into her own she was 15, but she had been depicted as a 12-year-old when the character was seen on the show six months earlier.

Carl Grant of "AMC" exited as an infant and returned shortly thereafter as a five-year-old. Dottie, who returned to "AMC" in mid-83, had left a few years before as a child of perhaps six to eight and she is now old enough to work in the Steampit disco and to have a crush on Jesse Hubbard.

The other side of the miraculous aging quality discussed above is the tendency of some characters to remain forever young—or even to get younger! Even if it is physically possible, most intelligent viewers are hard-pressed to believe that so many soap characters are busy having babies at the same time as their soap children have pre-adolescent children, but it happens all the time just to keep all the characters active.

An interesting sidelight to this is the "grandmother clause" elicited by Eileen Fulton. Upon renewal of her "ATWT" contract, Fulton insisted that a clause be added guaranteeing that her character not become a grandmother for as long as Fulton wished. That way the character of Lisa could be eternally youthful.

Reincarnation

One of the funniest twists that soap opera fans have learned to live with is the mysterious reincarnation of characters who have supposedly died. The most oft-used way of reintroducing a "dead" character is that old standby, amnesia. Countless numbers of characters have reappeared after a long hiatus with the explanation that they hadn't actually died; they'd just been injured and in a daze that left them with no memory. Or they'd been in a coma for months. Or they'd been bravely recovering from a debilitating injury on their own to spare their loved ones the pain. Or they hadn't actually been killed at all; it had been their twin who bit the big one! Soap operas will go to any lengths to restore a character they really want reinstated. There are many reasons for this machination:

- The characters whose lives would be affected the most by such a return from "the dead" need something new and exciting in their lives.
- A character is just about to be rewarded with happiness after much sorrow, and the show needs something with which to pull the rug out from under them.
- A popular star who previously left the show is now willing to return, and the network can't resist the potential ratings boost that would accompany such a surprise.

On the opposite side of the coin is the familiar purging of whole families from shows in recent years. To make way for a new look, many shows have indulged in mass murder of a sort to get rid of what they feel are stale characters. The audience isn't so gullible, however, and ratings almost invariably drop when producers axe the core families that longtime fans love. An unusual departure from the usual purge took place on "The Young and the Restless," which survived and then some when its two major families were recently joined by new families.

THE LIFE OF A SOAP STAR

What really goes on behind the scenes of a soap opera? Many viewers wonder what it's like to live the dual life of real person and fictional character. And a tough life it is, no matter how rewarding.

A typical soap actor's day, for instance, begins at dawn and ends after dusk, and the actors must learn long scripts for shows that will be aired every single week day of the year. How do these stalwarts keep their own personalities separate from those of their characters? How do they carve out a personal life at all with so little time left over? The answer often is, with much difficulty. Some soap stars appear to be incredibly energetic, pursuing second and even third careers as commercial actors, in business ventures, and as activists. Others say it's all they can do to go home and fall into bed at the end of the day. And almost all of them have had to make some sacrifices in their own personal lives—just like their characters do. In some notable examples, actors and actresses from the same show have wed (at least they see each other during the day). In others they have studiously avoided such relationships to give themselves a life separate from soaps.

At least three couples have married as a result of playing parts on "OLTL." Andrea Evans (ex-Tina) married Wayne Massey (ex-Johnny Drummond), Gerald Anthony (Marco Dane) married Brynn Thayer (Jenny Janssen), and Stephen Schnetzer (ex-Marcello Salta) married Nancy Snyder (Katrina Karr). In addition, Judith Light (ex-Karen Wolek) fell in love with Robert Desiderio (ex-Steve Piermont) while they were both on "OLTL." Back in the early '70s, Erika Slezak, still an unmarried woman at the time, dated fellow castmate Tony Ponzini, who created the role of Larry Wolek's brother Vinnie. For a brief time Robert Woods (Bo Buchanan) dated Kristen Meadows, when she was appearing on the show as Mimi King. Currently, Erika Slezak's real-life husband Brian Davies appears on the show as Scott Edgar.

One of the most amusing, and disturbing, problems these actors and actresses have to deal with is the much-discussed identity crisis that arises when one spends at least half of one's time being someone else. Most of the successful actors have learned to deal with this through a sense of humor and ability to remove themselves from their work roles. Long-time stars such as Steve Beradino (Steve Hardy on "GH") have gotten used to receiving an occasional frantic call from a fan who wants to warn them of some impending doom that is about to befall their characters. Others haven't

Soap stars who are together off-screen (left to right): Marcia McCabe of "Search for Tomorrow" and Chris Goutman of "Texas"; Sherry Mathis of "Search" and husband Jerring Lanning of "Texas" worked together on "Search for Tomorrow"; and Chris Rich and fiancee Nancy Frangione, both from "Another World."

An example of soap interrelationships: Candice Earley (Donna, "All My Children") and Clint Ritchie (Clint Buchanan, "One Life to Live") are what the gossip columnists used to call an "item." Candice is a veteran stage actress who was starring in the Broadway play Grease at the time she signed on with the soap some eight years ago. Clint is a horseman who competes annually in California's rugged Tavis Cup race. In New York he rides in Central Park. Photo by Bob Deutsch.

been so lucky. Eileen Fulton of "ATWT," for example, had to be protected by a guard from righteous viewers who actually began to attack "Lisa" on the street for all her evil deeds. Rosemary Prinz finally had to leave her role as Penny Hughes for the sake of her health. And other actresses have found themselves automatically picking out clothing that their characters would wear, rather than that they would choose.

On the happy side, what are the rewards of starring in a soap opera? Many stars find this type of role more fulfilling than any other because they have so much input into their roles. Unlike movies or the stage, soap operas often allow the actors to contribute as much direction and development to their characters as the writers and directors. In addition, there are very few other roles that would allow an actor to portray so many different facets of a character. Bitches mellow; wayward types reform; virtuous people become dissolute; the virgin loses her virginity; the priest is defrocked; the heiress loses all her wealth, and so on *ad infinitum*. To their credit, the fact that the audience still believes in the characters, despite all these major changes, is due to the actor's knowledge and understanding of their characters. When Dorian (Robin Strasser) on "OLTL" was mellowed by the reappearance of her daughter Cassie and the loyalty of her husband Herb, she did not make a complete turnabout; rather, we saw Dorian from a new angle that tended to explain in part why she'd been such a rat in the past.

The monetary rewards are nothing to sneeze at, either.

Money Matters

The salary levels for daytime actors range from the merely respectable (something over union scale) to the very generous. The average payments are arranged as follows:

For an actor who has not yet built up "pulling power" (the ability to get viewers over to the soap merely on his or her name) the basic payment may be about $400 a show, perhaps even $500 if the budget allows. If the actor can swing a clause in his or her agreement that says no fewer than two appearances a week will be required, that actor can expect to make up to $1,000 a week. With such an agreement signed and sealed, the show can still make adjustments in the schedule. However, union rules would then require

that they pay the actor a portion of the amount he or she would have received if work had been required that week.

Some actors may earn as much as $5,000-$7,000 per show.

The truly elite among the daytime acting community can command payment by annual fees rather than by show. Some can earn a half million dollars a year; some have reportedly already signed the first million-dollar-a-year contracts in daytime television. (Anthony Geary is rumored to be among these serial Croesuses.)

The unions that support actors include such craft groups as SAG (Screen Actors Guild), AFTRA (American Federation of Television and Radio Artists), and AGVA (American Guild of Variety Artists). In most instances daytime performers may belong to both SAG and AFTRA. When dealing with television, of course, it's AFTRA's rules that apply.

Under union scale (scale is the minimum payment for an actor in the union) a daytime performer can receive $331.25 for a half-hour show and about $446.00 for an hour's performance.

There are day players—those actors who are not under contract—and they're paid by show.

There are also "under fives," actors who have less than five lines of dialogue; their minimum is $185 per show.

SOAP OPERA'S UNSUNG HEROES

You'll never see them on your TV screen, but they're there nonetheless, creating the atmosphere you've come to identify with "RH's" New York, "Y&R's" Genoa City, or "GL's" Springfield. They're the people who create the musical and set backgrounds that complete the soap opera picture. Set designers, for example, may not earn as much as some other soap workers (perhaps $700 a week), but they're very important to the success of their shows.

Soap opera sets have come a long way since the good old days. Remember when all soap living rooms and kitchens looked the same (like something out of the Sears catalog), and all the characters were dressed for PTA meetings? Remember, not more than a few years ago, when characters who were supposed to be less-than-well-to-do ran around in designer clothes looking like they just left the hairdresser? Well, today, soap opera producers insist on a more realistic look, and the set designers are there to provide it. Once-immaculate children's rooms are now filled with the toys and other trappings of childhood. "Ryan's Hope" is notable for the realistic look of Ryan's Bar but even more for the kitchen behind it, which looks functional and funky at the same time.

Long gone are the days of simple backdrops. Today most soaps use three types of sets and spend several thousand dollars a week on props alone. There are a few permanent sets—usually the large mansions featured, for example—along with "swing" sets that are brought onstage only when needed (these are usually the smaller apartments or single rooms that are shown slightly less frequently). Finally there are the one-time sets used when a character makes a single foray into unknown territory. These days there are also numerous locations shots, pioneered by such shows as "Search for Tomorrow" to be spliced in with the studio shots. The number of these expensive location shots used today is obviously a testament to the amount of money the soaps can now afford to spend.

If the set designers make the soaps visually appealing and believable, the music engineers give each show its own audio personality. Gone are the days of live organ music, thank goodness. Today, studios employ several experts and much modern equipment to give the soaps the proper musical accompaniment. Those in charge of the music must learn almost as much about their characters as the actors. They can choose the proper style for each character or situation. Sometimes existing recordings are used; in other cases new music is commissioned specifically for a show. One thing is certain: the variety and quality of music used on soap operas has done much to bring them up to date.

16

Where Are They Now?

On the following pages you'll find the past and present credits of many soap actors and actresses as well as background information on soaps no longer on the air.

TO THEIR CREDIT

It would be impossible to list them all, but it's interesting to take a look at the accomplishments of some past and present stars of daytime dramas. Which series have your favorite soap actors appeared on in the past? What major stars of stage and screen once graced the casts of today's soaps? Where have some of yesterday's soap actors gone? Read on.

- William Gray Espy (Mitch on "AW") has a habit of disappearing for long periods when he is between soaps. After leaving "Young and the Restless," and

Tony Geary and Ruth Warrick entertain at Soap Alive, Atlantic City. Photo by Ed Geller.

before appearing on "Another World" the first time (he left and came back once more), he was rumored to be (1) in a monastery, (2) in Tibet, (3) working for the CIA, or (4) working under another name.

- Fred J. Scollay (ex-Charlie Hobson, "AW") was one of the original cast members of "The Doctors" and has appeared on "Edge of Night," "Search for Tomorrow," and "Somerset." Between soaps he does theater and films and lots of commercials.

- Cleavon Little (Captain Hancock, "AW") is recognized as a brilliant acting talent (he costarred in *Blazing Saddles*), and is seen on stage and in films and nighttime television.

- Howard Rollins, who won raves for his work in *Ragtime*, and later appeared as Ed in "Another World," goes on to appear in important television and theater productions and continues to win raves.

- Robert Christian (Bob Morgan, "AW") who died in January at the age of 42, was an Obie winner for his Off-Broadway work. A scholarship was founded in his memory to benefit the Negro Ensemble Company.

- Besides doing "All My Children," Dorothy Lyman costars in the nighttime sitcom, "Mama," and directed theatrical productions in New York, including *A Couple of White Chicks*, which starred Susan Sarandon.

- "Edge of Night" famous grads have included Celeste Holm, Larry Hagman, Ruby Dee, Tony Roberts, John Cullum, Barry Newman.

- "Guiding Light" has graduated several important actors including Kevin Bacon, the young man who went on to appear in *Diner*, the hit sleeper film of 1983, and the Broadway play, *The Slab Boys*.

- Other recent departees who have achieved success in other areas include Cindy Pickett, who went to Paris and became the favorite actress of Roger Vadim, the man who made stars out of two of his wives (Brigitte Bardot and Annette Stroyberg) and married another already established star, Jane Fonda. Cindy didn't marry Vadim but did make an important film with him.

- Others who left "Guiding Light" to light up marquees on Broadway and movie houses are: Barnard Hughes, Lilia Skala, Sandy Dennis, Gerald S. O'Laughlin, Jan Sterling, Ruth Warrick, Joseph Campanella, Cicely Tyson, Ruby Dee, Christopher Walken, James Earl Jones, Blythe Danner, Billy Dee Williams, Chris Sarandon, Larry Gates, Nancy Malone, and writer-producer James Lipton.

- John Hodiak of "GL's" radio days went on to do a considerable amount of theater and achieved screen stardom in such films as *Lifeboat* and *Mrs. Miniver*.

- Mercedes McCambridge of "GL" (radio) was one of the most successful radio actresses. She carried her success through to films where her smoky voice lent interest to her roles in such movies as *All the King's Men*, *A Farewell to Arms*, *Giant*, *Suddenly Last Summer*, *Cimarron*, and others.

- Anthony Geary, who went on to commit an act of rape on "General Hospital," was a rapist on "The Young and the Restless."

- Among other famous male graduates of "The Young and the Restless" are Tom Selleck and David Hasselhoff. Selleck went on to win a new large following via his successful nighttime series, "Magnum, P.I." Hasselhoff (who co-owns a French restaurant in Georgia with his sister and French brother-in-law), scored high ratings marks with his nighttime show, "Knight Rider."

- John Gibson, who played Cash on "Y&R," was a male strip dancer before he joined the show—did ditto while on the show—and continues to make a name for himself as one of the best interpreters of this newly popular dance form.

- Dennis Cole (Lance, "Y&R") began his television career co-starring in a TV series with Howard Duff. He insisted on doing most of the show's difficult stunts himself. No wonder. Cole began his show business career as a Hollywood stunt man. He's since gone on from "Y&R" to do nighttime TV and films.

- Wings Hauser (Greg, "Y&R") is now making movies and is on nighttime TV.

- For years, "ATWT's" executive producer was Fred Bartholomew, the former child actor. Some of the show's graduates include Richard Thomas, Swoozie Kurtz, film director Mark Rydell, Martin Sheen, Joyce Van Patten, and James Earl Jones.

- In 1983 Kate Mulgrew returned to "Ryan's Hope" to play Mary's ghost. She first left it several years earlier to star in the nighttime series, "Mrs. Columbo." She later made a film with Richard Burton (not as yet released) on the Tristan and Isolde legend. She also starred in a mini-series, "The Mansions of America," written by Agnes Nixon.

- John Gabriel (Dr. Seneca Beaulac, "RH") started his career as a singer and considers himself a singer who acts, not an actor who also sings.

- Other "RH" graduates include: Gordon Thompson, who went on to do "Dynasty"; Daren Kelly, who

Marie Cheatham (Stefanie, "Search for Tomorrow") in exotic dress. Photo by Bob Deutsch.

went into theater; Daniel-Hugh Kelly, who has landed a nighttime TV series; Richard Muenz, who toured in a revival of *The Most Happy Fella* and then was chosen to play Sir Lancelot in a tour of *Camelot*.

- Joseph Papp used to be stage manager on "Search for Tomorrow" in the mid-50s.
- Many of the actors who have appeared on "SFT" have gone on to achieve fame in other media. Among them: Lynn Loring (who played Joanne's daughter, Patty); Robert Benson (who played Jo's son); Don Knotts; Lee Grant; Sandy Duncan; Susan Sarandon; Roy Scheider; Barbara Baxley; Jill Clayburgh; Trish Van Devere; Constance Ford (now in "Another World"); Henry Morgan; Morgan Fairchild; Earle

Hyman; Patricia Harty; the late Ross Martin; George Maharis; Wayne Rogers; James Coco; Kevin Kline; and "Soap's" fine star, Robert Mandan.

- Sherry Mathis, who plays Liza Sentell on "SFT," is also a singer. She met her husband, Jerry Lanning (who appeared on the soap once as a gangster and later starred in "Texas") while both were costarring in a regional production of *Camelot*. She made her film debut opposite Burt Reynolds in *W.W. and the Dixie Dance Kings*.
- Marie Cheatham (Stephanie Wyatt, "SFT") is of American Indian descent and is working on a project that will include a book, a film, and a TV production on the life of an American Indian chief, Quanah Parker, whose mother was a white farm girl. She owns a large collection of American Indian and Western artifacts, including wagon wheels and other ranch miscellany that belonged to her Texas grandparents. (She was born in Tulsa, Oklahoma.) She also raises exotic orchids in her New York apartment.
- Few people move from soaps to superstardom. Among those who have made the move, most of

Christopher Reeve, who soared to fame as Superman, started his move out of soaps when he toured with Katharine Hepburn after being seen on the now-cancelled series "Love of Life." Photo by Tony Rizzo.

them—like Roy Scheider, Christopher Reeve, Warren Beatty—are men.

An occasional exception does occur. The most recent of such exceptions is Morgan Fairchild, who seemed to zoom from "Search for Tomorrow," in which she played murderer Jeniffer Pace Phillips for three years, to other media fame.

Morgan did a few nighttime guest shots after leaving "Search." Then she was cast for the sexy nighttime series, "Flamingo Road." Instantly, Morgan was a front cover star whose face looked out from magazines around the country and everywhere else where "Flamingo Road" was shown.

The lovely lady also made a movie, *The Seduction*, and although it didn't set box office records, it certified her as a bona fide film star.

- Helen Gallagher, who has played Maeve Ryan since "RH" began, is a Broadway star. She's been center stage in such productions as "Pal Joey," "No, No Nanette," and "Hazel Flagg." She also appeared in "Sugar Babies" with Mickey Rooney. Gallagher teaches singing to aspiring actors. "You should be able to know how to do it all when you decide on a career in theater or in any area of show business," she says. "Act, sing and dance as if your career depended on it. It just might."
- Bernard Barrow (Johnny Ryan, "RH") is a doctor. He holds a PhD in drama and until recently taught at Brooklyn College. He left his teaching chores to concentrate on doing plays between "Ryan's Hope" appearances.
- Mary Stuart's film career before "SFT" included costarring opposite several important actors. She worked with Clark Gable and Errol Flynn.
- Larry Haines (Stu Bergman, "SFT") is a two-time Emmy winner who has more than 15,000 radio performances to his credit. He also appeared on Broadway, in films, and on prime time TV.
- Judy Lewis, formerly the producer of the now defunct series, "Texas," is the daughter of actress Loretta Young. Judy appeared on several soaps as an actress before deciding she liked working behind the scenes best.
- Dack Rambo, starring as Steven Jacoby on "All My Children," costarred, along with his late identical twin brother, Dirk, on "The Loretta Young Show."
- Anthony Call (Herb Callison, "One Life to Live") began his career as a child prodigy pianist.
- Lynn Loring, who was in the original cast of "Search for Tomorrow" playing Patti Barron, Joanne's

daughter, is now a producer. She is married to actor Roy Thinnes who was the original Dr. Phil Brewer in the original cast of "General Hospital."

- Elizabeth Harrower, one of the fine writers for "The Young and the Restless," is the mother of one of soap opera's most popular stars, Susan Seaforth Hayes (Julie Williams in "Days of Our Lives").
- Constance Towers (Clarissa, "Capitol"), is the wife of John Gavin, the U.S. Ambassador to Mexico. She spends her weeks on the soap and her weekends in Mexico City as the Ambassador's Lady. She is a veteran of the Broadway musical scene, and costarred for years both on Broadway and on tour with Yul Brynner in *The King and I*.
- Richard Egan ("Capitol") made his movie debut in 1949. His studio groomed him as the successor to Clark Gable. His career, however, took him into rugged films for the most part and his original romantic impact became one of swords, saddle, leather, and gunpowder instead.
- Rory Calhoun of "Capitol" was once considered the sexiest man in movies. He made his film debut in

Larry Haines and Mary Stuart, veterans of "Search for Tomorrow." Photo by Bob Deutsch.

Dack Rambo is Steve Jacobi on "All My Children." Photo by Ed Geller.

1942 and became one of the more popular movie cowboys.

- Ed Nelson ("Capitol") made his most vivid impact on video audiences as the principled Dr. Rossi of "Peyton Place."
- Kimberly Beck-Hilton, stepdaughter of singer Tommy Leonetti, was part of the "Peyton Place" cast, joining the then controversial nighttime soaper as a small girl, before starring on "Capitol."
- Macdonald Carey ("DOOL") became one of the first daytime drama actors to win an Emmy when the Academy of TV Arts & Sciences finally established a category for daytime programming. Macdonald Carey began his career in the '40s and starred in the classic film, *Wake Island*, in 1942. A gifted poet, he recently had his first book of poetry published.
- "DOOL" boasts the presence of Robert Clary, who was a Broadway actor before moving to California and marrying one of Eddie Cantor's daughters. Clary plays the part of Robert LeClair. In his own life, Clary has lived through experiences that no soap could hope to approach for drama and courage. As a youngster in his native France he was arrested by

the Nazis and sent to certain death in a concentration camp. A series of fortunate happenstances kept him alive until he was finally liberated by the Allies. Today, Clary travels the country talking to young people in school about the Holocaust as he, personally, lived it.

- Gregg Marx, who plays David Banning on "DOOL," is a Marx Brothers descendant. Groucho was his granduncle; as were Harpo and Chico. His granddad was Zeppo Marx.
- The very dapper, distinguished Forrest Compton (Mike Karr, "EON") once appeared in cowboy movies.
- Lois Kibbee, who plays the wealthy Geraldine Whitney Saxon ("EON"), is a cousin of several distinguished Kibbees, including a former Chancellor of Higher Education in New York and a writer/director. She is also the niece of the great screen actor, Guy Kibbee. Lois has written several of the soap's scripts in recent years under the direction of the series' former longtime writer (13 years) Henry Slesar and new writer Lee Sheldon.
- The original actress who played Laura Baldwin on "GH" was not Genie Francis but a young girl named Stacy Baldwin. At that time Laura had not yet met

Constance Towers is "Capitol's" Clarissa McCandless.

Father and daughter, 1978: Walter and Erika Slezak.

and married Scotty Baldwin; that would happen in 1979.

- The actress who played Barbara Vining on "GH," the woman who adopted Lesley's daughter, Laura, was Judy Lewis, who later became a producer of "Texas," on which Kin Shriner appeared after leaving "General Hospital." Kin later returned to the "Hospital" when his role on "Texas" seemed mired in a plot line muckpile.
- Ellen Holly, who plays Carla Hall on "OLTL," was the first black actress to create a major daytime television character.
- Al Freeman, Jr. ("OLTL"), appeared in the controversial film, *Dutchman*, by Leroi Jones, in 1967, establishing himself as a powerful actor. He later went on to play Malcolm X in "Roots II." He's now Ed Hall.
- Anthony George, who plays Dr. Will Vernon on "OLTL," was one of the three stars of the series, "Checkmate," which made its debut in 1959. The other stars were Sebastian Cabot and Doug McClure.
- Erika Slezak, Viki Lord Riley Buchanan on "OLTL," is the daughter of the late actor, Walter Slezak, and the granddaughter of the opera singer, Leo Slezak.

- Eric Braeden, who plays Victor Newman on "Y&R," was born in Germany towards the end of World War II. His father was an officer with the German army. Eric's real name is Hans Gudegast and it was as Gudegast that he made his TV debut in the United States in the 1960s series, "Rat Patrol." He later made a film which has become a cult movie with college students, *Colossus: The Forbin Project*. Braeden once played soccer with an Israeli team.
- Steven Ford (Andy on "Y&R") is the son of former President Gerald R. Ford and Mrs. Betty Ford. A rodeo performer before he became an actor, he now owns a horse-breeding ranch. As an actor, he made all the rounds and auditioned "just like every other actor" before winning his role on the soap.
- Jaime Lyn Bauer (Lauralee Prentiss on "Y&R") was absent from the series in 1983 when she joined the cast of the unsuccessful nighttime series, "Bare Essence."

Jaime Lyn Bauer. Photo by Bob Deutsch.

• Perhaps the first time a major film personality worked in a soap as a guest star occurred in 1968. A talented young actress named Christina Crawford had to bow out of *The Secret Storm* because of emergency surgery. Her mother, Joan Crawford, called producer Gloria Monty and asked to appear in her daughter's place. Gloria, of course, agreed, and for four episodes the legendary Joan Crawford held forth on a daytime soap opera.

Prize Winners

Among those who appeared on soaps, several of these former suds-factory stars won important awards over the years. Some of those include the following.

• Lee Grant won an Oscar for her role in the film, *Shampoo*; she played Rose Peabody on "Search for Tomorrow."
• Ellen McRae played Dr. Kate Bartok on "The Doc-

tors." She later changed her name to Ellen Burstyn. In 1974 she won an Oscar for her work in the movie *Alice Doesn't Live Here Anymore*.
• Ernest Thompson played Tony Cooper in "Somerset." He went on to write a prize-winning hit Broadway play that then became a prize-winning movie, *On Golden Pond*.

WHAT EVER HAPPENED TO . . . ?

There are always people who remember the old shows and wonder why—if they liked them so much and if their neighbors liked them so much, and if the stars were forever being interviewed in fan magazines—the series were yanked from the air.

The rule of thumb almost always applicable to these cases is simple: ratings. It's not always the size of an audience that counts for a sponsor as much as the share of an audience a show gets. It's not always the

Kim Hunter can be called a soap graduate, for she went through the makeup mill during her "witchy" guest stint on "Edge of Night."

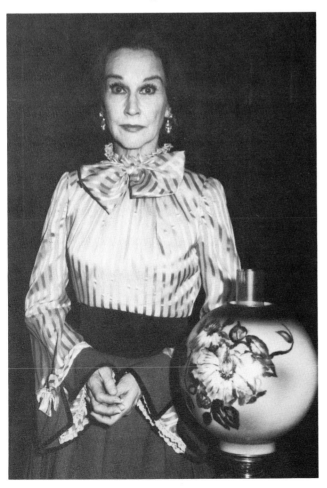

Armand Assante (right) and Steve O'Brien, who played Dr. Steve Aldrich on "The Doctors." Photo by Bob Deutsch.

Three stars from "The Doctors" (left to right): James Pritchett, Gerald Gordon, Steve O'Brien. Photo by Bob Deutsch.

share either. It's the type of audience as well. For example, if the sponsor is after a youthful consuming group, the soap that attracts those potential customers will stay on the air; the soap that doesn't doesn't remain air-borne.

Several soaps languished for lack of competitive strength (in ratings, share, audience, etc.). Among the more recent departees were "The Doctors," which lasted nearly 20 years, and "Texas," which stayed on for only three years. In the latter instance, there was the complicating factor of a loss of outlets. The fewer places a series can be seen, the fewer numbers who will see it. There was also the matter of the show's time slots across the country. "Texas," for example, might be seen early in the morning in one area and at night in another.

Glenn Corbett, once Jason on "The Doctors," also played James Lake on "Route 66." Photo by Bob Deutsch.

Tina Johnson and Charlie Hill from "Texas."

Above: "Texas" star Pam Long, who played Ashley Linden, relaxes aboard a sailing yacht in New York Harbor. She had virtually no acting experience when she was awarded the part of the ambitious Southern belle on "Texas."

New York Met catcher John Stearns touches up for the cameras for his appearance on "Texas."

John McCafferty, from "Texas."

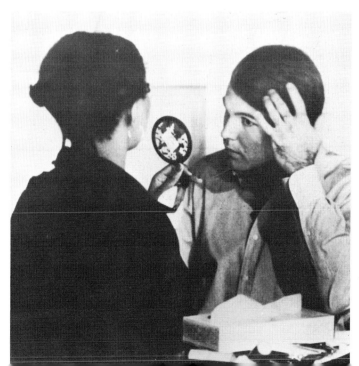

Robert Burton is a soap veteran. On "Texas" he played a character who touched a mysterious Indian artifact and turned into a mummy. Photo by Ed Geller.

Among the more popular late and still-lamented shows are "Somerset," "Where the Heart Is," and "Secret Storm." Probably the all-time most popular canceled series is "Love of Life." From time to time fans ask if the show will ever be revived. Chances are good that it won't be. Sponsors and networks alike are wary of starting backward, as they say. Even if the series had a totally new set of storylines, experience has shown that revivals tend not to last beyond the early curiosity stages.

Above: Barry Jenner and Fawne Harriman of "Somerset," before it ended its run.

Below: Ron Tomme played Bruce Sterling on "Love of Life." Photo by Howard Gray.

Left: "Somerset" star Audrey Landers. She's since gone on to star in "Dallas" as Afton Cooper. Photo by Bob Deutsch.

Ed Kemmer ("Somerset") and Fran Sharon ("Edge of Night") are married in real life. Photo by Howard Gray.

Birgitta Tolksdorf and Rick Weber, formerly on "Love of Life." Photo by Bob Deutsch.

Left: Diana Greg and Walker Abel appeared on "Where the Heart Is." Photo by Howard Gray.

Above: Conrad Fowkes, whose soap credits include "Love of Life," "As the World Turns," "Edge of Night," "Search for Tomorrow," and "The Doctors."

Above: Donna Mills, currently starring on "Knots Landing," once played Laura Donnelley Elliott on "Love is a Many Splendored Thing." Photo by Howard Gray.

Leslie Charleson, now Monica on "General Hospital," used to play Iris Donnelly Garrison on "Love is a Many Splendored Thing." Edward Power played Spencer Garrison. Photo by Howard Gray.

Below: Two of the stars of defunct "Love is a Many Splendored Thing": David Birney (Mark Elliott) and Gloria Hoye (Helen Elliott Donnelly). Photo by Howard Gray.

The other show that might have compared as most popular canceled series, "Dark Shadows," recently proved to the networks that it's best to let the dead stay dead. When "Dark Shadows" was reintroduced via a syndicated deal, audiences flocked to their televisions to recapture the old menacing moods. New viewers rushed to see what all the fuss was about. Within weeks, "Dark Shadows' " ratings were so low the show was pulled from non-prime time to mid-morning—2:00 A.M. for example—exposure and then, finally, the plug was pulled for good.

Above: Nancy Addison plays Jill Coleridge Ryan on "Ryan's Hope" and occasionally does plays. Photo by Bob Deutsch.

Below: Loanne Bishop is Rose Kelly on "General Hospital." She also regularly appears off-Broadway and owns her own hair-accessory company. Photo by Ed Geller.

Above: Joan Bennett, who starred on "Dark Shadows," with Lisa Brown, of "Guiding Light."

Below: Lisa Brown of "Guiding Light" has also appeared in the Broadway show 42nd Street. Photo by Bob Deutsch.

John Wesley Shipp (Kelly, "Guiding Light") is a singer. His father is a minister. Shipp combines his singing and his religious faith when he entertains (or simply visits with) older people in old age homes. Here he introduces some of the elderly guests to the joys of pet ownership. Photo by Ed Geller.

Diedre Hall of "Days of Our Lives." Diedre makes regular appearances on several game shows. Photo by Ed Geller.

Lori Cardille was "Edge of Night's" Winter Austin in 1978.

As Dr. Rick Webber, Chris Robinson feels that his character's decisions involve morality as well as medical judgment. Chris is an amateur archaeologist and a collector of American Indian artifacts. He has a ranch near the Colorado border and an art gallery in Sedonia, Arizona.

Above: Rose Alaio recently left the cast of "Guiding Light." She regularly visits New York schools to talk and answer questions children have about acting. Photo by Ed Geller.

Below: "Guiding Light's" Kathleen Cullent (Amanda Wexler) has left the soap and is working on an HBO film; she is also active in the ERA movement.

Above: Michael Tylo as Quint McCord brought youthful, mysterious drama to "Guiding Light." Tylo recently appeared in a Pennsylvania production of The Importance of Being Earnest.

Below: Louise Shaffer, with her Burmese cat named Paris. She plays Rae Woodward on "Ryan's Hope," and she and her husband Roger Crews (a "Ryan's Hope" writer) are hoping to do a radio show in the near future.

"Soaps—An American Celebration" took place in Los Angeles in 1982. At the tribute to the 50th anniversary of the soap opera, Doug Davidson, left ("The Young and the Restless") and John Stamos ("General Hospital") entertain the crowds.

Left to right: Susan Lucci (Erica), Debbie Goodrich (Silver), and Cheryl Tiegs on a recent "All My Children" episode.

Rock star Rick Springfield played Dr. Noah Drake on "General Hospital." Photo by Ed Geller.

Tommy Lee Jones, now one of the hottest film talents, started his career on soaps ("Search for Tomorrow"). Photo by Bob Deutsch.

Left: Asa Buchanan of "One Life to Live" is played by Phil Carey, who spent most of his career appearing in action films. Photo by Ed Geller.

Jameson Parker played Brad Vernon on "One Life to Live," but he left the series to make films for nighttime TV. Photo by Bob Deutsch.

Jennifer Cooke played Morgan Nelson, restless young wife of doctor Kelly Nelson, on "Guiding Light." She left "Guiding Light" and is currently up for a role in the new Warren Beatty movie Mermaid *and for a Broadway role. Photo by Ed Geller.*

"All My Children's" Mark LaMura portrays Mark Dalton. In his spare time he is writing a screenplay.

Lawrence Lau plays Greg Nelson, a star-crossed lover on "All My Children." He is currently up for a movie role as well as a part in a Broadway show.

Soap opera stars gather in Milwaukee on the set of Plaza Suite *as part of a summer tour. Standing from left are Tom Hallick ("The Young and the Restless"), Emily McLaughlin ("General Hospital"), John Lupton ("Days of Our Lives"), Jaime Lyn Bauer ("The Young and the Restless"), and Jim Sikking ("General Hospital"). Seated is Jeanne Cooper ("The Young and the Restless").*

Pam Long and Jerry Lanning once shared costarring duties on "Texas." Since then Pam has gone on to write "Guiding Light" and Jerry (who is married to Sherry Mathis, the woman who appears as Liza Sentell on "Search for Tomorrow") is rumored to be on the verge of signing a very important soap contract. His mother is the famous singer, Roberta Sherwood (once said to be the only singer who, when she appeared on stage, could make Walter Winchell stop taking notes about what everyone around him was doing and listen). Lanning met his future wife, Mathis, when they costarred in a theatrical production. Photo by Bob Deutsch.

Right: Lisa Peluso (Wendy on "Search for Tomorrow") combines school, modeling, and acting. Petronia Paley (Quinn, "Another World") combines soaps with films. The ladies take time to do charity shows. Photo by Ed Geller.

Terry Davis played April Cavanaugh Scott on "Edge of Night" before tiring of the role and moving to "Another World" to play Stacy Winthrop. Photo by Ed Geller.

Anthony Herrera is writing a screenplay and has appeared in movies.

Brenda Dickson returned to "The Young and the Restless" as Jill Foster after a lengthy hiatus. She has appeared on many game shows, on "Dinah," on "Love, American Style," and in many theatrical productions.

Above: Lori Loughlin stands between two ex-"Edgers," blond Mark Andrews (Chad) and dark-haired Mark Arnold (Gavin). Loughlin is still an active model who does TV commercials and appears in the movie Amityville III. Photo by Ed Geller.

Pictured at the Stork Club in 1943 are Frances Heflin (Mona Tyler of "All My Children") and her brother Martin, the siblings of actor Van Heflin.

Gloria Loring, who played Liz on "Days of Our Lives," is also a professional singer.

Georgeann Johnson, formerly of "Another World" and "Somerset," left the soaps to do films and nighttime TV. Photo by Bob Deutsch.

17

Complete Emmy Lists

The Daytime Emmy Awards were not always with us. For years, the Academy of Television Arts & Sciences did not have a separate daytime category. Indeed, for much of the Academy's existence, the daytime genre was all but ignored. In 1967-68 Joan Bennett ("Dark Shadows") and Macdonald Carey ("Days of Our Lives") won awards for Outstanding Achievement. In 1970, the series "Love is a Many Splendored Thing" won an award for technical achievement.

In 1973 Mary Fickett (Ruth Martin, "All My Children") won an Emmy in the newly created daytime category. The response from the television audiences was so overwhelmingly positive that the Academy enlarged the scope of the soap awards the next year.

The following is a listing of award winners from 1974 through 1982.

Val Dufour and Helen Gallagher. Photo by Bob Deustch.

OUTSTANDING ACTOR IN A DAYTIME DRAMA SERIES

1974: *Macdonald Carey (Tom Horton, "Days of Our Lives")*

1975: *Macdonald Carey (Tom Horton, "Days of Our Lives")*

1976: *Larry Haines (Stu Bergman, "Search for Tomorrow")*

1977: *Val Dufour (John Wyatt, "Search for Tomorrow")*

1978: *James Pritchett (Matt Powers, "The Doctors")*

1979: *Al Freeman, Jr. (Ed Hall, "One Life to Live")*

1980: *Douglass Watson (Mac Cory, "Another World")*

1981: *Douglass Watson (Mac Cory, "Another World")*

1982: *Anthony Geary (Luke Spencer, "General Hospital")*

Tony Geary ("General Hospital") and Robin Strasser ("One Life to Live") in 1982. Photo by Ed Geller.

Irene Dailey ("Another World"). Photo by Bob Deutsch.

OUTSTANDING ACTRESS IN A DAYTIME DRAMA SERIES

1974: *Elizabeth Hubbard (Althea Davis, "The Doctors")*

1975: *Susan Flannery (Laura Horton, "Days of Our Lives")*

1976: *Helen Gallagher (Maeve Ryan, "Ryan's Hope")*

1977: *Helen Gallagher (Maeve Ryan, "Ryan's Hope")*

1978: *Laurie Heineman (Charlene Watt, "Another World")*

1979: *Irene Dailey (Liz Matthews, "Another World")*

1980: *Judith Light (Karen, "One Life to Live")*

1981: *Judith Light (Karen, "One Life to Live")*

1982: *Robin Strasser (Dorian, "One Life to Live")*

Judith Light won the Best Daytime Actress award twice, in 1980 and 1981, for her portrayal of Karen Wolek. She left the series in 1983 to make a TV movie with Tony Geary. Photo by Ed Geller.

OUTSTANDING ACTOR IN A SUPPORTING ROLE FOR A DAYTIME DRAMA SERIES
(Category started in 1979)

1979: *Peter Hansen* (Lee Baldwin, "General Hospital")

1980: *Warren Burton* (Eddie Dorrance, "All My Children")

1981: *Larry Haines* (Stu Bergman, "Search for Tomorrow")

1982: *David Lewis* (Edward Quartermaine, "General Hospital")

OUTSTANDING ACTRESS IN A SUPPORTING ROLE IN A DAYTIME DRAMA SERIES

1979: *Suzanne Rogers* (Maggie Horton, "Days of Our Lives")

1980: *Francesca James* (Kelly Cole, "All My Children")

1981: *Jane Elliot* (Tracy Quartermaine, "General Hospital")

1982: *Dorothy Lyman* (Opal Gardner, "All My Children")

Peter Hansen ("General Hospital") and Suzanne Flannery ("Days of Our Lives"). Photo by Bob Deutsch.

BEST DAYTIME SERIAL

1974: "The Doctors"
1975: "The Young and the Restless"
1976: "Another World"
1977: "Ryan's Hope"
1978: "Days of Our Lives"
1979: "Days of Our Lives"
1980: "Guiding Light"
1981: "General Hospital"
1982: "Guiding Light"

Agnes Nixon has had a soap on television every day for more than 20 years. Photo by Bob Deutsch.

Douglass Watson (Mac Cory, "Another World") and Judith Light (Karen Wolek, "One Life to Live") at the Emmys. Photo by Bob Deutsch.

DAYTIME EMMY UPDATE: 1983 Awards

Award Category	*Actor*
For Outstanding Achievement in a Starring Role: Male	Robert S. Woods (Bo Buchanan, "One Life to Live") (ABC)
For Outstanding Achievement in a Starring Role: Female	Dorothy Lyman (Opal Gardner, "All My Children") (ABC)
For Outstanding Achievement in a Supporting Role: Male	Darnell Williams (Jesse Hubbard, "All My Children") (ABC)
For Outstanding Achievement in a Supporting Role: Female	Louise Shaffer (Rae Woodard, "Ryan's Hope") (ABC)
Best Writing	"Ryan's Hope" (ABC)
Best Daytime Drama	"The Young and the Restless" (CBS)

Robert Woods started his show business career in earnest after leaving the Green Berets. He plays Bo Buchanan on "General Hospital." Photo by Ed Geller.

Dorothy Lyman, "All My Children." Photo by Bob Deutsch.

NOTES ON EMMY

"Ryan's Hope," though only eight years old, has won 13 Emmys—a record for a soap of that relatively short on-air duration.

Dorothy Lyman won as Best Supporting Actress for the same role last year. This sometimes happens; it did with Larry Haines whose role as Stu Bergman on "Search for Tomorrow" once won him a Best Actor Award, later a best supporting actor.

Susan Lucci at the Emmys.
Photo by Ed Geller.

18

Soap Trivia

SOAP OPERA QUIZ

The answers to the following questions are at the end of this chapter.

True or False?

1. Erica's full name on "All My Children" is Erica Martin Brent Cudahy Kingsley.

2. Actor Douglass Watson was featured on "Days of Our Lives" before his tenure as Mac Cory on "Another World."

3. The nefarious Dr. Ivan Kipling of "OLTL" showed up, uninvited, at the lavish costume ball thrown by Asa and Samantha Buchanan dressed as an executioner.

4. Helen Gallagher, who played Maeve on "Ryan's Hope," is the only actress who has won the Emmy for outstanding actress in a daytime drama series two years in a row.

5. "Y&R's" Genoa City is based on a resort town in Florida.

Susan Lucci as the beautiful but difficult Erica Kane of "All My Children."

6. During the fabled "Summer of Luke and Laura," Tony Geary of "GH" won the Emmy award for best actor in a daytime serial.

7. The late Carolyn Jones, who originally played Myrna Clegg of "Capitol," once starred in the TV show "The Munsters."

8. Joanne of "Search for Tomorrow" has been married four times.

9. Police chief Bill Marceau is the one character who was part of the original Monticello citizenry who remains on "Edge of Night."

10. Eileen Fulton, who played Lisa on "ATWT" for 20-plus years, left the series because she was sick and tired of playing the soap's resident bitch.

11. Julie Olson Banning Anderson Williams and her best friend Susan ("DOOL") each bore a child by David Martin.

12. Charita Bauer created the role of Bert (Bertha) Bauer on "GL."

13. The third marriage of Delia on "Ryan's Hope" was to the dashing Prince Albert, an expatriate from a fictional middle-European country.

14. Forrest Compton (Mike Karr on "Edge of Night") is the spouse of one of ABC's top execs.

15. Kyle was the name of the movie producer who kept sabotaging his own film in one of "Another World's" recent plots.

16. The engagement of Julie and Tyler on "Capitol" was called off when Julie discovered that Tyler was having an affair with Sloane Denning.

17. Llanview of "One Life To Live" and Pine Valley of "All My Children" are neighboring towns.

18. One of former president Jimmy Carter's children plays a role on "The Young and the Restless."

19. The first black actress to play a major daytime role was Lillian Hayman, who plays Sadie Gray on "OLTL."

20. Tommy Hardy ("GH") is Steve's illegitimate son.

21. Procter & Gamble used the 1951 debut of "Search for Tomorrow" to introduce to Americans not only the Barron family but also two new toothpastes that have since become household names.

22. Susan Martin of "Days of Our Lives" was played by the same actress who later played Dr. Monica Quartermaine on "General Hospital."

23. The Bauers of Springfield have been "Guiding Light's" core family ever since the program's radio debut in 1937.

24. Famous child actor Jackie Cooper later served as executive producer on one of CBS's daytime dramas.

25. Dr. Joe Martin's "other son," Bobby, was killed in a car accident during the first year of "All My Children."

26. Mark Denning of "Capitol" is a senator from New York.

27. When "Y&R" debuted in 1973 it adopted the "General Hospital" look to gain instant popularity.

28. Steve Frame was "killed" twice on "Another World" before his final and permanent demise several years ago.

29. That stoical sentinel of the second-floor nurses' station on "General Hospital," nurse Jessie Brewer, has been married only once in the 20-plus years she has been on the show.

30. "Guiding Light" is the only current TV soap opera to have made the transition from radio to TV.

31. Bonkers is Daisy Cortland's (alias Monique Jonvil) pet name for ex-husband and current lover Palmer Cortland "AMC".

32. Gregg Marx (David Banning on "Days of Our Lives") is the grandson of Groucho Marx.

33. One of "Search for Tomorrow's" early cast members can now be seen in reruns as a bumbling country sheriff's deputy.

34. Monticello of "Edge of Night" is based on the city of Cleveland.

35. Jacqueline Courtney and George Reinholt, who captivated "Another World" fans as Alice Matthews and Steve Frame, went on to play another pair of lovers in "As the World Turns."

36. "Ryan's Hope's" Delia has been married to three different Ryan men.

37. Lewis Edmonds, who plays the part of Langley Wallingford on "All My Children," once played a part on the defunct occult-theme soap called "Dark Shadows."

Ann Flood, veteran actress of "Edge of Night."

38. The Montague-Capulet feud between the McCandlesses and the Cleggs ("Capitol") began long ago and is still going strong because Sam Clegg II is really in love with Clarissa McCandless.

39. Out of three children he and Diana Taylor called theirs ("GH"), none of them was Peter's.

40. When the Bauers and company of "GL" moved from Selby Flats to Springfield the medical-profession characters were transferred to a new hospital.

41. In the early '80s, in a move to compete with other soaps that had boosted their ratings with outlandish plots, "Search for Tomorrow" ran a story that featured an expatriate samurai.

42. When Kay Chancellor of "Y&R" realized that her husband Phillip had tricked her into signing divorce papers while she was drunk, she proceeded to poison him.

43. Monticello's glamor girl, Raven ("EON"), has been married six times.

44. In a landmark storyline on "ATWT," John Dixon went to jail for raping his wife Dee.

45. In real life, Bill Hayes and Susan Seaforth, who play major characters Doug and Julie Williams on "Days of Our Lives," are happily married.

46. Devout Catholic Maggie was Phoebe Tyler's cook on "AMC."

47. The Ice Princess on "General Hospital" was the name given to Helena Cassadine, played by the legendary Elizabeth Taylor.

48. Jumbo is the name of the Ryans' dog on "RH."

49. Brynn Thayer (Jenny Janssen of "One Life to Live") is married to the real-life Brad Vernon.

50. "Search for Tomorrow" was the first TV daytime drama to feature a pregnancy.

51. Bill Bauer ("GL") died of cirrhosis of the liver.

52. When nighttime soap "Bare Essence" was conceived both Genie Francis of "GH" and Victoria Mallory of "Y&R" left daytime to do the new show.

53. Faith's former husband Tom ("RH") died as a result of Roger Coleridge's professional negligence.

54. Will Vernon's wife is no longer on "One Life to Live" because she returned to her home in the northwestern United States after divorcing Llanview's premier shrink.

More Trivia Questions

1. What was "Papa" Bauer's first name on "Guiding Light?"

2. What was the name of Joe Novak's fishing boat on "Ryan's Hope?"

3. One of Henderson's most notorious beauties stood trial for murder during the mid-70s. Who was she?

4. True or False?
   In soap terminology, an "under-five" is the term given to children under age five, who rarely have any lines or active parts.

5. "One Life to Live" was not the original title intended for the show when it was in the planning stages. What was it?

6. True or False?
   Popular Doug Williams was a con artist when he made his debut on "Days of Our Lives."

7. Which longtime TV star is such a fan of "All My Children" that she asked for a temporary role on the show?

8. Since 1974, only three daytime actresses have won an Emmy in two consecutive years. Who are they?

9. The writer for which daytime drama won the coveted Edgar award?

10. Which star of the comedy film Blazing Saddles once played a role on "Another World?"

11. True or False?
    Brad Vernon of "One Life to Live" once was jailed for raping his own wife, Jenny.

12. Star of the movie Alice Doesn't Live Here Anymore, Ellen Burstyn, once played a doctor on what serial?

13. Ernest Thompson, once Tony Cooper on "Somerset," made the transition from actor to writer successfully. What is the name of his prize-winning play turned prize-winning movie?

14. Once considered the sexiest man in movies, this veteran actor now plays a major role on a daytime series. Who is he?

15. The part of Dorian on "One Life to Live" has been played by four different actresses. Who was the second Dorian? Hint: She was recently seen as another bitch on nighttime TV's 1982–83 comedy surrounding a wacky, wealthy Southern family.

16. An underlying rivalry often has stood between Jill and Faith Coleridge of "RH." What secret from the past helped the sisters understand and reconcile these differences?

17. Nearly every daytime drama has featured a child custody battle in the late '70s or early '80s. Whose child was the object of a civil suit on "Edge of Night?"

18. Which former "Days of Our Lives" writer now owns and writes "The Young and the Restless?"

19. In what widely acclaimed movie did "GL" graduate Kevin Bacon star?

20. Agnes Nixon is considered by most insiders to be the queen of the daytime dramas. How many different series has she had a significant hand in?

21. How many times did Phil Brent disappear from Tara Martin's life on "AMC?"

22. True or False?
    For "GH's" Luke and Laura, it was love at first sight, and the character played by the inimitable Tony Geary immediately launched a campaign to break up Laura and Scotty.

23. Which soap opera has won the greatest number of Emmy awards in the shortest period of time since 1974?

24. True or False?
Lee and Tom Baldwin of "GH" were both at one time in love with Lee's wife Meg.

25. True or False?
Jenny Gardner and Tad Martin, brother and sister modeling team on "All My Children," are the children of Opal Gardner by two different husbands.

26. Kate Mulgrew (once "RH's" Mary Ryan) left daytime drama to portray the wife of what famous TV detective?

27. True or False?
Greg Nelson and Jenny Gardner broke up their "AMC" teen romance because Greg blamed Jenny for the accident that caused his paralysis.

28. True or False?
The late '70s and early '80s were the heyday of ABC daytime drama, and the high ratings the ABC soaps received were matched by the Emmys awarded to these shows.

29. The Rileys used to be one of the core families on "One Life to Live." What ever happened to the late Joe's sister Eileen?

30. True or False?
Brooke English broke up the romance between "AMC's" Erica Kane and Mark Dalton during the days before she married Tom Cudahy.

31. True or False?
"OLTL's" Edwina Lewis experienced one of her most traumatic moments when it was revealed to her that Dr. Ivan Kipling was her natural father.

32. How many times has Joanne of "Search for Tomorrow" been plagued by blindness?

33. True or False?
"One Life to Live's" Samantha Vernon was married to Tony Lord before she married Asa Buchanan.

34. True or False?
Jesse Hubbard of "All My Children" is the long-lost son of the late Frank Grant and a former wife, who gave their son her maiden name.

35. Why did Brian Kendall of "OLTL" run frantically into the street, where he was killed by a hit-and-run driver?

36. True or False?
Estelle Sego left Benny on "AMC" when she found

Model Kim Delaney plays sweet Jenny Gardner on "All My Children." Photo by Bob Deutsch.

out that her husband was having an affair with Brooke English.

37. When Genie Francis left "GH" the void left in the Luke and Laura romance threatened to swallow up the remarkable ratings the pair had helped the show garner. Until Holly Sutton appeared in Port Charles it seemed that ABC would never be able to come up with a new love for the passionate Luke. How many lucky ladies were given the assignment of capturing the hearts of Luke and the "GH" audience?

38. Which famous psychologist appeared as herself on "One Life to Live" in the early 1970s?

ANSWERS TO THE SOAP OPERA QUIZ

1. **False.** Try as she might, the alluring Erica was unable to wrench Brandon Kingsley away from his loving and long-suffering wife of 20 years. The reconciled Kingsleys flew happily off to Hong Kong, where Brandon had found a job after leaving Sensuelle. Erica's husbands were Jeff Martin, Phil Brent, Tom Cudahy, and . . . who knows?

2. **False.** Watson played a part in the Canadian-based drama called "Moment of Truth," launched by NBC at the same time as "Days of Our Lives," along with two other soaps. After a year, only "Days of Our Lives" had survived.

3. **True.** No one knew that the crazed Dr. Kipling had slithered back into Llanview, but several of the guests felt familiar chills run up their spine upon sight of the hooded doctor. [They were, by the way, given plenty of chances to notice him, since the party to end all parties lasted a full two weeks (two months?)!] That's a lot of champagne and caviar, even for the likes of Asa Buchanan.

4. **False.** Judith Light also has that distinction. Gallagher won the award in 1976 and 1977; Light (Karen Wolek on "OLTL") captured the honor in 1980 and 1981.

5. **False.** While the "Y&R" setting is a pretty racy place, it's definitely in the midwest. In fact, it may be based on Chicago-area resort Lake Geneva, which is just over the border in Wisconsin.

6. **False.** Geary won the award in 1983, long after Genie Francis and Laura had disappeared from Port Charles.

7. **False.** Jones was the slinky Morticia in "The Addams Family."

8. **True.** Joanne's name in 1983 was Joanne Barron Tate Vincent Tourneur. Joanne was introduced to TV audiences as the young widow of Keith Barron whose second marriage was to Arthur Tate, who also left Joanne a widow. She then had an eventful romance with Sam Reynolds that never worked out, and she married Tony Vincent. Again Joanne was widowed, and her most recent marriage was to the flawed Martin Tourneur. Legally separated as of 1983, the couple showed signs of an impending reconciliation.

9. **False.** Attorney Mike Karr, the backbone of Monticello, has been on the show since its birth in 1956.

10. **False.** *Au contraire,* Fulton left because she felt the writers had mellowed the character of Lisa too much.

11. **True.** Both children were conceived out of wedlock, but Susan's baby was born after David had married her. Julie's son was put up for adoption and became Brad Banning.

12. **False.** Identical last names notwithstanding, Charita didn't become Bert until 1950. The original radio Bert was Ann Shepherd.

13. **False.** Prince Albert was the Central Park Zoo ape who snatched Dee and carried her to the top of the park's Belvedere Tower, in one of "RH's" most way-out plots ever. Delia's third husband was Roger Coleridge, the surgeon who loved Delia as she really is.

14. **False.** It's his "EON" wife, played by Ann Flood, who is married to an ABC VIP.

15. **False.** Kyle was the name of the culprit on an almost-identical plot used by "One Life to Live" during the same period. Milo was the two-faced producer on "Another World."

16. **True.** However, it proved to a be a setup by Myrna, and when Julie realized there had been no affair, they were reengaged.

17. **True.** "All My Children" was actually conceived by Agnes Nixon before "OLTL's" 1968 premiere and it seems that Ms. Nixon submitted "OLTL" because she didn't feel confident in proposing the older script. Both towns are fairly obviously along the Philadelphia Main Line, with characters hopping by car to Philadelphia and by commuter plane to NYC all the time. To reinforce the connection, "AMC's" Paul Martin several times has been called on to put his legal expertise to work to save one of "OLTL's" characters from taking a trip up the river.

18. **False.** Steven Ford, son of former President Gerald Ford, plays Andy on "Y&R."

19. **False.** Ellen Holly, who plays Carla Hall Scott on "One Life to Live," was given that honor.

20. **False.** Jeff Webber proved to be Steve's illegitimate son by Mrs. Lars Webber. Tommy is Audrey's son by Dr. Tom Baldwin.

21. **False.** Joy dish detergent and Spic & Span cleaner were unveiled to the public courtesy of Joanne Barron and company.

22. **False.** Denise Alexander was Susan Martin and now plays Dr. Lesley Webber, the ever-understanding wife of Dr. Rick Webber and mother/guardian of Laura, Mike, and Amy. (Mrs. Dr. Quartermaine has been Lesley's nemesis in the past.)

23. **False.** In the original radio series, the focus was

on the Rutledge family, headed by the Reverend Dr. Rutledge, who would have been shocked by the goings-on in Springfield. (Actually, he may not even have been interested in the doings of Springfield; the original "Guiding Light" was set in a town called Five Points.)

24. **False.** Fred Bartholomew (formerly known as Freddy) produced "As the World Turns" for many years.

25. **False.** Bobby Martin took off on a ski trip 6 months after "AMC's" debut and has never been seen—or mentioned—again, an omission that has delighted its cast for years.

26. **False.** Denning, played by Ed Nelson, is the senior senator from Virginia.

27. **False.** It actually happened the other way around. "Y&R" took the young and sexy approach at a time when "GH" was still an "old-fashioned" soap. It was "General Hospital" that caught on to "Y&R's" formula for success and adapted it to its own situation.

28. **False.** Steve's story wasn't quite as unlikely as that. He was believed dead after an accident in which his body fell into the water and was conveniently impossible to find. Several years later he was bumped off for good in another accident, but this time everyone knew he'd never reappear because his body was found.

29. **False.** One of the two remaining original cast members on "GH" (the other being John Beradino, who plays Dr. Steve Hardy), as Jessie Brewer Emily McLaughlin has been put through the romantic wringer many times. Today's "GH" fans may find it hard to believe, considering the background role the now-single Jessie plays, but Ms. Brewer has been married four times! Marriage number one was to Phil Brewer, a man younger than Jessie whom she supported while he was in medical school. Number two was to the dying Dr. Prentice; number three was Phil Brewer again. Number four was the late Dr. Peter Taylor, but this marriage was annulled when it was revealed that Phil Brewer, who was presumed dead, was actually (horrors!) alive and well. Jessie returned to Phil, but again the marriage failed. Jessie then fell for another younger man, who jilted and bilked her in one fell swoop. These experiences subsequently made her wary of another involvement, and when kindly Dan Rooney, "GH" administrator, came along, Jessie was forced to admit to herself that she may not be capable of giving true love to any man again.

30. **True.** "Guiding Light" is not the oldest TV daytime drama (that distinction belongs to "Search for Tomorrow"), but it is the only one to have made the big move successfully. "Guiding Light" made its radio debut in 1937 and its TV debut in 1952.

31. **False.** Bonkers is the name of the Persian pedigree cat that Palmer gave to Daisy. (Bonkers, by the way, is in real life the pet of "AMC" producer Jackie Babbin.)

32. **False.** He's the grandson of Zeppo, which makes him Groucho's grandnephew.

33. **True.** Don Knotts, who later played Andy Griffith's sidekick Barney Fife, was once on "SFT."

34. **False.** It is said that the hometown of "Edge of Night" is modeled after Cincinnati, headquarters city of sponsor Procter & Gamble.

35. **False.** After Reinholt was fired from his job at "AW" he and Courtney moved to ABC and "One Live to Live," where they played star-crossed lovers Pat Ashley and Tony Lord.

36. **False.** Delia has been married to both Ryan brothers, Frank and Pat, and had an affair with cousin Barry Ryan, from the Chicago branch of the family, but Barry's propensity for bending the truth ironically was too much even for Delia.

37. **True.** Professor Wallingford, who is in actuality Lenny Vlasik, former carny con man, used to play Roger Collins on the 1960s "Dark Shadows," which enjoyed popularity before fading out in 1970.

38. **False.** The fight began when Clarissa McCandless married the only man that Myrna Clegg, Sam's wife, ever loved.

39. **True.** The first two children Diana bore were Phil Brewer's. The third baby was theirs via black-market adoption, and the fact that the baby was Heather's set off one of "GH's" hottest mystery plots of recent years.

40. **False.** Miraculously, Selby Flats' Cedars Hospital was transplanted along with the characters.

41. **False.** This plot, which was panned by viewers, involved a Japanese ninja, the deadly assassins trained from birth to carry out all kinds of underworld and underground activities.

42. **False.** The wealthy but tipsy Mrs. Chancellor did kill her husband, but she did so by driving him over a cliff in her car. She survived, and Phil lived long enough to marry Jill anyway.

43. **False.** As of this writing, the dark-haired Raven has been married five times: Her first marriage was to Kevin Jamison (though she was still having

an affair with Logan Swift). Husband number two was Logan Swift, whom she wed after Kevin's death but soon lost interest in. Raven's third marriage was based on a lie: she thought she was marrying Schuyler Whitney, richest man in Monticello, but actually it was one Jefferson Brown, who'd had his face changed to match Sky's through plastic surgery and was impersonating him. Number four was Ian Devereaux, whom she agreed to marry to further government investigations into Ian's espionage dealings. Finally, Raven has married the real Sky Whitney.

44. **False.** In a conclusion that was perhaps truer to life, the assaulted wife bowed under pressure from outsiders and dropped the charges.

45. **True.** Contrary to their "Days of Our Lives" counterparts, who have been married, divorced, and remarried, the couple has been married since the early '70s, when they met on the show.

46. **False.** Maggie was the motherly Center City lady who treated then-hooker Estelle like her own daughter. (Estelle told Maggie that she was a maid at the Tyler mansion so that Maggie wouldn't discover her real profession.)

47. **False.** The Ice Princess was a gargantuan diamond that set off "GH's" famous (or infamous) "mystery island" plot. The diamond, as fans will remember, was much more valuable than it seemed.

48. **False.** The Ryans' Irish wolfhound is named Finn. Jumbo was Jack Finelli's friend and substitute father.

49. **False.** Brynn Thayer is the spouse of Gerald Anthony, who plays the irresistible con artist Marco Dane (and also at one time played his own twin brother, Mario Corelli). (Do you know whether they met on the show?)

50. **True.** In the mid-50s Joanne Tate bore a son by husband Arthur.

51. **False.** Troubled Bill had kicked the alcohol habit but later supposedly died in a fall from a Chicago hotel room window.

52. **False.** Genie Francis starred in the short-lived "Bare Essence" along with Genoa City expatriate Lauralee Prentiss, who plays Jaime Lyn Bauer.

53. **True.** The somewhat amoral Roger was preoccupied with his new wife Delia and consequently gave Tom's attending nurse the wrong instructions for Tom's care. (Faith eventually found out about Roger's deadly mistake, but the two have since reconciled.)

54. **False.** Mrs. Vernon, who had "cried wolf" once too often, took a drug overdose and then, ironically, was unable to phone for help once she'd changed her mind.

Answers to More Trivia Questions

1. Frederick. "GL" fans didn't learn this fact until Papa's great-grandson was born and was named after him.

2. The Nova. Joe's first gift to Siobhan when he began courting her was a huge fish, courtesy of the Nova, and a single rose.

3. Temptress Jennifer Pace Phillips, played by Morgan Fairchild, was the accused. Fairchild has since played a gorgeous baddie on prime-time's "Flamingo Road."

4. False. "Under-five" refers to actors who have fewer than five lines of dialogue in any given soap episode—the "bit" parts of soaps.

5. Originally, the show was slated to be called "Between Heaven and Hell," but the network nixed this title as too racy.

6. True. The suave Mr. Williams was originally after Susan's money but soon fell in love with Julie. His part on the show has been a major one ever since.

7. None other than Carol Burnett played the long-lost daughter of Lenny Vlasik (alias Langley Wallingford), with the expressive name of Verla Grubbs.

8. Helen Gallagher (Maeve Ryan, "Ryan's Hope") won the award for outstanding actress in both 1976 and 1977. Judith Light won the same award in both 1980 and 1981. Dorothy Lyman won the award for outstanding actress in a supporting role (Opal Gardner, "All My Children") in 1982 and then won the award for a starring role in 1983. It is to the actress's credit that her role on "AMC" was expanded to a major part.

9. The Edgar is awarded by the Mystery Writers of America, and—you guessed it—it was presented to Henry Slesar, who wrote for "The Edge of Night" for years. (Year of award?)

10. Cleavon Little was cast as Captain Hancock.

11. False. Brad was tried for raping his sister-in-law, Karen, while Jenny was in the hospital because of a difficult pregnancy. (The only charge that stuck, by the way, was assault.)

12. Ellen Burstyn, then Ellen McRae, played "The Doctors'" Dr. Kate Bartok.

Elizabeth Taylor played Helena Cassadine during "General Hospital's" Ice Princess caper.

13. Thompson wrote *On Golden Pond.*
14. He's Rory Calhoun, and he plays Judson Tyler on "Capitol."
15. The second Dorian was Dixie Carter, who was featured on CBS's "Filthy Rich."
16. Maeve Ryan revealed to Jill that she was actually the daughter of her father's mistress of long ago, not of his wife. When Jill's real mother died, Ed Coleridge brought his illegitimate daughter home to be raised with his other children. Jill and Faith were often at odds as children because neither of them understood why Faith and Roger's mother was so cold to Jill, and why their father treated Jill as if she were special.
17. Jamie, son of Raven and attorney Logan Swift. The child was conceived while Raven was engaged to Kevin Jamison. Jamie's true parentage was revealed when matriarch Geraldine Whitney,

Kevin's aunt, told Raven that Kevin was sterile.
18. The vaunted William Bell wrote for "Days of Our Lives" for many years, up until the late '70s.
19. The movie was *Diner*, released in 1983.
20. Seven: She created "One Life to Live," "Search for Tomorrow," "All My Children," and the 1980s' "Loving," as well as cocreating "As the World Turns." She also served "Guiding Light" and "Another World" as headwriter.
21. Twice. Reported MIA in Vietnam, Phil returned from the assumed dead to find Tara married to Chuck Tyler and the happy couple raising the son Tara had borne as a result of Phil and Tara's high school affair. The second time, Phil was "lost" overseas on a secret government mission, only to be found, only to die in a plane crash on his way back to Tara and little Charlie.
22. False. Luke's original reason for wanting to end the romance between Scotty and Laura was to allow his sister Bobbie to step into Laura's shoes. When introduced to the series in the mid-70s, the Spencers' wrong-side-of-the-tracks waterfront upbringing urged them to use all kinds of nasty means to get what they wanted.
23. The critical acclaim that was bestowed on "Ryan's Hope" was backed up by 13 Emmys, and the show has been on only since mid-1975.
24. False. Lee and Tom both fell for Jessie. Tom was the only brother who ever married her.
25. False. Both Jenny and Tad were sired by the evil Ray Gardner, but Tad was adopted as a boy by the saintly Martins, Ruth and Joe.
26. Kate Mulgrew went from being Mrs. Fenelli to being "Mrs. Columbo" on a spinoff that went nowhere.
27. False. Greg never stopped loving Jenny, but his blueblood mother, who strongly objected to the rich boy-poor girl match, convinced him that giving her up was a much more loving move than allowing her to commit herself to living with "half a man."
28. False. Although ABC's plots and characters seemed all the rage during this time period, only two ABC series have been named best daytime serial since 1974: "Ryan's Hope" in 1977 and "General Hospital" in 1981.
29. Long ago, Eileen and daughter Julie moved to Florida, where they've apparently been ever since. As often happens in daytime drama, they have been treated as nonexistent ever since, and they weren't even notified of Joe's death!

30. False. The budding romance between Erica and Mark was nipped by Erica's mother, Mona, who was forced to reveal the long-kept secret that Mark is Erica's half-brother (both of them were sired by Eric Kane, Mark illegitimately with his secretary while Mona and Eric were still married.)

31. False. Although the groundwork was laid for this event, "OLTL's" producers/writers apparently decided not to follow up on this offshoot of an already sensational story line. Will Edwina ever learn the awful truth? Who knows?

32. As of 1983, twice. Fortunately, she also recovered twice.

33. False. Samantha stunned the residents of Llanview when she made a hasty exit from her wedding before the vows could be exchanged. At the last minute Samantha decided that, despite months spent in dogged pursuit of the dashing Tony, she didn't really want to marry a man who wasn't truly in love with her.

34. False. Jesse is the son of Frank's long-lost sister, who died of heart problems. Frank had only two previous marriages before his marriage to Nancy: A first marriage to Nancy, followed by a marriage to Caroline, who left him when she found out that Nancy was pregnant as a result of a one-night-stand between Frank and Nancy during Frank and Caroline's marriage.

35. Brian was overwrought by the news that Tony Lord, not Paul Kendall, was his real father. Mother Pat had a difficult time reconciling her guilt over having told him after Brian died.

36. False. Estelle was killed in a car accident. Benny and Brooke did indulge in occasional interludes when she, as a spoiled rich teen was attracted by the animal magnetism of chauffeur Benny. Since those days, however, both characters have mellowed and remain good friends.

37. After Francis's departure, nubile young actresses popped up in such rapid succession as to suggest that ABC had a large harem lying in wait for the demanding Luke Spencer. After Laura "disappeared" from the screen, Luke kept seeing her everywhere. The first phantom Laura was an accident victim who may have also been mistaken for Laura by the David Gray bad guys. The second Laura was Laura Templeton, another hapless blonde who was unwittingly mixed up with David Gray's strange scheme. She also was phased out of the show. Soap opera magazines began to promote Laura T's sister, Jackie Templeton, as Luke's next love, but she also has been phased out (at least for now). Finally, the lovely Holly Sutton, played by Emma Samms and touted as an Elizabeth Taylor look-alike, was introduced, and while it wasn't love at first sight for the viewers, it was for Luke, and the viewers soon were as charmed by the new character as was Luke.

38. Dr. Joyce Brothers made the first such appearance on a daytime drama when she was called to Llanview to help Meredith Lord Wolek with postpartum depression.

Appendix:

Scrapbooks and Crystal Balls

For those who are nostalgic, here are lists of some of the most memorable radio shows named for their main characters and a complete list of all soap operas to appear on television.

Among soaps named for their core characters were:

"Name of Soap"	Year of Debut
"Vic and Sade"	1932
"Clara, Lu 'n' Em"	1932
"Judy and Jane"	1932
"Betty and Bob"	1932 (Arlene Francis played Betty.)
"Marie, the Little French Princess"	1933
"Just Plain Bill"	1933
"The Romance of Helen Trent"	1933
"Ma Perkins"	1933
"Peggy's Doctor"	1934
"The Gumps"	1934 (Agnes Moorehead played Min.)

"Name of Soap"	*Year of Debut*
"Life of Mary Sothern"	1934
"The Story of Mary Marlin"	1935
"Mrs. Wiggs of the Cabbage Patch"	1935
"Five Star Jones"	1935
"Backstage Wife"	1935
"The O'Neills"	1935
"Molly of the Movies"	1935
"The Goldbergs"	1936
"Pepper Young's Family"	1936 (Mason Adams of the "Lou Grant Show" starred as Pepper.)
"Dan Harding's Wife"	1936
"David Harum"	1936
"John's Other Wife"	1936
"Big Sister"	1936 (Martin Gabel, Arlene Francis' husband, starred in this soap opera as Dr. John Wayne.)
"Myrt and Marge"	1937
"Pretty Kitty Kelly"	1937
"Our Gal Sunday"	1937
"Lorenzo Jones"	1937
"Arnold Grimm's Daughter"	1937
"Kitty Keen, Inc."	1937
"Jenny Peabody"	1937
"Terry Regan: Attorney at Law"	1938 (The late Jim Ameche, Don Ameche's brother, played Terry.)
"Stepmother"	1938 (The silent screen star Francis X. Bushman starred as the Stepmother's husband.)
"Joyce Jordan, Girl Interne"	1938
"Young Widder Brown"	1938
"Stella Dallas"	1938 (MacDonald Carey, film veteran and star of the soap opera, "Days of Our Lives" was the young male lead, Dick Grosvenor.)
"Those Happy Gilmans"	1938
"Houseboat Hannah"	1938
"Jane Arden"	1938
"Her Honor, Nancy James"	1938
"Doc Barclay's Daughters"	1939
"The Life and Loves of Dr. Susan"	1939
"The Carters of Elm Street"	1939
"Manhattan Mother"	1939
"When a Girl Marries"	1939
"Caroline's Golden Store"	1939
"The Man I Married"	1939 (The late Van Heflin, film, TV, and stage actor and brother of "All My Children's" Fran Heflin, played Adam Waring.)
"Woman of Courage"	1940
"Meet the Dixons"	1940 (starring Richard Widmark as Wesley Dixon)
"Brenda Curtis"	1940 (Costarring the late Hugh Marlowe, film, stage, and TV star. He was last in "Another World" as Jim Matthews.)

"Name of Soap"	*Year of Debut*
"Ellen Randolph"	1940
"My Son and I"	1940
"Society Girl"	1940
"Young Dr. Malone"	1940
"Martha Webster"	1940
"Amanda of Honeymoon Hill"	1940
"Portia Faces Life"	1940 (Portia was played by Lucille Wall who later became the first "older" bride to have a white wedding on a soap, "General Hospital.")
"We, the Abbots"	1940
"Kate Hopkins, Angel of Mercy"	1940
"Mother O'Mine"	1940
"The Johnson Family"	1941
"Charlie and Jessie"	1941
"The Story of Bess Johnson"	1941
"The Bartons"	1941
"Front Page Farrell"	1941 (Richard Widmark appeared, as did Virginia Dwyer, who would create the role of Mary Matthews on "Another World" in 1964.)
"The Second Mrs. Burton"	1941 (No, not Elizabeth Taylor. Teri Keane, later to appear on "Edge of Night," costarred.
"Kitty Foyle"	1941
"Second Husband"	1942
"Woman of America"	1943
"Lora Lawton"	1943 (Jan Miner, later a TV soap stalwart and later also to gain fame as Madge the Manicurist for Palmolive Dishwashing Liquid commercials, was Lora.)
"Perry Mason"	1943 (Yes, it was a soap and it starred many who would go on to star in TV soaps. Among them: John Larkin who would become "Edge of Night's" first Mike Karr played Perry. Mandel Kramer, also to join "Edge" later on was Lt. Tragg.)
"Tena and Tim"	1944
"Rosemary"	1944
"Barry Cameron"	1945
"Rose of My Dreams"	1946
"Katie's Daughter"	1947
"Wendy Warren"	1947 (Douglas Edwards, the veteran newscaster, played himself.)
"The Story of Holly Sloan"	1947
"This Is Nora Drake"	1947
"Marriage for Two"	1949
"Nona from Nowhere"	1950
"Dr. Paul"	1951
"Woman in My House"	1951
"The Doctor's Wife"	1952
"One Man's Family"	1955 (A daytime version of a successful evening show)
"The Affairs of Dr. Gentry"	1957 (The distinguished actress Madeleine Carroll was Dr. Gentry.)

The listing of daytime dramas on television follows:

Soap	Year of Debut	Network
"The First Hundred Years"	1950	NBC
"Search for Tomorrow"	1951	CBS (Now on NBC)
"Love of Life"	1951	CBS
"The Egg and I"	1951	CBS
"Hawkins Falls"	1951	NBC
"Miss Susan"	1951	NBC
"Guiding Light"	1952	CBS
"The House in the Garden"	1952	NBC
"Valiant Lady"	1953	CBS
"The Bennetts"	1953	NBC
"The World of Mr. Sweeney"	1953	NBC
"Three Steps to Heaven"	1953	NBC
"Follow Your Heart"	1953	NBC
"The Brighter Day"	1954	CBS
"Portia Faces Life"	1954	CBS
"Road of Life"	1954	CBS
"The Secret Storm"	1954	CBS
"The Seeking Heart"	1954	CBS
"Woman with a Past"	1954	CBS
"A Time to Live"	1954	NBC
"One Man's Family"	1954	NBC
"The Greatest Gift"	1954	NBC
"Concerning Miss Marlowe"	1954	NBC
"First Love"	1954	NBC
"Golden Windows"	1954	NBC
"Date with Life"	1955	NBC
"The Way of the World"	1955	NBC
"As the World Turns"	1956	CBS
"The Edge of Night"	1956	CBS (now on ABC)
"The Verdict is Yours"	1957	CBS
"Hotel Cosmopolitan"	1957	CBS
"Kitty Foyle"	1958	NBC
"Young Dr. Malone"	1958	NBC
"Today is Ours"	1958	NBC
"From These Roots"	1958	NBC
"For Better or Worse"	1959	CBS
"House on High Street"	1959	CBS
"Road to Reality"	1960	ABC (The network's first
	1960	soap)
"The Clear Horizon"	1960	CBS
"Full Circle"	1960	CBS
"Our Five Daughters"	1962	NBC
"Ben Jerrod: Attorney at Law"	1963	ABC
"General Hospital"	1963	ABC
"The Doctors"	1963	NBC
"The Young Marrieds"	1964	ABC
"Another World"	1964	NBC
"Never Too Young"	1965	ABC

Soap	Year of Debut	Network
"The Nurses"	1965	ABC
"A Time for Us"	1965	ABC
"Days of Our Lives"	1965	NBC
"Moment of Truth"	1965	NBC
"Morning Star"	1965	NBC
"Paradise Bay"	1965	NBC
"Confidential for Women"	1966	ABC
"Dark Shadows"	1966	ABC
"Love Is a Many Splendored Thing"	1967	CBS
"One Life to Live"	1968	ABC
"Hidden Faces"	1968	NBC
"Where the Heart Is"	1969	CBS
"Bright Promise"	1969	NBC
"All My Children"	1970	ABC
"A World Apart"	1970	ABC
"The Best of Everything"	1970	ABC
"Another World (Somerset)"	1970	NBC
"Return to Peyton Place"	1972	NBC
"The Young and the Restless"	1973	CBS
"How to Survive a Marriage"	1974	CBS
"Ryan's Hope"	1975	ABC
"Lovers and Friends/For Richer For Poorer"	1977	NBC
"Texas"	1980	NBC
"Capitol"	1982	CBS
"Loving"	1983	ABC
(In Development: "Scruples")		NBC
(In Development: "The Young Loves of General Hospital")		CBS

CRYSTAL BALL

Far be it from anyone to dare to predict what will happen to soap operas in the future. (Surely, it would be ludicrous to attempt such a task for individual shows or characters, considering the nature of the soap opera.) However, some current trends can give us some hints as to what we might see in the future.

Many people feel that the soaps have gone as far as they can with the sensationalism, youthfulness, and glamor of the '80s soaps. And viewers of this era may notice that many soap operas were, in mid-1983, exhibiting a growing trend toward returning to traditional plots. Whether this continues to be the trend of the future is anybody's guess.

New Soap Operas

Certainly there are plenty of soap operas on tele-vision now, but that doesn't seem to stop the networks from spewing forth new ones with great regularity. As we've discussed, many of the new shows, like their failed predecessors, won't last. But some may. Let's look at a few of them.

Who Said CBS and ABC Don't Have "Scruples?"

Well, the people in these networks are certainly fine folk with high regard for the same moral values you and I cherish, but it's NBC who scored the coup in getting the rights to the sizzling novel *Scruples* by Judith Krantz, for a daytime series.

No less a veteran writer than Pat Falken-Smith, who has at least 20 screenplays behind her and has written for such soaps as "Where the Heart Is," "Guiding Light," and "General Hospital," heads up the team that was to turn out this newest daytime drama.

Says Smith about "Scruples": "It's full of the stuff that makes each of us human beings interested in one another. There's every sort of relationship any of us might have experienced."

Well and good. But towards the end of 1983, NBC decided it didn't want to put any of these fictional relationships on its daytime roster. As a matter of fact, NBC gave indications of moving from soaps toward alternative programming. TV insiders call this a "noble experiment," but most say the network will eventually put some sort of drama back on its afternoon schedule; if not a soap, then something soap-like. Meanwhile, "Scruples" will be offered to other networks.

Can the Future Be Found in Cable TV?

Only time will answer this question. Producers of new cable TV soap operas hope that the freedom that the new medium allows will create a whole new form of soap opera—and that TV viewers will pay to see it. The cable TV medium opens the door to these changes in soap operas:

- More revealing sex scenes and looser dialogue: The constrictions of network TV don't affect cable, which can and does employ nudity, explicit language, and more explicit sex.
- Length of episodes: Some of the cable entries into the soap genre have employed a combination of serial and film techniques to produce shows that are connected by continuing characters but can stand on their own because they are movie length and can wrap up a storyline within an episode.
- Fluidity: In daytime dramas today, one character cannot appear in two scenes in a row in different

places without raising the question of how he or she had time to get there. Cable, on the other hand, can do so, cutting from scene to scene as in film.

Cable television is providing a new outlet for soap operas. Already well established in the medium are Douglas Marland's "A New Day in Eden" and the Christian Broadcasting Network's "Another Life." Ted Turner, the pioneer in cable broadcasting introduced his series, "The Catlins," over TBS in April, 1983.

Generally, the cable soaps are still in the process of being widely accepted. In some instances the newcomers were fueled by a lot of steamy, passionate sex scenes. Indeed, on cable, a producer can get away with a lot less—less, that is, on the bodies of his in-bed stars.

The one exception is "Another Life," which projects the theme that no matter what else happens, there is, for everyone, another life; that is, there is salvation for even the most sinning character.

A decade ago "The Young and the Restless" introduced bed scenes on TV. The series showed half-naked young people—the bottom parts of their anatomies below the waist were always covered by sheets for the males, while the ladies had their sheets drawn up to their breasts—cuddling close. A position called "the soap position" was created in which the woman lay across her partner's bare chest.

On the cable soaps, the woman's chest is often bare and it's her partner who lies across her convex contours, more often than not.

Already there is talk that sex alone won't sell soaps on cable. So the question arises—is there a future for soap operas on this medium?

The answer must lie with the response from audiences as cable becomes a more pervasive medium across the country with the lowering of costs for use of satellite technology.

Bibliography

Edmondson, Madeline, and Rounds, David. *The Soaps.* New York: Stein and Day, 1973

Fireman, Judy (editor). *TV BOOK.* New York: Workman Publishing, 1977.

Fulton, Eileen (as told to Brett Bolton). *How My World Turns.* New York: Taplinger Publishing Co., 1970.

Halliwell, Leslie. *The Filmgoer's Companion.* Third Edition. New York: Avon Books, 1970.

Lackmann, Ron. *Remember Television.* New York: G.P. Putnam's Sons, 1971.

Lackmann, Ron. *TV Soap Opera Almanac.* New York: Berkley, 1976.

LaGuardia, Robert. *Wonderful World of TV Soap Operas.* New York: Ballantine Books, 1974

Lemay, Harding. *Eight Years in Another World.* New York: Atheneum, 1981.

Levin, Martin. *Hollywood and the Great Fan Magazines.* New York: Arbor House, 1970.

Stedman, Raymond William. *The Serials.* Second Edition. University of Oklahoma Press, 1977.

Stuart, Mary. *Both of Me.* New York: Doubleday, 1980.

Warrick, Ruth (with Don Preston). *The Confessions of Phoebe Tyler.* Englewood Cliffs, NJ: Prentice-Hall, Inc., 1980.

Index*

*Italicized page numbers indicate information contained within a photograph or its caption. Italicized names listed indicate names of fictional characters in daytime dramas.

Dumonde, Renee, 71, 72
Dumont, Paul, 28
Duncan, Sandy, 183